PRISONS AND PRISON LIFE

Costs and Consequences

Joycelyn M. Pollock

Texas State University–San Marcos

Roxbury Publishing Company

Los Angeles, California

BAS PS

Library of Congress Cataloging-in-Publication Data

Pollock, Joycelyn M., 1956–
Prisons and prison life: costs and consequences / Joycelyn M.
Pollock.
   p. cm.
Includes bibliographical references (p.) and index.
ISBN 1-931719-09-8
   1. Prisons—United States. 2. Imprisonment—United States. I. Title.
HV9471.P648 2003
365'.973—072—dc21   2003014691
                                            CIP

Prisons and Prison Life: Costs and Consequences

Publisher: Claude Teweles
Managing Editor: Dawn VanDercreek
Production Editor: Monica K. Gomez
Copy Editor: Pauline Piekarz
Cover Design: Marnie Kenney
Typography: SDS Design, info@sds-design.com

Printed on acid-free paper in the United States of America. This book
meets the standards of recycling of the Environmental Protection Agency.

ISBN 1-931719-09-8

ROXBURY PUBLISHING COMPANY
P.O. Box 491044
Los Angeles, California 90049-9044
Voice: (310) 473-3312 • Fax: (310) 473-4490
Email: roxbury@roxbury.net
Website: www.roxbury.net

44.95   1/11/07

Contents

Chapter 9:
'Doing Time Eight to Five' 215

Chapter 10:
'We Shall Be Released' 253

Preface

This book is intended for use as a supplemental text for corrections courses or in an upper-level penology class. It could also be used for a social problems class because this country's overdependence on prisons has been and continues to be a problem, both for those who are incarcerated and for the rest of us who have to pay for it, at the expense of education and other public services. The goal of the book is to present up-to-date figures on the incarceration rate, numbers in prison, and current issues and controversies. This book also tries to incorporate the "voice" of prisoners and correctional workers through the liberal use of quotes.

After presenting a short history of prisons for historical context, the first chapter provides the latest figures on numbers as well as a comparison of rates over the last several decades to show that the incarceration "binge" started in the mid-1980s and has only recently abated somewhat. The second chapter presents a historical and current look at the nation's "drug war," since our policies toward drug offenders have been largely responsible for the imprisonment binge. Other chapters look at types of prisons, prisoners, subculture, prisoners' rights, and programming opportunities in prison. I devote a separate chapter to women's prisons and, also, to correctional officers. The final chapter discusses the reality of parole and the challenges of release, and the book closes with some final thoughts on the "prison industrial complex."

The book may carry a stronger tone of advocacy than is usual in academic books. This is justified, I believe, by the overwhelming evidence that prisons are harmful to those who live and work within them. It is also clear to me that there are good things that sometimes happen in prison. Inmates find enlightenment through programs or receive support for the first time in their lives from a caring staff member. Unfortunately, for every story of success, there are many more where a prison sentence serves only as an impediment to a successful life. Has incarcerating two million people contributed to a reduced crime rate? Perhaps—although evidence does not support this conclusion. What is clear is that if we continue to incarcerate everyone who commits a crime, we will end up taking that money away from our schoolchildren and teachers. Other public services must be curtailed in order to pay for the prison industrial complex. This is not hyperbole, it is fact.

Acknowledgments

I would like to thank the graduate assistants who collected and checked sources for me over the last year: Victoria Quintana, Rosa de la Garza, and Autumn Hanna. The anonymous reviewers provided by Roxbury provided me with helpful criticism that was much appreciated and I want to thank them: Kelly Asmussen (Peru State College), Delores E. Cleary (Central Washington University), Terri Earnest (Arkansas Tech University), Charles Hanna (Duquesne University), William E. Harver (Widener University), Christopher Hensley (Morehead State University), Kathy Johnson (University of West Florida), Gordon M. Robinson (Springfield College), Barbara Sims (Penn State University), and Peter J. Venturelli (Valparaiso University).

I would especially like to thank Noel Pinero and the Center on Crime, Communities and Culture. I have been lucky enough to be on his listserve and benefit from his electronic "clipping service." It has been an invaluable resource for spotting trends and identifying national issues of justice concerns, including prisons. The Soros Foundation and their Center on Crime, Communities and Culture has been one of the most active supporters of prison alternatives and re-examining this nation's priorities in crime and drug policy making. Their support has assisted grassroots advocates such as "Critical Resistance" and policy and research activities such as Marc Mauer's research at the Sentencing Institute. I thank the community of scholars, too numerous to name, who continue to contribute to prison literature and provided much content for this book. If policymakers and politicians would read the good works of these people, we might see smarter policy choices.

Finally, I thank my husband, Eric Lund, for putting up with my manic schedule when finishing this book, and Brooke Miller who helped with the index.

Chapter 1

Prisons

Then and Now

The United States incarcerates five to eight times more citizens per capita than any Western European nation (Abramsky 2002). There are over 2 million inmates in this nation's prisons and jails (King and Mauer 2002a, 2002b). How did this happen? To understand our use of imprisonment as a form of correction, it is important to briefly revisit the history of prisons in the United States and to look at the goals that have been assigned to prisons since the birth of this country.

What Are Prisons?

The use of imprisonment as punishment is a relatively recent occurrence. Historically, communities punished offenders through the use of corporal punishment, fines, or banishment. In this country, people were held in jail for debt, until fines could be paid, or until some form of corporal punishment could be carried out. Imprisonment as punishment was not "invented" until late in the eighteenth century. Thus, prison is a punishment that is scarcely over 200 years old.

In the colonial era, communities were small and close-knit. Offenders were usually dealt with through some form of public humiliation; for instance, the stocks and pillory, whipping, the ducking stool, and so on were used to inflict injury and humiliate the offender. If this shame did not reform the offender, the individual was banished. Death was used as a punishment only when other methods failed, or when the offense was extremely serious. The offender might be incarcerated, but only until some other form of punishment was carried out, or until the individual, or his relatives, paid the fine imposed (Barnes and Teeters 1952).

In the late 1700s, older forms of punishment, which depended on public humiliation, became less effective. Cities were too big, communities were less cohesive, and populations were mobile— new forms of social control were necessary. The congregate care facility was born from the need to control and provide services to larger numbers of people (Rothman 1971/1990). Orphanages were used to house orphaned or abandoned youngsters; hospitals were created to house the sick and infirm; and mental institutions were opened to take care of those who were unable to function. Workhouses or poorhouses ("almshouses" in England) were used to control and house indigents who had no work or means of making a living.

The workhouse and jail housed a similar and overlapping population. Since the poor would never be able to pay a fine, keeping them incarcerated became the punishment itself. Street people ended up in a workhouse or a jail, and sometimes there wasn't much difference between them. Houses of Correction supposedly taught a trade and "corrected" the poor of their life of idleness (Durham 1994). In effect, this practice made it a crime to be poor, with the punishment being incarceration and forced labor.

In the late 1700s, Benjamin Rush and others transformed the Walnut Street Jail in Philadelphia from a typical jail that held debtors and those awaiting punishment into a place of "reform." The new institution included such concepts as classification and reformation through penitence (Durham 1994; Garland 1990). Women and men were separated, children were kept separate from adults, and the sick were isolated so they did not infect the healthy. Furthermore, some attempt was made to have those incarcerated work at some craft. With these changes, the jail took a giant step toward the institution we now call a prison or a penitentiary.

Clergymen, politicians, and educators all believed that this institution was the perfect place to instill the characteristics of sobriety, regularity, and piety in the wayward inmates found within. The only influence permitted was the Bible and a religious guide to aid in finding salvation. After a due period of "penitence," the individual was expected to emerge as a new person (Johnson 1997; Durham 1994). Unfortunately, management problems such as overcrowding and corruption displaced the idealism and goals of the reformers within the space of a few years. Indeed, the history of all prisons seems to be a period of idealism and optimism followed by overcrowding and corruption. More recent history indicates that this cycle continues.

The Philadelphia and Auburn Models

The concepts of the Walnut Street Jail were transplanted to Eastern Penitentiary, built in 1829. Each inmate lived in a separate cell with a separate exercise yard. The individual was kept completely separate from outside influences and from other inmates. Meanwhile, in 1817, Auburn Penitentiary was built in New York (Barnes and Teeters 1952). This facility adopted some of the principles of the Pennsylvania model and rejected others. The biggest difference was that inmates worked, ate, and exercised together, and cells were smaller. Industrial manufacturing replaced individual handcrafts.

Similarities between the "Philadelphia" (or "separate") system and the "New York" (or "congregate care") system existed as well. In both institutions, outside influences were kept to a minimum and silence was maintained to reduce "contamination" from other inmates. In Pennsylvania, this was done physically by isolating the prisoner's body; in Auburn, it was done through a harsh punishment system that deterred talking, even when inmates worked side by side. Neither method was entirely effective in preventing prisoners from communicating (Conley 1992).

The Pennsylvania model and the New York model were compared and contrasted, becoming the topic of editorials, debates, and public speeches. For traveling Europeans, the two prisons were as much a part of the "American Grand Tour" as the buffalo, "wild" Indians, and the transcontinental railroad (Rothman 1971 / 1990). The Civil War interrupted the ongoing controversy over which system was better at reforming inmates; however, after the war, newfound interest in the debate led to the National Prison Congress in 1870. There reformers and practitioners met and created a Declaration of Principles that would be the agenda for corrections for the next 100 years.

Whether one system or the other was "better" at reforming inmates was not the factor that ended the debate—it was economics. The New York (Auburn) model was cheaper to build and cheaper to maintain. Further, it could actually be profitable, since the inmates could be put to work at something other than handicrafts. Some early prisons were income producers for the state. Most were at least self-sufficient, at least in the early years.

At the 1870 Prison Congress, a new model for imprisonment was born—the reformatory (Reichel 1997; Walker 1980). Zebulon Brockway implemented the idea of classification, in which the inmates earned privileges of liberty, education, and training, at the Elmira Reformatory in Elmira, New York, in 1876 (Sullivan 1990). Young offenders, who could benefit from a strict regime of disciplined living and education, were targeted for the new reformatory. Discipline was harsh. Brockway believed in earning liberties, but he was known for inflicting harsh punishments as well (Sullivan 1990). These two models—the penitentiary and the reformatory—are still with us today.

While the penitentiary and reformatory became the models for prison architecture in the North, the southern states followed a different course. Because so much of the South's economy depended on agriculture, the prison "farm" emerged. Northern prisons were also built in rural areas with a great deal of cultivated acreage, but prison industry was the more important economic contribution. Northern states either produced goods for sale or leased the institution and prisoner labor to private industry. In the South, prisoners were much more likely to work in fields than in prison "factories." After the Civil War, prisoners, in effect, took the place of slaves and the prison farms became the new plantations (Johnson 1997). "Leased labor" was a contract between landowners and the state whereby landowners would feed and house prisoners in return for their labor. As can be imagined, in some cases conditions were horrific, with landowners literally working the prisoners to death. In fact, the average life span of a prisoner during this time was no more than six or seven years (Johnson 2002, 44). Periodic exposés of the terrible conditions that these prisoners lived under spurred some oversight and change, but the system continued well into the 1940s (Stone 1997).

From Then to Now

Prisons during the early 1900s and through the 1950s enjoyed some improvements in conditions, but virtually no public attention was directed to them throughout both World Wars. Typically, prison wardens were expected to keep the prisons out of the paper. If they managed to do that, they were considered successful. Inside the prisons, nothing much was happening. According to Robert Johnson, "Big Houses," his term for this era's penitentiaries, were "a world populated by people seemingly more dead than alive, shuffling where they once marched, heading nowhere slowly" (Johnson 1997, 41; 2002, 42).

In the 1950s, a rash of prison riots brought prisons to the front pages of newspapers. It was also during this time that the disciplines of sociology, psychology, and psychiatry began to influence prisons. By the late 1960s and 1970s, prisoners in some states underwent rudimentary "diagnoses" and were classified according to their problems and their degree of security risk. In many states, inmates started their prison terms in "classification centers," where they took a multitude of educational, aptitude, and interest tests and medical examinations. These tests were then used to determine what prison they would be sent to and the appropriate mix of educational, vocational, and treatment programs to which they would be assigned (Spencer 1997). By the 1970s, in addition to basic and advanced education, a prisoner might partake of group therapy, transactional analysis, or behavior modification; even transcendental meditation and yoga were offered in some prisons. The Big House of the 1940s and Jimmy Cagney films had been replaced by the "correctional institution," and psychology replaced religion as the agent of reform (Durham 1994; Pollock 1997c).

It should be noted that even at the height of the rehabilitative era, not all prisons operated as described above. The South was particularly known for brutal prisons where rehabilitation was a foreign word. For instance, a prisoner's petition from the notorious Tucker and Cummins prison farms in Arkansas was the impetus for a federal district court to overturn the "hands-off" doctrine that had insulated prison authorities from court scrutiny for years. Court testimony, unrefuted by the state of Arkansas, documented individual cases of torture with the "Tucker telephone," an electrical apparatus that transmitted electric shocks to the inmates' genitals and other body parts. Inmates were made to work in the fields without coats or shoes in the winter, they had to pay for medical care, and some were kept in the "hole" without light despite damage to their retinas. The court, clearly shocked at the level of brutality, wrote a holding that included a stern warning—if a state chose to run a prison system, then it must run it in a way that met basic constitutional protections (*Holt v. Sarver*, 309 F.Supp. 362 [E.D. Ark. 1970]).

The agricultural model continued in the South well into the 1980s, at which time the winds of change finally began to reach "plantation prisons." Some argue that though there were abuses, there were also some good elements to farms such as Parchman in Mississippi, where inmates were housed in "camps" of less than 200 and were kept out in the fresh air rather than caged 23 hours a day. An ex-warden notes that the Parchman he came back to in the 1980s was very different from the one he left in the 1970s (Cabana 1996, 131–132):

> The way the original camps were organized was a prison adminis-
> trator's dream. . . . The smallness of the camps also permitted a
> sense of informality that simply did not exist in most correctional
> facilities. The camp sergeants knew their inmates, and they got to
> know their families as well. . . . The institution had truly been trans-
> formed in the last dozen years to just another prison. . . . Not only
> was Unit Twenty-Nine [a new building] a concrete monolith sur-
> rounded by double fences, razor ribbon, and motion detectors—it
> housed fifteen hundred inmates.

As mentioned, the early 1950s was a time of great change in the purpose and programming of this nation's prisons, but at the same time, several serious riots occurred across the country. In the 1970s, too, this combination of reform and riots occurred. The Attica riot in 1972 brought prisons into every living room. Citizens watched live footage of prisoners holding knives to the throats of hostages on the evening news. The nation waited as negotiations continued over the course of many days until New York state police regained control after a bloody assault. Public opinion, which had been relatively supportive of rehabilitative programs and treatment, shifted to a less tolerant view toward prisons and prisoners. It was hard to see prisoners wielding machetes and other crudely lethal weapons as a group that would be able to benefit from education and other programs. Further, the politicalization of prisoners, especially African-American prisoners, made the treatment ethic (that the individual needed to be diagnosed and treated for his "problem") less relevant. For many social reformers and activists, the concept that the individual needed to be changed was replaced with the concept that it was society that was the cause of crime, either because of poverty, racism, or capitalism.

Another blow to the rehabilitative trend was the Martinson Report of 1974 (Martinson 1974). This report, paid for and then suppressed by the New York State Department of Corrections, was a meta-analysis and evaluation of over 200 prison and correctional programs across the country. According to the first articles published from this study, no correctional program was successful in reducing recidivism. Actually, the findings were a little more complicated and Martinson attempted in later articles to modify his original harsh stance, but the damage had been done. Politicians interested in the bottom line of reducing the budget and/or wanting to appear "tough on crime" promoted the ethic of punishment first, and treatment not at all. Academics offered philosophical justification for retribution (von Hirsh 1976). Despite pundits, politicians, and public opinion continuing to call for the abandonment of rehabilitation in the 1990s, the rehabilitative era was pretty much already dead by the mid-1980s.

In fact, prison administrators were struggling with a much more immediate problem than rehabilitation in the 1980s—a massive influx of offenders. A spike in crime rates and the federal "War on Drugs" led to a rapid rise in incarceration rates, which soared in the 1980s and throughout the 1990s. Prisons met and exceeded their maximum capacity levels. State-sentenced prisoners were held back in jails awaiting space, and even then jails were filled to capacity and beyond. Prisoners were housed in cafeterias, gyms, and in some cases tents in the prison yard. State legislatures increased prison budgets, doubling, tripling, and then quadrupling the amounts allocated for departments of correction. States went on building binges to meet the ever-expanding numbers. In fact, the dizzying numbers led to an incredible surge of a profitable new industry—private prisons. Multitudes of small private companies were created to meet the need of states for quick construction and management agreements. The biggest companies, such as Wackenhut and Corrections Corporation of America, boasted exponential growth and even began trading on the New York Stock Exchange. Incarceration rates (the number of people incarcerated per 100,000 in the population) doubled and then tripled nationally.

The 1990s and Beyond

In the 1990s, politicians outdid each other in their anticrime platforms. Democrats co-opted the traditionally Republican mantra of "toughness" and President Clinton signed the Violent Crime Control Law Enforcement Act in 1994. This sweeping legislation sent money to the states for prison construction, created a federal "three strikes" law, and expanded the federal death penalty. Other legislation mandated eviction for any public housing tenant convicted of any type of drug crime, even if it was for a first offense. This eviction policy has affected countless families of drug users as well as the users themselves, and was recently upheld by the Supreme Court (2001).

Obviously, during a time when prison administrators are struggling simply to find beds, programs are purely a luxury item. Thus, once again, the cycle is repeated. The idealism and optimism of the 1970s was replaced with overcrowding and cynicism. Prisons again have became warehouses, albeit modern ones. Of course, there are differences between the prisons of the 1940s and today—there is not the pervasive brutality and racism that occurred in earlier years, basic education now exists in almost all prisons, legal rights give prisoners some modicum of due process and protection against arbitrary actions of administrators, and the facilities themselves are often newer and cleaner. But for all the public concern about crime during the 1980s and 1990s, very little attention has been directed to the inside of the prison, or to those who live there. Prisons, once built, rarely are the subject of news reports, and "success" is still defined as when the prison stays off the front page, just as in the 1940s.

Incarceration Rates: A War on People

The increased rate of incarceration in this country is nothing short of phenomenal. In 2002 there were a record 2,019,234 people in state and federal prisons and jails (Harrison and Karberg 2003, 1). The annual increase between 2000 and 2001 slowed to 1.1 percent, the smallest annual increase in three decades, but it appears to be rising again, with a 5 percent increase in the first six months of 2002 (Salant 2002; Cernetig 2002, A9; Harrison and Karberg 2003, 2).

In the early 1980s, some academics and some policymakers warned against the increasing prison rates. They had no idea that their concerns would be completely ignored and incarceration rates would double and then double again before the century came to a close. In 1972, the incarceration rate was 93, meaning that for every 100,000 people, 93 were incarcerated. In 2001, it was 472 per 100,000 (Beck, Karberg, and Harrison 2002, 3). As Table 1.1 shows, the largest increases in the rates of imprisonment have been seen in the last 20 years.

Table 1.1 Incarceration Rates

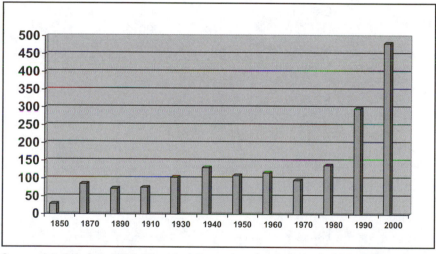

Source: M. Cahalan, 1986. *Historical Corrections Statistics in the United States, 1850–1984* (Rockville, MD: Westat); Bureau of Justice Statistics, *Sourcebook of Criminal Justice Statistics* (Washington, D.C.: Department of Justice, 1997); Bureau of Justice Statistics, *State and Federal Prisoners, June 30, 1998* (Washington, D.C.: Department of Justice, 1998); P. Harrison and J. Karberg, *Prison and Jail Inmates at Midyear* 2002 (Washington, D.C.: Department of Justice, 2003).

Table 1.2 compares the United States with other countries (the rate is higher than that discussed in the previous section because this rate also includes the number sentenced to jail as well as state and federal prisons). No western nation approaches the United States in its rate of imprisonment. More recent statistics than those used for the table indicate that, like the United States, most countries have seen increases in their rate of incarceration; for instance, Belarus went from 505 to 575 per 100,000, South Africa from 265 to 400, and Spain from 105 to110. Russia was one of the few countries where the imprisonment rate decreased (from 690 to 675 per 100,000) (Sentencing Project 2001, 8).

Table 1.2 Incarceration Rates—Selected Countries

Country	Rate of Incarceration
Russia	690
United States	600
Belarus	505
Ukraine	390
Singapore	287
South Africa	265
Poland	170
South Korea	137
Canada	115
Spain	105
China	103
England	100
France	95
Germany	85
Norway	55
Japan	37
India	24

Adapted from: M. Mauer, *Race to Incarcerate*, (New York: New Press, 1999), 23.

In some states, the increases have been dramatic and have strained state budgets. Texas went from 38,000 inmates in 1988 to 158,131 in 2002 (Hendricks 2000, 1; Harrison and Karberg 2003, 1). California's prison population was about 160,315 prisoners as of midyear 2002 (Harrison and Karberg 2003, 1). Table 1.3 presents 2001 and 2002 rates for selected states. It appears that some states have successfully lowered their incarceration rates, whereas others continue to see rising rates.

Table 1.3 Incarceration Rates: Highest and Lowest

State	Rate per 100,000 2001/2002	State	Rate per 100,000 2001/2002
Louisiana	795/799	Maine	126/137
Texas	731/685	Minnesota	131/139
Mississippi	689/728	North Dakota	158/167
Oklahoma	669/672	Rhode Island	179/184
Alabama	592/593	New Hampshire	184/197
Georgia	540/552	Vermont	221/211
South Carolina	526/542	Nebraska	225/227
Delaware	505/557	West Virginia	225/246
Missouri	500/531	Utah	235/226
Nevada	485/499	Massachusetts	247/240

Source: A. Beck, J. Karberg, and P. Harrison, *B.J.S. Bulletin: Prison and Jail Inmates at Midyear 2001* (Washington, D.C.: Department of Justice, 2002), 6; P. Harrison and J. Karberg, *B.J.S. Bulletin: Prison and Jail Inmates at Midyear 2002* (Washington, D.C.: Department of Justice, 2003), 3.

There are tremendous regional differences in incarceration patterns. While southern states have very high rates, northern states incarcerate far fewer of their citizens. One correlate of incarceration rates is the percentage of minorities in the state population (Irwin and Austin 1994; Sorensen and Stemen 2002).

As can be seen in Table 1.4, there are tremendous differences in the size of state systems. The size of a state's system is largely due to the size of the population. Obviously, larger states have larger prison populations. While some states incarcerate over 100,000, others incarcerate about 1,000. In addition to the population, however, there are sentencing practice differences that account for the different incarceration rates, irrespective of crime rates. Some states, especially in the South, are simply more punitive. That does not necessarily translate to lower crime rates, only to larger prison populations.

Table 1.4 Size of Prison Systems: Five Largest and Five Smallest

Highest	
Federal Bureau of Prisons	161,681
California	160,315
Texas	158,131
Florida	75,553
New York	67,131
Lowest	
North Dakota	1,168
Wyoming	1,732
Vermont	1,784
Maine	1,841
New Hampshire	2,476

Source: P. Harrison and J. Karberg, *B.J.S. Bulletin: Prison and Jail Inmates at Midyear 2002* (Washington, D.C.: Department of Justice, 2003), 3.

Incarceration and Race

African-American men are imprisoned at a rate that is almost 100 times higher than that of white women and about seven times higher than that of white men. An amazing fact that cannot be explained by crime rates is that this nation's prisons went from being 70 percent white in the 1950s to nearly 70 percent African-American and Latino by 2000 (Sampson and Lauritsen 1997). The total rate of about 690 people incarcerated in prison or jail for every 100,000 hides the true story of who is most likely to end up incarcerated. Broken down by groups, the incarceration rate, from lowest to highest, is as follows (Harrison and Karberg 2003, 12–13).

(per 100,000)	
White women	68
Hispanic women	137
African-American women	349
White men	649
Hispanic men	1,740
African-American men	4,810

Austin and Irwin (2001, pp. 4–5) point out the following:

- Almost one in three African-American men in the age-group 20 to 29 are either in prison or jail, or on probation or parole.

- More than one of every 10 Hispanic men are under some form of correctional supervision.

- Sixty years ago, less than one-fourth of prison admissions were nonwhite; today nearly three-fourths are.

- African-Americans and Hispanics constitute about 90 percent of all persons sent to prison for drug possession.

- African-American women have experienced the greatest increase in correctional supervision, rising by 78 percent from 1989 through 1994.

Cole (1999) and others document the tremendous toll imprisonment has taken on the African-American community. One of out every 14 African-American children has a parent who is incarcerated (Cernetig 2002, A9). In fact, about 12 percent of African-American men in their twenties and thirties are in prison, compared with 4 percent of Hispanic men and 1.6 percent of white men (Harrison and Karberg 2003, 1).

Statistics from specific states are even more troubling. The Justice Policy Institute reports that nearly four in 10 African-American men in their twenties are under some form of criminal justice control in California. While African-Americans constitute about 20 percent of all felony arrests, they make up 43 percent of third-strike defendants. In New York, more than 90 percent of the people doing time for drug offenses are African-American or Latino. It is reported that there are more African-Americans and Hispanics locked up in prison in New York than attending colleges and universities. In Maryland, since 1990, nine out of every 10 new inmates imprisoned are African-American (Kaplan, Schiraldi, and Ziedenberg 2000, 1).

In Texas, one out of three young African-American men are in prison, jail, or some form of community supervision. African-Americans are incarcerated at a rate seven times higher than that of whites in Texas (Kaplan, Schiraldi, and Ziedenberg 2000, 3). Many believe that these figures are evidence of a pervasive racism that permeates not only the criminal justice system but the entire socioeconomic system, relegating minorities to second-class citizenship. In this view, consciously or unconsciously, prisons are used as a tool for controlling excess and disenfranchised groups (Rusche and Kirchheimer 1939; Foucault 1977; Mauer 1999; Parenti 1999).

Although most information available gives us figures for African-Americans, other minority groups are also overrepresented in this nation's prisons. Unfortunately, it is more difficult to see trends because, historically, Hispanics and Native Americans have not been identified and counted separately. Native Americans, especially, are probably underrepresented in state figures because of reporting practices (Archambeault 2003).

Crime Rates and Prison

Are more people being sentenced to prison because more people are committing crime? It doesn't seem so. According to the Uniform Crime Reports (UCRs), crime has been steadily declining for about 10 years. Between 1993 and 1999, violent crime declined 32.7 percent. Property crime has been declining for 25 years (Leary 2000). During this same time period, we've seen incarceration rates continue to rise. Some argue that the crime decline is due to increased use of incarceration; however, Mauer, Chesney-Lind, and Clear (2001, p. 7) point out that in the 1980s, just the reverse was true. Incarceration rates climbed quite dramatically, but so did crime rates. More telling, there doesn't seem to be much correlation between the rate of the crime decline and the imprisonment or enforcement patterns of states. Further, the National Research Council of the National Academy of Sciences has estimated that the impact of imprisonment on violent crime rates is minimal, and preventative strategies are more important (Mauer 1999, 87).

For instance, the prison population of Texas increased five times faster than New York's prison population during the 1990s, but New York experienced a 26 percent greater decline in crime for the same period. In 1998, Texas incarcerated 1,014 compared with New York's 574 per 100,000; but the crime rate was 42 percent higher in Texas (5,111 compared with 3,588 per 100,000) (Greene and Schiraldi 2002, 3; Kaplan et al. 2000). New York City's declining crime rate was attributed by some to the New York Police Department's zero tolerance policy of arresting petty criminals, but similar rates of decline occurred in cities that did not employ zero tolerance. In fact, criminologists attribute the crime decline to a mix of factors, including the decreasing numbers in the crime-prone age years, the stabilization of the crack markets, lower unemployment, and perhaps even "creative reporting" by agencies that felt pressure to match the nation's decline with local figures (Blumstein and Wallman 2000; Parenti 1999, 82). Crime rates declined in most states between 1993 and 1999, but not necessarily those states with three strikes laws or harsher sentencing (King and Mauer 2001, 8).

It should be remembered that the UCRs, the most common source for crime rates, can present only those crimes reported to (and counted by) police. They are the best indicators of crime rates we have, but they are only reports of crime and are influenced by the reporting agencies' practices as well. There is virtually no way to tell accurately whether changes in the UCR are changes in actual crimes or changes in reporting (or counting) practices. In other words, the crime increase in the 1980s or the crime decrease in the 1990s may bear only a rough approximation to reality; however, the National Crime Survey, which is a victim survey, also registered declining reports throughout the 1990s. Thus, rising incarceration rates cannot be explained by increases in crime rates.

It should also be noted that our ravenous use of prison has evidently not made us much safer compared with other countries. Although property crime rates between the United States and West European countries and Australia and Canada are fairly comparable, our violent crime rates are vastly different. Americans are still many more times likely to be victimized by homicide than citizens in most other countries, most of which have much lower prison rates than we do (Mauer 1999). Table 1.5 shows the homicide rate of the United States as compared with other countries.

The dramatic decline of both violent and property crime over the last decade may be over. The most recent reports present less clear evidence that crime continues to decline. The UCR released for 2001 indicated that violent crime rates remained stable (a 0.1 percent increase was reported from June 1999 to June 2000), whereas the National Crime Victimization Survey (NCVS) indicated a 15 percent decline in violent crime over the same period (Butterfield 2001). The reason for the discrepancy is no doubt in the methodology of the two reports; the NCVS does not measure

Table 1.5 Homicide Rates—Selected Countries

Country	Rate of Homicide/100,000
United States	7.4
Finland	3.1
Switzerland	2.8
Scotland	2.6
Canada	2.1
Northern Ireland	2.1
France	2.0
Australia	1.9
England/Wales	1.3
Japan	1.0
Norway	0.9

Adapted from M. Mauer, *Race to Incarcerate* (New York: New Press, 1999), 28.

homicide, and the UCR does not measure non-serious assault. Simple assaults probably accounted for the decline observed in the NCVS. Further, the NCVS measures crime through victim responses to surveys; these crimes may not have been reported to police and it is police reports that are the source of the UCRs. The most recent report of the UCR (for 2002) reflected only a slight decrease of crime rates between 2001 and 2002. There was a 1.4 decrease in violent crime and virtually no change in property crime (UCR 2003).

The decade-long trend of declining crime rates has only recently seemed to affect incarceration rates. As noted below, we have seen the incarceration rate level off in recent years, and in some states there are decreasing numbers of prisoners admitted to or sent back to prison. Only time will tell whether this trend will continue.

Reasons Why We Incarcerate

What accounts for our increased use of imprisonment over the last two decades? One study asked prison administrators that question. They responded that four factors contributed to the phenomenon: increased sentence length, the "drug problem," legislative response to the drug problem, and the public's desire to "get tough" on crime (Vaughn 1993, 15–16). Actually, these issues are all interrelated and if one were to choose one factor over any other in accounting for our overcrowded prisons, it would be the "War on Drugs." Like any other, this war has many prisoners. The trouble is, of course, that the so-called enemies we incarcerate are our sons, daughters, wives, husbands, mothers, and fathers, a topic that will be covered in the next chapter.

> It has been said that you can tell a lot about a culture by its great public works. If this is true, then America at the end of the twentieth century will be at least partially remembered as the society of imprisonment. The days of building public works like Grand Central Station, Hoover Dam, and the Golden Gate Bridge have given way to two decades dominated by building structures surrounded by razor wire. (Dyer 2000, 15)

Others note that the use of imprisonment in this country has risen to unprecedented levels and is part of a trend of "getting tough" on marginalized groups. This trend started with the Reagan White House and has continued fairly unabated since. Beckett and Western (2001) proposed that reduced welfare benefits and increased incarceration rates are not mere coincidence; they illustrate the government's shift in the philosophy and manner in which those at the fringes of economic self-sufficiency are handled. While welfare benefits have been drastically reduced over the last 25 years, government spending has not. The dollars have been transferred from Aid to Families and Dependent Children (AFDC) and other welfare benefits to bricks and mortar for prisons. In fact, Beckett and Western found that states' welfare spending was negatively associated with the incarceration rate. In other words, states with generous welfare benefits had lower incarceration rates, and states that had very low welfare spending had the highest incarceration rates. They also found that the percentage of African-Americans in a state's population was positively associated with the state's incarceration rate (2001, 45).

In a sentencing study conducted in conjunction with the Vera Institute of Justice, it was found that crime rates, the proportion of African-Americans in the population, and the ideologies favored by a state's citizens were the most influential factors affecting incarceration rates. Having a sentencing guideline system (a method of guiding a judge's sentencing decisions) was also an influential factor. It was found that a presumptive sentencing guideline system lowered a state's incarceration rate by 72 per 100,000 (Sorensen and Stemen 2002). Other variables, although less influential, included the percentage of the population in the age-group 18 to 34 and the poverty level. On the other hand, determinate sentencing, mandatory sentencing policies, and truth-in-sentencing legislation did not seem to have much effect on prison admission rates, contrary to what many believe (Sorensen and Stemen 2002). Note, however, that prison admission rates are different from incarceration rates (which factor all those in prison against a base population figure). Laws that increase sentences will affect imprisonment rates because more people will serve longer sentences.

In addition to an increase in the number of people sentenced to prison, what has also occurred in the last 30 years is that sentences are getting longer and/or there is a decrease in the use of discretionary release and parole. In Texas, for instance, the state's Criminal Justice Policy Council showed that prisoners in 1998 served over half of their sentence, compared with an average of less than a quarter 10 years earlier (Hendricks 2000).

Three strikes laws sentence offenders, sometimes young offenders, to 25-year or life sentences. Over half of all states now have some type of three strikes or habitual offender laws, but only a few states have used their laws to any great extent. King and Mauer (2001) note that as of mid-1998, only California has used such a law to sentence a substantial number of offenders. As of 2001, about 40,511 had been sentenced under California's three strikes law. Georgia (942), South Carolina (825), Nevada (304), Washington (121), and Florida (116) all use their laws much less frequently than California.

California's law is perhaps the best known. Passed in 1994 as a direct reaction to the horrifying killing of Polly Klaas, the three strikes provision provides for a 25-year to life sentence for a third felony. Less known is the law's "two strikes" provision, which doubles the offender's sentence upon conviction of a second felony. The two strikes provision impacts many more offenders than the three strikes punishment (Clark, Austin, and Henry 1997; King and Mauer 2001).

Critics argue that the law is not only unjust but also unwise because it ties up state resources for those offenders who are already beginning to decrease their criminal activity (the so-called maturation effect, which refers to the fact that all offenders drastically curtail criminal activity after age 35). King and Mauer (2001) argue that the three strikes law will age the California prison population and result in extreme costs connected with housing an older prison population. It is estimated that by 2026 there will be 30,000 inmates serving sentences of 25 years to life in California prisons at an annual cost of $750 million (Zimring, Hawkins, and Kamin 2001, 71).

> The first thing a convict feels when he receives an inconceivably long sentence is shock. The shock usually wears off after about two years, when all his appeals have been denied. He then enters a period of self-hatred because of what he's done to himself and his family. If he survives that emotion—and some don't—he begins to swim the rapids of rage, frustration, and alienation. When he passes through the rapids, he finds himself in the calm waters of impotence, futility, and resignation. It's not a life one can look forward to living. The future is totally devoid of hope, and people without any hope are dangerous—either to themselves or others. (an ex-inmate, Martin and Sussman 1993, 259)

These laws are not necessarily reserved only for violent offenders. In fact, large numbers of offenders sentenced under habitual felon laws have committed nonviolent felonies. A California report indicated that 85 percent of those imprisoned under the law committed a nonviolent third felony (Butterfield 1996, A14). A study of those convicted under Florida's habitual felon law found that in 87 percent of the cases, there was no injury to the victim (Austin and Irwin 2001, 42). In Clark, Austin, and Henry's review of California's and Washington's three strikes laws in 1997, they noted that 98 percent of those sentenced under Washington's law had committed a "crime against a person," while only 25.5 percent of California offenders sentenced under the three strikes law had committed such a crime. In fact, close to three-quarters had committed either a property or a drug crime.

California's law has led to draconian results. One author described some of the third "strikes" that resulted in life sentences—robbing four men of their pizza, stealing five bottles of liquor, and selling marijuana (Cole 1999, 147). Others noted these examples of third felonies that resulted in life sentences: theft of a pair of sneakers, attempted breaking and entering, and theft of a jar of instant coffee (King and Mauer 2001, 10). While the three strikes law promised to keep violent offenders off the streets, it has cast a much broader net than perhaps many voters intended.

Another troubling aspect of California's three strikes law is that African-Americans tend to be disproportionately affected by such laws. In California, African-Americans make up 7 percent of the population but 43 percent of those sentenced to prison under the three strikes law in 1996 (Cole 1999, 148).

Researchers have begun to publish reports detailing the effects of three strikes laws. King and Mauer (2001) examined 50,000 California inmates sentenced under the law and found no link to the drop in crime California had experienced along with the rest of the country. California legislators disagree, arguing that their 41 percent drop in crime was twice the national average (Sherman 2001). Austin and Irwin (2001, p. 212) compared three strikes states (California, Georgia, and Washington) with states without three strikes laws but with similar crime rates before such laws were passed (Massachusetts, Michigan, and Texas) and found that there was little difference between three strikes states and those without in their levels of crime decline. All states experienced a crime decline between 1991 and 1996. Further, they looked at counties within California and found that those that vigorously pursued three strikes prosecutions experienced no greater decline than other counties that used three strikes convictions more sparingly. A Rand study of Oregon's mandatory minimum laws (Measure 11) found no evidence that the harsh law was responsible for Oregon's declining crime rate (Associated Press 2002).

It may be that three strikes laws are falling out of favor with policymakers and the public. Such laws have also seen challenges in court. In *Andrade v. Attorney General of the State of California* (November 2001; No. 99-55691), the Ninth Circuit ruled that a three strikes sentence of 50 years to life for two petty theft convictions was cruel and unusual. In another case, the court had held that a three strikes sentence was disproportional and remanded the convicted person for resentencing. Upon resentencing, the offender still received 50 years to life for stealing videotapes worth $153. In another case, the defendant had attempted to steal a $25 steering wheel alarm and was sentenced under the three strikes law to life in prison. Even though this offender did have violent crimes on his record, the court held that the sentence could not be "grossly disproportional" to the crime. Although the Ninth Circuit ruled that California's three strikes law was not unconstitutional *per se* but only in its application in these cases, California's attorney general appealed and the consolidated cases were heard by the U.S. Supreme Court in the October 2002 term.

The Supreme Court, in a five-to-four decision, upheld California's three strikes law. Ruling that the long sentences were not disproportional, even for minor property offenders, the Court's opinion seems to have forestalled any other challenges to habitual felon laws (*Ewing v. California,* No. 01-6978, and *Lockyer v. Andrade,* No. 01-1127). However, change may come from the legislative branch. There is also a California ballot initiative pending that would restrict the use of three strikes to violent or serious felonies (Kasindorf 2002).

'If You Build It, They Will Come'

In the 1990s, states built their way out of their overcrowding problem—temporarily at least. In Texas, for instance, the number of prison beds increased by 154 percent between 1990 and 1998 and the state can now house over 160,000 inmates (Verhovek 1996; Kaplan, Schiraldi, and Ziedenberg 2000). No other state comes close to Texas's building binge, but most states built new prisons and all states substantially increased their prison capacity in the 1990s.

States were not the only ones building prisons in the 1990s. Many counties built huge new jails with the expectation of filling them with state prisoners and paying for them with state "per diems" (cost per day to house inmates). Many of these county jails now sit empty because states built their own prisons and stopped paying the counties to house state inmates. In Texas, counties continued to receive state money in 2002 for state prisoners, even though the prison system had thousands of empty beds. The amounts were not small—in 2001 Limestone County received $11 million, and Newton County $10 million, among others. Why would the state of Texas pay counties (or private contractors) to house state prisoners when it had empty beds? The answer is politics. Counties have expensive jails to pay for and do not want to lose the revenue; and county officials have a powerful lobby. According to some figures, the state could save $100,000 a day by stopping payments to counties (M. Ward 2002a, A13).

Some counties have resorted to marketing their cells to other states. It is not unusual to have Hawaiian inmates serving time in county jails in Texas, or Indiana prisoners in Louisiana. Serving time so far away from one's home state causes problems for the inmates. Visitation is either extremely difficult or impossible. Pursuing any legal action is more difficult. Liability issues have been raised. Who is responsible when violations occur? Is it the sentencing state or the vendor state, county, or private prison that is housing the prisoner?

The building boom in prison construction in the early 1990s was unprecedented. The effect of this out-of-control prison use has been felt in state budgets. Prison budgets are eating up increasingly greater and greater percentages of state budgets. In 1978, about $5 billion was spent on prison and jail incarceration. In 1990, correctional costs rose to $12 billion. They jumped to $22 billion in 1996. By 2000, the cost of incarceration for states and the federal government had ballooned up to $40 billion; and the latest figures available put the figure at $46 billion. California, not surprisingly, spends the most—about $3 billion—and North Dakota the least—about $10.7 million. States spend about 7 percent of their budgets on corrections (Butterfield 2002a, A15; Kaplan 1999; Greene and Schiraldi 2002, 2; Cernetig 2002, A9).

Some states spend much more. California was projected to spend 18 percent of its entire state budget on corrections in 2002, while directing only 1 percent of it to higher education (Zimring and Hawkins 1995, 7–8). In Ohio, state spending on prisons ($1,026 billion) grew at six times the rate of state spending on higher education ($670 million) between 1985 and 2000, even though it still spends more for higher education (Collins 2002). In 1999, it cost every man, woman, and child in the United States $103 to run state prisons (Kaplan 1999, 1). The average per inmate cost is about $20,100 per year. With about 2 million incarcerated, it is easy to see why corrections budgets are eclipsing other governmental priorities. Very little of the correctional budget goes to treatment—about 80 percent goes to simply maintaining prisons and personnel costs for custody staff. All the rest is divided among juvenile corrections, probation, parole, and community-based programs (Kaplan 1999, 2).

A Lull Before a Storm?

It may be that we have finally satiated the public's demand for imprisonment. Recent figures indicate that the incarceration rate is slowing. Although the number incarcerated rose in 1999 to a record 1.8 million people, the 4.4 percent annual increase between 1998 and 1999 was below the average annual increase of the preceding years. The increase slowed again from 1999 to 2000 to only 2.3 percent, and in 2001 the increase was only 1 percent. However, the rate of increase between 2001 and 2002 inched up again, to 1.5 percent (Harrison and Karberg 2003, 3).

Several states have seen declines in their prison populations. The latest report from the Bureau of Justice Statistics shows that Illinois (5.5 percent), Texas (3.9 percent), New York (2.9 percent), Delaware (2.3 percent), and California (2.2 percent) all experienced reductions in their prison populations (Harrison and Karberg 2003, 3).

In fact, several states have closed prisons. Ohio, Illinois, Florida, and Missouri are four of the states that have already closed or are planning to close one or more prisons because of declining numbers of prisoners and budget shortfalls (Greene and Schiraldi 2002, 4). Other states have canceled or delayed plans for building or canceled contracts with private vendors. Still others have taken steps to reduce the number of people entering prison. Iowa passed a law giving judges discretion whether to impose a prison sentence or not for drug crimes and some property crimes that had required mandatory sentences before the law. Mississippi passed a law allowing first-offense prisoners to be eligible for parole after serving 25 percent of their sentence instead of 85 percent, as had been the case since a 1994 "tough" law (Butterfield 2002a, A15). Alabama, Mississippi, North Dakota, Connecticut,

Utah, and Arkansas have either passed or are considering passing legislation that revises sentencing laws or mandates reviews of sentences in order to reduce the number of nonviolent and/or drug offenders spending long periods of time in prison (Greene and Schiraldi 2002, 11). New York has frozen hiring at 36 prisons and eliminated about 600 correctional officer jobs through attrition in 2001–2002 (Rohde 2001).

Some of the states with the highest incarceration rates are leading the nation in implementing plans to reduce these rates. Louisiana, North Carolina, and Texas have already seen the effects of their sentencing and parole changes (Schiraldi 2002b). In 2001, the Louisiana legislature, by a vote of 29 to 5, passed a law that ended mandatory prison time for certain nonviolent offenders; reduced sentences for drug possession offenders; set up a panel to review cases of certain inmates to see if they were good risks to be freed; and limited life sentences for multiple offenders to violent criminals (Shuler 2001). It is estimated that these changes will save the state $60 million per year (Schiraldi and Greene 2002, A2).

Unfortunately, the federal government seems to be going in the opposite direction. While some states have seen decreased rates of incarceration, the federal government rate has increased, and, in fact, is much higher than any state (double the state average for 2002) (Corrections Digest 2002, 1; Schiraldi 2002b). About 40 percent of the growth between 2001 and 2002 was accounted for by federal prisoners (Harrison and Karberg 2003, 3). This increase is due almost completely to drug laws that require mandatory terms of imprisonment and long sentences. Other contributors are the growing number of non-citizen offenders and immigration violators. The size of the Federal Bureau of Prisons has increased from about 25,000 in 1980 to over 161,681 in 2002—the largest prison system in the country (Schiraldi 2002; Harrison and Karberg 2003, 1).

Recent polls indicate that the public is more in favor of rehabilitation and less likely to support increased spending for prisons than has commonly been believed (Greene and Schiraldi 2002, 6). Even though a substantial number still believe in punishing nonviolent offenders, there is also support for rehabilitation, a growing belief that long mandatory prison sentences are not fair, and an unwillingness to take state monies from education to devote to corrections (Greene and Schiraldi 2002, 6). About 65 percent of those responding to a recent public opinion survey supported addressing the root causes of crime compared with 32 percent who favored strict sentencing (Open Society Institute 2002). Further, survey respondents were more willing to cut prison budgets than child care, terrorism protection measures, education and job training, or health care. About 63 percent agreed that drug addiction should be dealt with by counseling and treatment rather than punitive measures, and 70 percent believed that the current approach is a failure. In fact, the majority of respondents believed that prisons were only "warehouses" that provided little or no rehabilitation (Open Society Institute 2002).

The Open Society study also found that Americans were losing confidence in mandatory sentencing policies. Over half favored the elimination of three strikes laws; and most saw prevention as the most important function of the criminal justice system (Open Society Institute 2002). Interestingly, there was even less support for the three strikes law in California than elsewhere. In another study, it was found that only 13 percent of California citizens, for instance, support three strikes sentences for "less serious" property offenders (King and Mauer 2001, 8). The prevention program perceived to be most effective was teaching young people personal responsibility and moral values. Over three-quarters (77 percent) believed that expanding after-school programs would save money by reducing the need for prisons (Open Society Institute 2002).

Citizens opposing new prison construction have, in some cases, been successful in convincing legislators to vote down new construction proposals. Interestingly, some of the strongest support for programming comes from prison wardens and correctional officials. In a recent survey, 92 percent of wardens surveyed believed greater use should be made of alternatives to prison (cited in Greene and Schiraldi 2002, 7). Even conservative politicians and editorialists are beginning to express their discomfort with the gluttonous use of incarceration embarked upon over the last 20 years.

Even though the recent decline is encouraging, two factors may drive incarceration figures up again. First, the large group of inmates who were incarcerated for very long terms in the 1980s is now nearing release. In the next several years, large numbers of inmates who have served 15- and 25-year sentences will be released into the community. Policymakers and academics have recognized this fact and there is burgeoning interest in "re-entry." The fact of the matter is that these inmates received very little in the way of programming over the last decade and they are woefully unprepared to enter the workforce of the twenty-first century. It may be that their homecoming will be short-lived as they face economic problems and the temptations of drugs with no better economic or personal resources than they had before their imprisonment.

Second, our recent slide into an economic recession has thrown multitudes of people out of the workforce. Although the hardest hit were white-collar, technical workers, the trickle-down effect can be expected to affect crime rates and sentencing decisions (unemployed offenders are more likely to be sentenced to prison than probation). Crime rates have already slowed their decline and, in some areas, show an increase. If unemployment continues to rise, we may also see imprisonment rates start once again to climb.

In the wake of eviscerated public budgets and huge costs associated with imprisonment, some jurisdictions have gone back to charging inmates for their keep. A Massachusetts senator has proposed a bill that would mandate charging offenders up to $10 a day for their imprisonment and several county sheriffs in that state have already starting charging county jail inmates five dollars a day for their keep (Sutner 2002). Of course this begs the question of how indigent inmates would pay and whether it makes sense legally or morally to charge inmates' families (who are usually the source of any monies in the inmate's account) for their loved one's incarceration. However, the proposal will no doubt be popular with a punitive public and cash-strapped legislature. One thing is clear: As state and local governments begin to feel the pinch of the recession, the money to pay for prisons and jails will have to come from somewhere.

Conclusion

We have seen that prisons are a relatively new weapon in our arsenal against offenders. In a short 200-year history, they have risen to become the "first-choice" option for judges sentencing offenders (so much so, that now we are having difficulty paying for all the prisoners we have incarcerated). The history of prisons is cyclical. Periods of optimism and a belief that institutions can reform offenders are followed by periods of neglect, during which overcrowding and/or corruption is rampant until there is another cycle of interest. We may be seeing a new cycle of interest and reform in the recent attention paid to the problems of re-entry. This may lead to programs that will help inmates avoid recidivism. Such programs would have to include drug programs, vocational training, and education, to name a few. Prison programs are the subject of Chapter 6.

> Let me describe what prison is like for me. Prison is deep emotional pain with no release from the hurt. . . . Prison is the picture, etched in my memory, of my wife breaking down in convulsive wracking sobs for what I did. Prison is watching the tears run down my mother's face every day. My daughter was in high school and we used to enjoy working through her homework in the evenings. She was an A and B student. Prison is her report cards that came after I was locked up—with Ds and Fs because she was hurting so for what I did. I have these memories with me every day. . . . How do I show them that I do love them? I am in prison. That is prison. It is pain, deep, frequent, and daily. (an inmate; Rogers in Johnson and Toch 2000, 68)

One thing that all the numbers and charts cannot do is describe the effect these sentences have on families. Two million people is a hard concept to imagine; harder still are the many more millions affected outside of prison.

Study Questions

1. How many people are incarcerated in the United States? How does this compare with other countries? What are the regional differences in rates of incarceration?
2. What is the trend in incarceration rates? Are we incarcerating more or fewer people than in years past?
3. What are the reasons proposed for our patterns of incarceration?
4. Which states have the largest prison populations; which have the smallest?

5. What are three strikes laws? How do they affect incarceration rates?

Chapter 2

The War on Drugs

A Misguided Policy

One cannot explain what has happened in prisons without examining this nation's drug policy. The war on drugs and the concomitant sentencing of drug offenders has been perhaps the largest contributor to rising incarceration rates. In 1980, there were about 40,000 offenders in prison for drug crimes. In 2002, there were more than 450,000 (Cernetig 2002, A9). Drug offenders have filled federal and state prisons and changed the subculture inside. It is impossible to discuss prisons without also discussing the drug war.

History of the War on Drugs

The beginning of the modern drug war might be assigned to the Harrison Act of 1914. In the early part of the twentieth century, a wide variety of patent medicines were marketed, with no oversight or control by government. Many of these elixirs, which contained derivatives of morphine, cocaine, and/or alcohol, were touted as cures for everything from depression to bunions. Marijuana, cocaine, and heroin were also in use, although for the most part restricted to small segments of the population. The Harrison Act merely required that drug manufacture and sales be taxed and reported to the Treasury Department. It allowed physicians to prescribe, dispense, or administer narcotics to their patients for "legitimate medical purposes." For a variety of reasons, some obscured by the passage of time, the interpretation of the act led to enforcement that prohibited all uses of drugs and Treasury Department officials began prosecuting physicians who prescribed drugs. Upon a legal challenge, the Supreme Court upheld the absolute prohibition and drug prescriptions of narcotics were ruled illegal, even if they were being prescribed as part of withdrawal treatment (Inciardi 2002).

In the 1930s, federal attention shifted away from cocaine and heroin to marijuana, which was used by fringe groups and minorities. There seemed to be a clear racial tone in the campaign against marijuana. Evidence of this, for instance, is a *New York Times* article from 1927 that warned against the "devil weed" used by "blacks and wetbacks" (cited in Inciardi 2002, 32). Amid a spate of lurid news stories and warnings regarding how marijuana could make users go insane, various states passed legislation criminalizing marijuana use and possession. Harry Anslinger, appointed commissioner of the Treasury Department's Bureau of Narcotics in 1930, took up the campaign with a vengeance. Whether he truly believed that marijuana destroyed brains and was a huge threat to American youth, or whether he was an empire-building bureaucrat, his leadership led to pressure on Congress to pass the Marijuana Tax Act of 1937, which placed marijuana on the same list as heroin and cocaine and defined it as a controlled substance.

In the 1940s, the use of narcotic drugs was reduced substantially, but it was not because of the legislation prohibiting and criminalizing its use. World War II effectively shut down the trafficking routes from Southeast Asia and thus users lost their supply. Throughout the war, the number of users remained low, although morphine addiction as a result of battle injuries was recognized as a problem for American veterans. However, within a few years after the close of the war, trafficking routes had been reestablished and drugs were once again available in U.S. cities. Still, the problem was not perceived as pervasive. Hollywood offered a few movies illustrating the evils of narcotics addiction, including *To the Ends of the Earth* (1948), *The Man With the Golden Arm* (1955), and *The Pusher* (1959). Most explanations of drug use were psychological, in that users and addicts were seen as having weak ego functioning or other individual traits that caused their addiction.

In the 1950s, drug penalties continued to be severe, but drug use was, for the most part, confined to small fringe groups. Federal penalties for marijuana ranged from two to 20 years, depending on whether it was a first, second, or third offense. Then in the 1960s, white middle-class kids began using marijuana in greater numbers and many were convicted and sentenced under these laws. Suddenly public views changed—almost every state reduced criminal penalties between 1969 and 1972. For instance, by 1973 simple possession was a misdemeanor in all but eight states. Some states decriminalized small amounts completely (Cole 1999, 153).

Of course, the pendulum swung again, largely through the efforts of the federal government and Richard Nixon's White House, assisted by William Rehnquist, who was at the time a young White House lawyer. Efforts to expand police powers to no-knock searches and preventive detention were undertaken. In 1970, the Comprehensive Drug Abuse Prevention and Control Act was passed. It provided $189 million for various forms of treatment programs and $220 million for enforcement. The Bureau of Narcotics and Dangerous Drugs (later known as the Drug Enforcement Agency) hired 300 new agents. The Law Enforcement Assistance Administration received $3.55 billion to be distributed to local and state law enforcement (Parenti 1999, 28).

By 1976, the White House, under Gerald Ford, was taking a less rabid stance. The federal drug strategy emphasized addressing causes of addiction, such as poverty and hopelessness, and even called for the "serious" study of decriminalizing marijuana. Jimmy Carter continued the tolerant trend, and during his tenure 12 states decriminalized marijuana (Parenti 1999, 28). In fact, from 1976 to 1992, marijuana could be legally prescribed to a small number of patients for research and treatment of impending blindness and reduction of pain in cancer and AIDS patients (Bianculli 1997, 173).

'Just Say No'

The pendulum swung again when Ronald Reagan took office. Reagan's White House took an aggressive stance on drugs that went far beyond Nancy Reagan's much maligned "just say no" campaign. The Comprehensive Crime Control Act was passed in 1984. Part of this legislation was the Sentencing Reform Act, which abolished federal parole and created a Sentencing Commission to set guidelines for federal crimes. This act also allowed federal preventive detention and expanded the possibilities of asset forfeiture. After 1984, state and local police could have drug cases tried in federal courts and still keep as much as 90 percent of the drug-related property. These forfeitures could take place in civil courts, with lower burdens of proof (Parenti 1999, 51).

The expanded use of asset forfeiture in drug cases is troublesome, and critics argue that it has been the incentive for police to target individuals more for what they have than for what they've done. It is estimated that between 1984 and 1999, as much as $5 billion has been taken from private individuals in forfeiture proceedings. Although some property has been taken from big-time drug dealers, much of it has been in the form of cars and houses of middle-class individuals who have had the misfortune to be related to a drug user. For instance, Kevin Perry and his wife in Ossipee, New Hampshire, pled guilty to a misdemeanor charge of possession of four marijuana plants. The United States seized their $22,000 mobile home (Parenti 1999, 53). In fact, some descriptions of government plea bargaining, in which both sides are bargaining, at least partially, over how much money the defendant is going to forfeit to the government, seem perilously close to a government in pursuit of money rather than justice (Parenti 1999, 53).

Reagan's most lasting legacy, however, has been his appointments to the Supreme Court. Legal analysts point to the virtual about-face in the approach taken to constitutional questions, compared with the prior Court's reasoning. In fact, Fourth Amendment law is composed almost entirely of drug cases; and decisions by the Court have clearly expressed the dogma that in the war on drugs, the balancing test almost always weighs in the government's favor.

It seems that 1986 was a watershed year in the war on drugs. There was what can only be described as a media frenzy in pursuit of drug stories; for instance, the *New York Times* increased its coverage from 43 drug stories in the last half of 1985 to 220 in the last half of 1986. Len Bias, a Boston Celtics basketball star, died from a cocaine overdose. The "crack epidemic" and its related epidemics of abandoned "crack babies" in public hospitals, drug wars between dealers, and related crime gripped the nation. The public believed we were in the middle of a "plague," "epidemic," or, more appropriately, a "war." What was needed was an all-out defensive assault, and in 1986 Congress passed the Anti-Drug Abuse Act. This act imposed 29 new mandatory minimum sentences. One was the mandatory sentence of five years in prison for five grams of crack and the same sentence for 500 grams of powder cocaine. This disparity, because of the fact that it is mostly minorities who use crack and mostly whites who use powder cocaine, has been bitterly opposed by critics ever since. Even the Sentencing Commission itself has recommended to Congress that the sentences be equalized. However, no legislator as yet has been willing to risk his or her political career championing African-American drug offenders, and the disparity stands (Parenti 1999; Fields 2001). "Liberal states" that had resisted the drug war's monolithic approach to all drugs finally succumbed to federal pressure to take a harsher stance. Oregon recriminalized small amounts of marijuana in 1986, followed by Alaska in 1990 (Inciardi 2002, 58).

More resources were needed for the war, and so Congress also appropriated $124.5 million for the Bureau of Prisons, $60 million for the DEA, and $230 million each year for three years for state and local enforcement efforts (Parenti 1999, 58). States followed the federal government in passing their own mandatory minimum laws, and incarceration rates, which had already been rising as a result of other "get-tough" legislation, rose even higher. Federal funding for the drug war rose from $1.5 billion in 1981 to $6.6 billion in 1989. It continued its astronomical rise to $17 billion in 1999 (Mauer, Chesny-Lind, and Clear 2001, 6). In 2003, it is estimated to be over $19 billion, but the federal government has revised the method of calculating the cost, eliminating a major portion of the cost of prosecuting and incarcerating federal drug offenders, so that the reported figure of $11 billion appears to be a decrease from prior years (Common Sense . . . 2003).

The 1988 presidential campaign was a classic case of how politics utilizes the "race and crime card." President Bush was able to portray Michael Dukakis as an ineffectual liberal who would put all "good people" at risk by the infamous "Willie Horton" advertisement. Someone in the Massachusetts work furlough program made the mistake of furloughing Horton. Upon release, he raped a white woman. The facts of the Horton case destroyed any hope Dukakis had of winning the election, despite the fact that hundreds of inmates had been furloughed without risk to the public and that Dukakis had virtually nothing to do with the decision anyway. George Bush came into office on a wave of anticrime sentiment and the result was the Anti-Drug Abuse Act of 1988. This act created a federal death penalty for participation in "continuing criminal enterprises" or any drug-related felony that is related to the killing of another. The bill also created a "drug czar" position to coordinate the "antidrug" policy of the White House. Over $2 million was given to the Department of Defense to train police and $3.5 million to equip police with military gear. Over $1 billion was given to state and local law enforcement. Millions went to the DEA, FBI, U.S. marshals, customs, and federal prosecutors. War is expensive, so forfeiture laws were expanded in order for government to recoup some of its money (Parenti 1999, 61).

The 1988 bill was so successful that the Bush White House followed it up with the 1989 bill. Media hype was at a fever pitch, and there was a symbiotic relationship between politicians who needed the publicity and media competitors who needed the story. The cases of manufactured "news" reached ridiculous proportions at times, including the notorious drug buy across the street from the White House. Played up by "outraged" politicians, it was the ammunition needed to pass the new drug bill. Later, to the embarrassment of the DEA, it was revealed that the evil dealer who brought the war to the very steps of the White House was a 17-year-old high school kid who was enticed to the site by DEA agents and had to be given explicit instructions and a great deal of coaxing before they could get him there to be arrested in the glare of television cameras (Parenti 1999, 62).

Other misguided media events took place as well, such as a drug bust televised live by a local southern news crew who had been promised the drama of a big cache of drugs and the arrest of a big-time drug dealer. Instead, television viewers were entertained by the sight of a beefy sheriff (who probably hadn't participated in a raid in years) and his dozen officers breaking in on a very confused housepainter and his girlfriend. No drugs, no arrests, no glory. The ignominy of defeat didn't stop more "live" busts, not to mention a spate of "reality" television shows that put television crews in police cars. What was not found in the media coverage, however, was any detailed analysis of the drug problem or recognition that it was as much, if not more, a problem of how to stop our kids, neighbors, and coworkers from buying and using drugs as it was how to stop the drug dealers from smuggling and selling them. Television, especially, seems to require "bad guys" and "good guys." The line between cop shows and the news was irretrievably blurred, if not altogether lost.

Other non-televised raids based on misinformation resulted in more serious consequences than red faces. The DEA, FBI, and local officers have participated in dozens of raids over the years in which innocent homeowners were dragged from their beds amidst obscenity-laced threats, held at gunpoint, and even in some cases injured or killed because of a wrong address and/or bad information from an informant (1971).

Between 1980 and 1987, federal drug convictions jumped by 161 percent and the number of drug offenders sent to prison rose by 177 percent (Parenti 1999, 63). The war was taking prisoners. Between 1980 and 1990, California's inmate population jumped from 22,000 to 97,309. By the end of the 1980s the drug war was in full swing and the "other side" began fighting back. Los Angeles exploded in a race riot, spurred by the acquittal of the police officers who had assaulted Rodney King. Certainly many of the rioters were thugs looking for an opportunity to steal, rob, and plunder; however, there was also a groundswell of disgust and despair over the seemingly racist justice system.

The War Continues

As a Democrat, President Bill Clinton was perceived by some to be a new diplomat in this war who would soften the stance and put treatment ahead of interdiction and enforcement. Instead, he pledged to put 100,000 more police officers on the street and signed the 1994 crime bill that provided for 16 more federal death penalty crimes and overhauled the federal appeals process, making it harder for defendants to appeal capital cases. The bill also provided for $7.9 billion in grants for states to build prisons, directed the Sentencing Commission to eliminate parole for those who sold drugs near schools (it was of little account that these dealers were often close to being children themselves), created a three strikes provision, and paved the way for waiver provisions that would allow juveniles as young as 13 to be tried in adult courts. As mentioned in Chapter 1, the law that prohibits drug offenders from living in public housing has forced families to choose between eviction and welcoming back relatives who have served their prison terms.

Further, the Violent Crime Control Act required "truth in sentencing" of states. If states wanted federal money, they had to limit the amount of "good time" an inmate could receive (Rich 2002). Again, the war required resources and billions were allocated (Parenti 1999, 65).

Clinton refused to support the Sentencing Commission's recommendation to equalize the penalties for powder cocaine and crack. The incarceration rate expanded tremendously, partially due to federal incentives to build prisons. Latter-day analysts now opine that if President Clinton had taken a scintilla of leadership in reducing and reversing the incredible trend of incarceration, especially of minority men, the Democrats would not have lost the election to George W. Bush. His post-presidential office in Harlem is seen by some as a cruel joke and blatant hypocrisy to those whose future he abandoned (Robinson 2000).

As governor, George W. Bush slashed treatment budgets in the state of Texas and tightened sentencing laws. As president, he has mandated enforcing a federal law that denies financial aid and loans for college to those convicted of drug crimes. The ban is permanent for repeat offenders. Some question the logic of denying student loans to drug offenders when murderers or bank robbers may obtain them, but the federal law is being enforced (Schemo 2001).

Our latest battles in the drug war are fought in the courts. There seems to be no weakening of the federal governmental stance that drug users are enemies to be vanquished. After all the billions spent and the years wasted in prison, there is little evidence that the war has resulted in fewer users or less drugs (United States Substance Abuse and Mental Health Services Administration 2001). Some argue that cocaine and heroin are cheaper and more pure than ever before (Mallaby 2001).

Victims of War

In every war there are victims. The official stance is that the victims of the drug war are the crime victims who have been murdered, robbed, and burglarized by drug addicts and the parents and family members of those who have succumbed to addiction. And that's true. But there are also other victims—victims of injustice, victims of neglect, and also victims of personal weakness and personality. For the last group, the criminal justice system bears little responsibility; however, for the first two groups, it can be argued that the system's response has been ineffective and even unjust. The accompanying box describes a few of the other victims of the drug war.

Box 2.1 Victims of the Drug War

Shellie Langmade was convicted of conspiracy to manufacture methamphetamine. Because of two previous misdemeanors for passing bad checks totaling $83.50, her sentence under federal sentencing guidelines was 10 years. The judge refused to impose it and in a bitter retort called the sentencing guideline "patently unjust" and removed himself from the case. (Fields 2001)

- *Vanessa Wade* was 19 when she agreed to help her boyfriend sell 22 grams of cocaine. Even though she had no prior record, she was sentenced to 23 years for conspiracy to distribute and possession with intent to distribute. (reported in King and Mauer 2002b, 5)

Kevin Sherbondy was raised in an upper-middle-class home by his grandparents. He used cocaine, as did most of the kids in his social group, and was arrested for cocaine possession in 1982. That same year he received several other convictions, all involving the same group of acquaintances, a related set of incidents, and within a nine-month period. After serving a short prison sentence, he stopped his drug use, severed ties with his drug-using friends, and started college. In 1986, he was holding down two jobs and going to school full-time while on probation for one of the charges that was linked to the peer group he no longer associated with. When an irate girlfriend reported to his probation officer that he had a firearm (an antique collector's item with the firing pin jammed), the officer waited five days to search, until November 17, when a new federal career criminal law took effect. Then, along with ATF officers, the probation officer searched his house, found the vintage revolver, and arrested him on a federal firearms charge. Prosecuted under the career criminal statute, the 23-year-old received a 15-year prison sentence with no parole. (reported in Martin and Sussman 1993, 85–87).

- *Kemba Smith* and *Dorothy Gaines* were both imprisoned on federal drug conspiracy charges. Both were involved with drug dealer boyfriends but did not sell drugs themselves. Both had small children. They were both convicted solely on the basis of witnesses, who had sentences reduced in exchange for testimony. Smith received 24 years, Gaines received 20 years. Both spent more than six years in prison before President Clinton granted them executive clemency. (Bernstein 2001)

These stories are only a few examples of the hundreds of thousands of individuals who did not murder, rape, or rob but who are serving very long prison sentences. Would the public view these individuals as criminals who deserve long terms of imprisonment, or feel that their money is well spent by keeping them behind bars?

Patterns of Drug Use

Trying to get a handle on drug use patterns is like buying a car. You know that you don't have all the facts, you don't fully trust the numbers given to you, and it is impossible to make a reasoned decision without knowing what you don't know. Federal drug use figures are flawed because they are missing large portions of the population. The high school senior survey does not include those who have already dropped out. The national household sample does not include those who refuse to participate or can't because they have no stable household. Further, whether people honestly admit their drug use is problematic. On the other side, there are huge political stakes involved in such numbers. "Ever used" figures are the most common, but the number who have ever used a drug is obviously not the same number as those who use drugs weekly or frequently enough to affect their lives.

Austin and Irwin (2001, p. 165) use reports from the Office of National Drug Control Policy to show that, overall, drug use has not changed much over the last 20 years or so, and the change has been downward in many drug categories. According to these authors, in 1978, about 31 percent of those surveyed reported using any drug ever; 14 percent reported use within the last 30 days. In 1995, about 34 percent reported ever using, with only 6 percent using within the last 30 days.

By most accounts, marijuana use reached an all-time high in 1979, with about 60 percent of seniors reporting at least one use incident. About 10 percent reported daily use. Throughout the

1980s, however, marijuana use declined. In 1992, only about 33 percent of seniors reported ever having used marijuana and only about 2 percent reported daily use. However, use figures started inching up again, and by 1999 about 50 percent of seniors reported ever using and about 8 percent reported daily use (cited from information from the National Household Survey on Drug Abuse, 1998, in Inciardi 2002, 295). In the 2000 high school senior study, 53 percent of seniors reported ever using marijuana, but only 6 percent reported using marijuana on a daily basis (Monitoring the Future, 2002).

Heroin figures have always been quite low—only about 1 percent of survey respondents reported even one-time use of heroin in a national household sample, whereas daily use was reported by only 0.1 percent. About 11 percent of the respondents reported use of cocaine, but only about 2 percent reported using it within the past month. About 8 percent reported any use of LSD. Only a little over 10 percent of survey respondents reported using any illicit drug within the past year, although 64 percent reported using alcohol and about a third reported smoking cigarettes (cited from information from the National Household Survey on Drug Abuse 1998, in Inciardi 2002, 295). The most recent figures available, from the 2001 National Household Survey, show slight increases in most ever-used categories, although the number of current users remains substantially below the peak use years of the late 1970s (United States Substance Abuse and Mental Health Services Administration 2002).

Whereas heroin has been a longtime but minor player in the drug world, cocaine has a more recent history. Some identify the growth of cocaine use with the building of a highway into the Uallaga River Valley in Peru. Most of the world's coca cultivation is limited to a mountainous region of Colombia, Peru, Ecuador, Brazil, and Bolivia. The coca leaf had been used by natives for centuries as a natural sedative against hunger and fatigue. Before the highway was built in the early 1970s, the product had to be taken out by mules—a long and arduous journey that prohibited much worldwide distribution. The transnational road allowed coca leaves and manufactured cocaine to be transported easily to the border and, very quickly, production increased and drug overlords marketed their product worldwide. It is estimated, for instance, that the total cocaine production of Colombia went from 30,000 metric tons in 1991 to 521,400 in 1999 (cited in Inciardi 2002, 132).

Processing the coca leaves involves crushing the leaves, soaking and shaking them in alcohol mixed with benzol, draining that mixture and adding sulfuric acid, then adding sodium carbonate. When washed with kerosene and chilled, this creates a coca paste that is 90 times more potent that the coca leaf. Further processing is involved before the cocaine hits the streets, involving additional baths of kerosene and alcohol, filtering and drying, sulfuric acid, and the addition of ammonium hydroxide and hydrochloric acid. Cocaine may be cut with a variety of substances to reduce its potency and increase its yield and profit. Crack is made by mixing cocaine hydrochloride with an expander, baking soda, and water; cooking it into a hard gel; and breaking it up into rocklike crystals that can then be smoked (Inciardi 2002). Although the crack epidemic of the mid-1980s was widely reported, the substance had been around since the early 1970s. The big advantage of crack is that it is inexpensive. Users can buy "rocks" for as little as five dollars. Whereas powder cocaine is associated with Hollywood, crack is associated with street junkies and crack houses. It is not hard to figure out which group is more likely to end up in prison.

Other drugs come and go in popularity—quaaludes, ecstasy, ketamine, Ritalin, rohypnol, and "designer drugs" have all been the subject of news reports that allege waves or use increases of such drugs. Whether there are increased numbers of users, whether it is a media construct, or whether media attention spurs greater use is impossible to know.

Drug Use and Crime

Does drug use cause crime? The popular belief is that a large majority of crime is linked to drug use. This premise, however, is not easy to prove. From a variety of studies, it appears that although drug use may not cause an individual to begin a life of crime, those who engage in crime do so more frequently while using drugs and their criminality decreases or is eliminated altogether when they stop using drugs. These findings obviously lend support to those who plead for more treatment dollars (Inciardi 2002, 188).

Terry (2003) offers a phenomenological study of long-term drug users who have nevertheless stayed clean for a substantial period of time. He chronicles the link between drug use and different types of crime as well as the factors involved in the decision to attempt reform. Often it was when the individual realized his drug lifestyle was eventually going to kill him.

Drug offenders report high levels of drug use. For instance, two-thirds of state drug offenders in prison reported using drugs the month before their arrest and 41 percent were under the influence at the time of their offense. About 28 percent admitted they committed the offense to get money to buy drugs (King and Mauer 2002a, 9). However, it would be a mistake to imagine that the drug abusers in prison are necessarily dangerous. In a study of drug offenders in prison, it was found that 58 percent of incarcerated drug offenders have no history of violence or even a high level of drug sales. Almost a third were convicted of simple possession. Further, three-quarters had been convicted only of drug and/or nonviolent offenses (King and Mauer 2002a, 2).

This same study found that only about a third of inmates who were sentenced for drug crimes have attended any treatment. Probationers were even less likely to have had access to treatment programs; only about 20 percent reported that they had been through treatment (King and Mauer 2002a, 9). Obviously, not all offenders who are sentenced for drug crimes are addicts or even users; however, as noted above, a large percentage of drug offenders do need treatment as do many offenders sentenced for other crimes.

Minorities and Women

One fact that is missing in the national debate on drugs is that the percentage of minorities found in criminal justice populations is not reflective of their percentage of user populations. About 13 percent of drug users are African-American, about the same number as their population (Schemo 2001), yet looking at courtrooms and prisons, one would reach the conclusion that drugs are a problem only in African-American neighborhoods. In fact, white kids use drugs, sell drugs, and commit crimes to support their drug habits, but they are much more likely to end up in drug treatment programs than minority youth (Human Rights Watch 2000).

Regardless of the fact that kids of all racial or ethnic groups use drugs, it is mostly minority youth who end up in prison because of it. The perception that drugs are a problem only in minority communities is so pervasive that the fact that over 60 percent of all narcotics convictions are of African-Americans barely raises an eyebrow. More telling, 84 percent of crack defendants in 2000 were African-American (Fields 2001, 3). Can anyone seriously believe that African-Americans, who make up only 12 percent of the population, constitute 60 percent of the drug-using/dealing public (Parenti 1999, 57)? In fact, according to some studies, African-Americans make up about 13 percent of all monthly drug users but 35 percent of all drug arrests, 55 percent of all drug convictions, and 74 percent of all drug prisoners (Parenti 1999, 239). Four of every five drug prisoners are African-American (56 percent) or Hispanic (23 percent) (King and Mauer 2002b, 2).

Other studies point out gross disparities in drug enforcement and sentencing patterns in specific states. In the period from 1996 to 2001, 80 percent of all Maryland's drug offenders were African-American. Remember, this compares with use figures of about 13 percent (reported in King and Mauer 2002b, 11). A newspaper analysis found that 62 percent of those convicted for less than 1 gram of drugs in Harris County (Houston, Texas) were African-American, while only 37 percent were white; these percentages do not reflect the population of the city (Graves 2002).

Racial profiling, where police officers stop those who fit a drug dealer "profile," has been condemned and curtailed as racist. One Florida study videotaped officers stopping 1,000 motorists on traffic violations—fully 85 percent of those stopped were African-Americans. In another study of stops in Volusia County, Florida, between 1989 and 1992, it was reported that of those stopped, 85 percent were African-American. Although $8 million was confiscated using civil forfeiture laws, 75 percent of the stops did not result in any charges (Parenti 1999, 54).

Women. There is clear evidence to indicate women are more heavily affected by federal and state drug sentencing that reduces judicial discretion and imposes mandatory sanctions on users as well as distributors. In 1983, only about 11 percent of female prisoners were in prison for drug offenses; by 1998 that number had tripled to 34 percent. In federal prisons, drug offenses account for 72 percent of female offenders (cited in Pollock 2001, 54).

Further, some evidence indicates that female prisoners may have higher use rates of drugs than male prisoners, were more likely to have been under the influence of drugs at time of arrest, were more likely to have committed an offense to get money for drugs, and had a higher correlation between drug use and serious forms of criminality, such as robbery (Snell 1994). It should be noted that some women are in prison for being drug couriers. These women, often from other countries, don't necessarily have a drug problem but have been enticed or coerced into smuggling drugs. They receive very long prison sentences, even if it is their first offense (Raeder 1993).

Despite evidence that drugs may play an even more salient role in female offenders' lives than in men's, the number of drug treatment beds in prison does not meet the need. Women seem to appreciate and involve themselves fairly enthusiastically when such programs are available. We will discuss these issues more carefully in Chapter 8.

The Impact on Prisons

Only about 7 percent of all new court commitments to prison were for drug offenses in 1980, but by 1992, almost 31 percent of all new prison commitments were for drug offenses (Gilliard and Beck 1994, 7). In California, the total number of inmates quadrupled over 12 years, but the number of offenders incarcerated for drug offenses increased fifteen-fold. In 1998, 59 percent of all federal prisoners, 21 percent of all state prisoners, and 26 percent of all jail inmates were there for drug offenses (Zimring and Hawkins 1995, 162).

Assuming, then, that an average of one-third of all prisoners (both federal and state) are there for drugs, if we estimated that at least a good portion have committed no violent offense or have an extensive criminal history apart from drug use, we might reduce the third to a quarter of the total prison population; since there are about 2 million incarcerated, that translates into a half million people who could be released from federal and state prisons and jails today, if we changed our policies regarding drug offenders. At a cost of even $20,000 a year to incarcerate them (and it's much higher in the federal system and in some states), we could realize a cost savings of roughly $10 billion—each year! Given current economic realities, these numbers demand a reanalysis of this country's policies toward low-level dealers and users.

Drugs in Prison

Prisoners have always sought mind-altering substances. "Pruno," a substance more valued for its intoxication qualities than its taste or robust "bouquet," has been and continues to be made in prison from smuggled fruit and some form of yeast (usually bread). As drug offenders constituted greater and greater numbers of prisoner populations, drug abuse in prison soared. Drugs are smuggled in by visitors, staff, and correctional officers. There is the temptation of large amounts of money or the coercion of threats to make guards "pack." Inmates who were not affiliated with drugs on the outside and, therefore, are under less scrutiny by officials, are coerced to have their visitors bring them drugs. The drugs are then taken and sold on the prison black market.

Drugs cause management problems in a number of ways. Those prisoners who get high on some substances become belligerent or irrationally violent (actually, alcohol is more likely to make an individual violent than other illicit substances). Much more common, however, is the violence that exists in the drug trade itself. Competitors fight or kill each other; those who owe drug dealers money either are assaulted or hurt their creditors first. Drug stashes are stolen. Snitches are killed. Ironically, sometimes a prisoner who didn't use drugs on the outside begins drug use in prison or changes to a "harder" drug because it is available. Then the inmate is released with a drug addiction that virtually ensures criminal activity be undertaken to service his or her habit.

Mandatory, random drug testing has been helpful in identifying drug users. Some prisons employ a "patch" system for drug detection that is supposed to be more effective than urinalysis. In one state study, Pennsylvania reported great success in reducing inmate drug use through a combination of testing, treatment, and enforcement. Whereas 8 percent of inmates had at least one drug in their system in 1996, by 1998, after implementation of the aggressive program, only 1.8 percent of inmates tested positive for drugs. There have also been 41 percent fewer drug finds, 57 percent fewer assaults on staff, 70 percent fewer inmate-on-inmate assaults, and 35 percent fewer weapons found (Feucht and Keyser 1999).

Treatment Versus Prison

One report estimates that drug addiction costs state governments $81 billion in any given year. Most of the money goes to welfare, law enforcement, corrections and the courts, health care, and so on. Only a small fraction, $3.4 billion, is spent on prevention or treatment (Nagy 2001). The report, conducted by the National Center on Addiction and Substance Abuse at Columbia University, noted state spending related to drug use and abuse in several areas. For instance, 77 percent of criminal justice system expenditures were related to drug abuse; 10 percent of education spending; 25 percent of health costs; 32 percent of child and family assistance; 31 percent of mental health; and 26 percent of public safety (C.A.S.A. 2001). The comparison between what states spend "cleaning up after" drug abuse versus treatment and prevention is astounding. For instance, North Dakota and Colorado spend about six cents for treatment for every $100 spent on responding to drug abuse. Given the social and real economic costs to society of drug abuse, it is obvious that treatment should be a priority. Yet, as with alcoholism, the public seems torn between treatment and punishment (C.A.S.A. 2001).

About 62 percent of prisoners report regular drug use in the year prior to prison (Rouse 1991, 32), and at least one report estimated that 80 percent of prisoners have serious drug or alcohol abuse problems regardless of their crime of conviction (Inciardi 1999, 312). One 1997 report stated, however, that only 25 percent of inmates had been in a drug treatment program (Mumola 1999).

It is a puzzle, then, why, despite everyone's acceptance of the fact that drugs are a strong element in the criminal choices individuals make, drug treatment beds seem to be declining rather than increasing. Austin and Irwin (2001, 162) and Lock, Timberlake, and Rasinki (2002, 380) report that while there were 158,000 drug treatment slots in 1984 and 201,000 in 1993, there were only 99,000 in 1998. Other treatment programs are also in decline. This seems to be a wildly misguided policy, since huge numbers of offenders are nearing release.

Drug treatment intervention has always been politicized; or, rather, there are competing approaches taken regarding the causation of drug addiction/dependency. For some, addiction is seen as a disease, perhaps inherited, certainly unintentional, with those who suffer from it needing both medical and behavioral intervention in order to live a drug-free life. Like the disease model of alcoholism, this approach holds that no one is cured, they are just "in remission." On the other end of the spectrum are those who see drug addiction/abuse solely as a reflection of a weak will. Those who abuse chemical substances could stop if they wanted to; they just don't want to. In the middle are a range of positions and approaches. For instance, some propose a psychological predisposition to chemical addiction: a poor self-image, a dependent personality, or an addictive personality have all been offered as "explaining" addiction. Others see drug addiction/abuse as more of a biological predisposition; because of brain chemistry, some individuals simply cannot use alcohol or drugs to any great extent without becoming physically and/or psychologically addicted to them. They may not become addicted, but they are more likely to, given certain lifestyles. They could stop, but it is harder for them than for someone who is not predisposed. The analogy might be of someone whose body type is predisposed to create fat cells. They may escape obesity, but it is harder for them to do so than for someone who is genetically predisposed to be thin.

Given these different approaches, it is no wonder that drug treatment programs have a wide range of approaches also. Modalities include drug education, "shock" group therapy, behavioral modification, and "talking" therapy, among others. Methadone and Antabuse are not therapies per se, but they help control use.

Therapeutic communities are probably the most common treatment approach. These self-contained communities allow treatment staff to isolate, to some extent, participants from negative influences present in the general population and also to reduce the temptation and opportunity for acquiring drugs. Therapeutic communities typically employ some type of graduated structure whereby new participants must earn privileges by good behavior. They have daily group meetings during which participants' behaviors in the community are utilized in the treatment process, which typically involves improving personal responsibility and increasing self-esteem. Treatment is eclectic, utilizing a variety of methods and techniques.

It may be that we are beginning to see a shift in national policies and treatment will be considered as an alternative to punishment.

Drug courts have been around for about a decade now. They either give the offender the choice or mandate that he or she enter treatment programs instead of receiving punitive incarceration. Evaluations report recidivism reduction rates of 5 to 28 percent for drug court participants (King and Mauer 2002a). There were at least 400 of these special courts in 2000 (Greene and Schiraldi 2002, 17). Findings to date indicate that, along with cost savings, there is less chance of recidivism when the offender successfully completes a drug program (Greene and Schiraldi 2002, 17).

It seems that while few disagree with the proposition that treatment is more effective than punishment in combating drug addiction, there is no political will to fund treatment over interdiction and punishment efforts. Since the early 1980s, the percentage of federal dollars spent on drug treatment efforts as part of the total budget of the war on drugs has decreased from 31 percent to 18 percent. A Rand study recently reported that for heavy users of cocaine, treatment costs one-seventh as much as the traditional punitive approach (Rydell, Caulkins, and Everingham 1996).

> The answer is not imprisonment and legal attack. The answer lies in sentencing reform, treatment, harm reduction and education. . . . The days of the "Drug War" waged against our people should come to an end. (Governor Gary Johnson of New Mexico, cited in Nagy 2001, 2)

Evaluating Drug Treatment

Programs that combine cognitive-behavioral components and life skill training (vocational training or education) seem to be the most successful treatment modalities (Sung 2001). Yet others strike a more cautionary note. Austin and Irwin (2001), for instance, conclude that there are many issues to consider before committing appreciably more money to drug programs. They question the conclusion that drug treatment would reduce much crime and point out that there are troublesome issues in the delivery of drug treatment. Since most of the model drug treatment programs are based on the therapeutic community (TC) model, they point out that TC programs can, by their nature, provide only a small number of treatment slots. Further, such programs have high in-program failure rates; sometimes as many as 60 percent drop out. Evaluations have not used randomized experimental designs and, when done properly, do not show much difference between those who have been through a treatment program and controls (Austin and Irwin 2001, 176–179). Although they are not condemning drug treatment programs generally, the authors' point seems to be that drug treatment is not a panacea to recidivism either and that equal or greater efforts should be placed on improving service delivery of education, employment training, and job placement.

Terry (2003) discusses drug treatment and addicts who have managed to remain sober for many years. What is important, according to Terry, is a new self-concept that includes a healthy dose of self-respect. This is an important point because our current approach to drug offenders is designed to make them feel like bad people and criminals. We may, in fact, be providing exactly the opposite setting of one that might help users and addicts reclaim their lives.

> Something that surfaced repeatedly among the men who had been clean and sober for several years was their realization that they were not bad people. (Terry 2003, 111)

Declining Public Support for the War

Even some staunch conservatives have come around to the view that our current policies of interdiction and punishment make no sense. Some have always opposed them. The leading voices from the resistance have been the Drug Policy Foundation (created in 1987) and the Lindesmith Center (started in 1994 by Alfred Lindesmith). These merged in 2000 and are now known as the Drug Policy Alliance. The goals and objectives of this organization are to move the country toward a "harm reduction" policy, which would include decriminalization of some drugs to some degree, reducing penalties, and emphasizing treatment. Billionaire George Soros has supported decriminalization efforts in Arizona and a number of other states. He funds the Open Society Institute, whose mission is to promote democracy and social programs and alleviate poverty. "Harm reduction"—the policy whereby drugs are viewed as a problem, but treatment and education are viewed as more efficacious than punishment—is promoted by the Open Society and other similar organizations.

In fact, increasing numbers of Americans believe that the nation's war on drugs has been ill conceived and wasteful of public dollars. Although almost everyone agrees that drugs are a problem (81 percent in a recent poll), the public may not believe that prison is the only solution to the problem (Lock, Timberlake, and Rasinki 2002, 381). In a recent poll, 77 percent of respondents agreed with the statement "Many people in prison today are nonviolent drug addicts who need drug treatment, not a prison sentence" (Greene and Schiraldi 2002, 6). Further, there are declining numbers of Americans who believe that criminal justice policies are the most effective responses to drug use, decreasing from 41 percent of respondents in 1990 to 31 percent in 1995 (Lock, Timberlake, and Rasinki 2002, 384). In a more recent survey, while 83 percent supported maintaining funding for treatment efforts, and 92 percent supported maintaining funding for prevention efforts, a smaller number (61 percent) supported maintaining levels of funding for criminal justice responses (Lock, Timberlake, and Rasinki 2002, 391). Still another survey found that 76 percent of respondents favored mandatory drug treatment rather than prison for those convicted of possession and 71 percent favored mandatory treatment and community service for those convicted of sales of small amounts (reported in King and Mauer 2002b, 1).

After Arizona passed the Drug Medicalization, Prevention and Control Act in 1998, diverting nonviolent drug offenders into treatment, the state realized a savings of more than $6 million a year (Greene and Schiraldi 2002, 8). California followed with Proposition 36, the Substance Abuse and Crime Prevention Act, in 2000. An analysis by the California Legislative Analysts Office estimates that even after paying for drug treatment, Californians can expect to see as much as $1.5 billion savings over five years in reduced prison costs (Greene and Schiraldi 2002, 9). A study by the Health Policy Tracking Service for the National Conference of State Legislatures reported that California could save $40 million annually (Theis 2002). In 2002, there were proposals in Florida, Michigan, and Ohio for similar diversion programs (Greene and Schiraldi 2002, 8).

California may ultimately find that Proposition 36 is more cost-effective than the more widely known three strikes law. Claremont University researchers found that crime rates for property and violent crime went down substantially in California after the passage of the three strikes law (45 percent and 36 percent, respectively), but that drug crimes showed almost no decline (only 4 percent). The study's authors did not compare California's crime decrease to other states without the three strikes law, so they cannot state with any assurance that it was the cause of the crime rate decrease; however, the study obviously does not support incarceration as an effective response to drug crimes either (Wilkie 2002).

The state of North Carolina has lowered its incarceration rate over the last decade by having a sentencing guideline system that favors treatment for first-time drug offenders. North Carolina has enjoyed the same declining crime rates as the rest of the country in spite of their tendency not to incarcerate drug offenders. Dollars saved have been used for education and other necessary expenditures (Greene and Schiraldi 2002, 19).

Texas is an interesting case because of the rise and fall and rise again of an emphasis on treatment. During Ann Richards' term as governor (1991–1994), legislation was passed that would have created 12,000 treatment beds in state prisons at a cost of $160 million. Either the facilities would have been located in existing prisons or new facilities would have been built, designed, and managed to provide treatment for drug offenders.

In 1994, George W. Bush won the gubernatorial race and, in short order, the plans for the 12,000 beds were scaled back considerably. Eventually only 5,300 treatment beds ever existed, but prison commitments went up. In 1997, Bush signed a sentencing bill that increased prison sentences for those convicted of selling or possessing less than a gram of cocaine.

It is hard to explain why treatment beds were cut when the Criminal Justice Policy Council, a state agency, reported several years ago that the recidivism rate for those who completed the treatment programs was 20 percent lower than for those who did not participate (Bryce 1999; also see Knight et al. 1997). A recent report from the Texas Criminal Justice Policy Council stated that prisoners who participated in the In Prison Therapeutic Community Program (IPTC) had a two-year recidivism rate of 16 percent for the 1997–1998 releasees, compared with a recidivism rate of 21 percent for releasees who did not participate in the program. The Substance Abuse Felony Punishment program (SAFP) is a short prison-based residential program for drug-offending probationers. The two-year release recidivism rate for those who finished the entire two-year program was only 7 percent. Unfortunately, only about 44 percent of offenders finished the program (Eisenberg 2001).

George Bush is now out of Texas and in the White House, and the pendulum has swung back to treatment—slightly. In the 2001 legislative session, Texas House Bill 1287 required that drug courts be established in counties with populations over 500,000 (King and Mauer 2002a, 7; Graves 2002).

On the federal level, the U.S. Sentencing Commission has recommended addressing the vast disparity between convictions for powder cocaine and crack cocaine. Despite being identical in chemical composition, powder cocaine earns a much lighter sentence. The fact that most offenders sentenced for crack are minority and most offenders sentenced for powder are white has raised a storm of protest that has been largely ignored by Congress (Fields 2001). Mandatory minimums for drug offenses are also being reevaluated by Congress, and even President Bush has signaled his concern regarding their impact on nonviolent drug offenders (Fields 2001).

But the "warmongers" have had their victories, too. Even though California passed a bill legalizing marijuana for medical purposes in 1996, the federal government chose to fight the law in court. In May 2001, the Supreme Court ruled that federal drug laws, in effect, usurp California's law to legalize marijuana use by seriously ill patients. Thus, the patients' groups and doctors who issued referrals for marijuana were targets of raids by the DEA. Most patients are AIDS sufferers who find that marijuana is about the only pain reliever that gives them relief. If prosecuted under federal laws, AIDS patients and their doctors will be sentenced under the guidelines that are responsible for incredibly long sentences for drug crimes (Martin 2001). Many advocate marijuana use for medical purposes, including its use to control vomiting, anxiety, and pain by cancer patients, to improve appetite and the loss of lean muscle mass in AIDS patients, to reduce muscle pain and spasticity for multiple sclerosis sufferers, to prevent epileptic fits, and to aid in the treatment of glaucoma (although this is controversial).

Nine states have enacted laws allowing marijuana for limited medical use in some circumstances—they are California, Alaska, Arizona, Colorado, Hawaii, Maine, Nevada, Oregon, and Washington (Leduff and Liptak 2002). All of these laws evidently are problematic, given the Supreme Court's opinion that states have no power to decide for themselves whether to allow medical use of marijuana. The House of Representatives had a bill to consider that would legalize marijuana for medical use, eliminating the conflict between the federal law and some state laws, but they did not act on the bill in the 2002 session and the bill does not have strong support (Leduff and Liptak 2002).

> We are not California wackos. . . . We are normal. This is not an attempt to embarrass the D.E.A. but rather a compassionate gathering in support of sick people who need their medicine. (Santa Cruz mayor willing to be arrested in defiance of federal prosecution of a local marijuana cooperative, Leduff and Liptak 2002)

President Bush's federal drug czar, John Walters, has advocated prison time instead of treatment for drug offenders. Advocates of diverting federal dollars to treatment were disheartened by his appointment and expect to see little redirection in the federal emphasis on punitiveness (Sanger 2001). In fact, treatment spending has seen only modest increases since 1981, rising from about one-half billion to four (cited from information from the Office of National Drug Control Policy in Inciardi 2002, 271). This amount is a tiny fraction of the total cost, and the percentage of funding allocated to treatment continues to decrease.

Conclusion

We are at a crossroads in this nation regarding our approach to drug use. We can continue to characterize the problem as a war, but to do so makes enemies of our sons, daughters, and neighbors. Although we have spent billions of dollars to eradicate drugs, the number of people using drugs and the amount of drugs on the streets have not changed much in 30 years. What has changed is the tripling and quadrupling of the number of people in prison. We can continue to spend money doing exactly what we have been doing, or we can divert what is spent on the interdiction of drugs, prosecution, and imprisonment to treatment and educational efforts. To do so would require a major shift in the public's conception of drugs and crime and political leadership. In the end, if it happens at all, it will probably happen because of economics, not common sense or compassion. The fact is, we simply can't afford to continue filling this nation's prisons with drug users.

Study Questions

1. What were the first drugs controlled and criminalized by the federal government?
2. What has been the effect of the drug war on the incarceration rate?
3. What has been the effect of increased numbers of drug users in the nation's prisons?
4. What percentage of the federal budget for drug interdiction and control has been spent on treatment?
5. What are the trends in drug use?

Chapter 3

The New Bastille

Prisons Today

Prisons are hellholes. They are nothing but human warehouses for society's misfits, outcasts, and transgressors. For the prisoners, the loss of freedom is devastating. Everything they have taken for granted is gone. They have no control over their lives, no choices. Others decide when and where they wake, eat, work, and sleep. Their lives are fastened to rules and regulations that discourage and disregard normal impulses. They accept the rules and adjust to them, just as they do to the overcrowded conditions, body odors, lack of privacy, standing in lines, and the like. They have no choice. (an inmate, Patrick, in Johnson and Toch 2000, 141)

Some prisons today look, smell, and sound like their predecessors of 100 or even 200 years ago. Other prisons are the ultimate in modern technology. Steel and cement, cameras and computers do what stone walls and guard towers used to do. There are even some prisons that look like some type of boarding school, except for the razor wire fences that surround them. Ask any prisoner, however, and he or she will probably say that a prison is a prison is a prison.

There are over 1,500 prisons in this country (Austin and Irwin 2001, 65). About 5 percent of them are private, and the rest are state or federal institutions. Most states have different custody level prisons, from minimum security to maximum security. Minimum-security institutions might be work camps, forestry camps, or urban work release centers. Maximum-security institutions are the epitome of the big house prisons, with high walls, razor wire, and guard towers. A few are considered "super-max," the most secure facilities in the world, where inmates spend the majority of their sentence completely alone in a way that is very similar to the Pennsylvania system described in the first chapter.

Guards on horseback still watch inmates toil in fields, harvesting rice, cotton and corn from the rich, flat Delta land. (describing Cummins Unit, Arkansas; Nelson 2002)

Some prisons today are over 100 years old, and visiting them is like returning to the past. Most are newer, having been built in the "boom" of prison construction in the last 15 years or so. The towering brick or stone structures of the 1800s with massive high walls and small cells arranged down long tiers are the exception today. Newly built prisons are modular, "cookie cutter" buildings constructed in the same way as self-storage buildings—an appropriate analogy, actually, since some argue that they are no better than human storage facilities. "High tech" has replaced high walls as security, with remote cameras and chain link and razor wire serving as perimeter security.

In other ways, however, some prison administrators believe in punishment the old-fashioned way. Chain gangs have made a comeback. Indiana, Washington, Alabama, and Arizona all have instituted chain gangs in the past several years. Prison work crews can be seen clearing trash from roadways under the supervision of a watchful guard. In Wisconsin, inmates on work crews wear 50,000-volt stun belts to prevent escape (Parenti 1999, 176).

Prisons may be prison farms or a high rise in a city. Although the movie version of prison usually includes cells, prisoners today are more often housed in dormitories. They are no doubt cheaper to build and maintain, but not safer. Further, the spread of contagious disease in dormitory settings is said to be twice that of cells (Cox, Paulus, and McCain 1984, 1154).

Upon entering one of these makeshift dorms, I am struck first by the noise level, including constant shouting, secu-

> rity officers barking orders or calling out inmates' names,
> and the flushing of the ten or twelve toilets that have
> been installed along one wall of the gymnasium. The in-
> mates report that the noise never dies down, and there is
> always someone hassling you. The lights are usually left
> on all night, presumably for security reasons, and inmates
> tell me that they have a hard time sleeping. The men bring
> food to their bunks, so there are roaches and mice. Tem-
> pers flare, fights erupt, victimization is rampant. (Kupers
> 1999, 48, describing a gym made into a dormitory)

Keve (1991) chronicles the history of the Federal Bureau of Prisons, beginning with the congressional act in 1891 that provided the legal authority to build Leavenworth, Atlanta, and MacNeil Island, the first federal penitentiaries. Today, the federal system has a system of penitentiaries, medium-level correctional facilities, and camps. Whereas the federal system has had the reputation of operating "country club" prisons, with white-collar offenders spending their time grooming golf courses, more recently, federal facilities have been filled with drug offenders. The growth in the size of the system has been phenomenal, prompting federal officials to rely increasingly on private vendors to house federal prisoners and detainees.

Private Prisons

On June 30, 2001, 31 states, the District of Columbia, and the Federal Bureau of Prisons (FBOP) held 94,948 prisoners in private prisons (a slight increase from the year before) (Beck, Karberg, and Harrison 2002, 4). In 2002, the number dropped to 86,626 (Harrison and Karberg 2003). Private prisons hold about 5 percent of all prison beds in the country (Parenti 1999, 218). Texas rivals the federal government in the number of beds it has contracted for with private vendors (17,746 in 43 prisons for Texas and 18,185 for the FBOP), but in 2002 the state substantially reduced its reliance on private vendors, and the number of prisoners in private prisons dropped to 10,764 (Beck, Karberg, and Harrison 2002, 4; Harrison and Karberg 2003, 6).

Privatization is certainly not a new concept in corrections. Some of the very earliest places of confinement were run by private individuals who contracted with the state to run the facility. In the South, lease labor systems were contractual arrangements between the state and landowners whereby landowners fed and clothed inmates and paid the state a certain amount of money in return for the prisoners' labor. Many states continue to contract with private groups to provide treatment, medical, or other services; and private-public partnerships in prison industries are gaining momentum. What is capturing the attention of some critics, however, is the increasing prevalence and lack of oversight of private corporations that contract with a state to build and/or run a correctional facility (usually a jail or a prison). When correctional corporations such as Corrections Corporation of America and Wackenhut have their stock traded on the New York Stock Exchange, some say it is time to reexamine the practice of prisons for profit.

Sorry to be late clueing you to this great new money-making opportunity, but there may still be time to get in on the seminar that will show you how to imprison people for fun and profit. . . . If you're looking for something really reliable, what better to invest in than human misbehavior? It has been a sure thing since Cain and Abel. (columnist Tom Teepen 1996)

Corrections Corporation of America (CCA) is the largest player in the private prison industry, holding a little more than half of all private prison beds (over 60,000 beds in the United States alone). In late 1998, it merged into the Prison Realty Trust (PRT), an accounting move that allowed the entity to be exempt from tax liability as long as it distributed 95 percent of its earnings to its stockholders (Geis, Mobley, and Shichor 1999).

CCA has built prisons in 27 different states and in many foreign countries. Started in Tennessee, its owners are well connected politically and have even proposed taking over the whole Tennessee correction system. After their first public offering of stock in 1995, the value of the stock increased by over 400 percent in the first year. After this incredible growth the stock has declined, largely due to politicians' growing disenchantment with privatization. In 2001, CCA's stock lost 93 percent of its 2000 value

(Greene 2001, 26). This financial meltdown was partly caused by a decline in crime and prisoners and partly fueled by a rash of scandals that have plagued CCA's prison facilities (Parenti 1999, 219). Account after account of escapes, violence, undertrained officers, and understaffing has emerged from several sites.

In Youngstown, Ohio, CCA opened a facility supposedly intended for medium-security inmates. Medium- and maximum-security inmates from Washington, D.C., and other places were packed into the facility, with no attempt to classify or isolate violent prisoners. Consequently, in 15 months of operation, there were 44 assaults, 16 stabbings, and two murders. The culmination was an escape by six inmates. When inspectors arrived to investigate the situation, evidently they were turned away at the front gate (cited in Parenti 1999, 222). The litigation that resulted ended with a $1.6 million settlement offer from CCA to affected inmates (Perez 2001). Other reports document incidents such as an escape by two inmates from a CCA facility in Bartlett, Texas, through a door that was left unlocked; two guards pleading guilty to severely beating a handcuffed and shackled inmate; and a $3 million judgment against CCA for the beating of a juvenile inmate in Columbia, South Carolina (Greene 2001, 23–24).

More recently, the CCA has been the target of a loosely organized, global organization of students and reformers that seek to persuade college campuses to drop their contracts with Sodexho Marriott Services, a corporation that owned about 48 percent of CCA stock. Students, upset that their money was being used to fund a corporation that "violat[ed] the human rights of prisoners and prison employees by sacrificing health and safety to improve the corporate bottom-line," have been successful in getting several large campuses to drop their contracts with Sodexho (Pranis 2001). The giant corporation has bowed to the threat and sold its shares in CCA (Ward 2001).

Wackenhut's prison division is a spin-off of the older company's private security business. Holding over 25,000 beds at several dozen facilities across the country, it comes in as number two among the private prison providers. It holds 11,000 prison beds internationally (57 percent of the international market of private prisons) (Austin and Irwin 2001, 66; Perez 2001). It also runs mental health facilities and addiction treatment centers. Since going public in 1994, Wackenhut's stock price has increased by 800 percent. Wackenhut has also had a series of incidents reported in its facilities that have affected its reputation and financial standing (Greene 2001). In New Mexico, Governor Gary Johnson threatened to move all state prisoners out of Wackenhut-run facilities because of four murders that occurred between 1998 and 1999 (compared with only two since 1986 in state-run facilities) (Fecteau 1999). Lawsuits and investigations in other states concern the use of tear gas (Louisiana), failing to prevent sexual abuse (Texas), and paying $3 million to a member of the state's prison policy panel (Florida) (Solomon 1999).

We've learned our lessons in the last decade. . . . We're not going into speculative building, and we're not being overly aggressive in pricing. (George Zoley, CEO of Wackenhut, cited in Perez 2001)

In addition to the big two, there are over a dozen smaller companies across the nation that compete for the private prison bids put out by the states. Replete with allegations of bribes, sweetheart deals, and other forms of corruption, the private prison industry has been criticized for having crooks on both sides of the bars.

Evaluations of Private Prisons

Issues regarding the propriety of private prisons include the following: Should the government (whether it be county, state, or federal) delegate its responsibility to incarcerate? Do these private institutions cost less as promised? Even if they cost less than public facilities, is it at the expense of quality, either in security or service? Does the profit motive encourage more imprisonment? Does the private sector respond more quickly with more flexibility to changing needs? Does the private sector have the legal authority to ensure security? Who is liable—the state or the private vendor or both—over issues of violation of rights of prisoners or victimization if there is an escape? Is the private sector better or less able to control corruption (Logan 1987)?

Proponents argue that private corrections can save the state money. Arguments include the idea that private corporations are more efficient, they can build faster with less cost and less red tape, and they have economies of scale (i.e., they can obtain savings because of their size). It may be true that private prisons can be built faster because private corporations are not bound by restrictions placed on government. For instance, a state would most likely have to go to voters to pass a bond in order to build new prisons; however, the state can contract with a private provider without voter approval. Unlike private corporations, state and local governments are bound by a myriad of bidding and siting restrictions.

In a Government Accounting Office meta-analysis, it was concluded that private and public institutions cost about the same (GAO 1996). Any profit realized by a private entity being "leaner and meaner" is offset by the profit margin private companies maintain and a regulatory system the state must put in place to make sure contract specifications are adhered to. Another meta-analysis of 33 evaluations concluded that the per diem cost of the prison has more to do with the security level and size of the prison than whether it is public or private. This study did not support the idea that private prisons were cost-effective (Pratt and Maahs 1999).

A private study of a CCA facility in Minnesota compared with similar state prisons found many more operational problems in the CCA prison, including program deficiencies, classification problems, and lack of trained personnel (Greene 2001). Greene further reports that other evaluations found 49 percent more inmate-on-staff assaults and 65 percent more inmate-on-inmate assaults in private facilities, 41 percent higher officer turnover, and 37 escapes (compared with eight in a state system of a similar size to all the private prisons in the country) (Greene 2001).

Some studies have concluded that private prisons produce results equal to state institutions at lower cost. Bourge (2002) describes Segal and Moore's study that examined 28 governmental and institutional studies comparing public and private facilities and found that 22 of the private prisons showed cost savings of 5 to 15 percent. They concluded that there is "significant evidence" that private facilities can provide comparable quality to state institutions. However, critics argue that studies that ignore higher assault rates in private prisons and other indexes of quality of service, and look only at cost, are flawed.

There have been issues concerning the evaluators as well. The evaluation by Segal and Moore, for instance, was funded by a libertarian think tank that arguably would promote private enterprise over government involvement (Bourge 2002). The biggest scandal in private prison evaluation research concerned Charles Thomas, a University of Florida professor who published many articles and books as "objective" evaluations of private prisons. Thomas testified before Congress and state legislatures considering private prison contracts. He consistently promoted the effectiveness and efficiency of private prisons, arguably as an independent, objective evaluator. His objectivity was called into question, however, when it was discovered that he was a highly paid consultant to CCA and owned over $500,000 worth of CCA stock. He was sanctioned by the state of Florida for violating their conflict of interest laws in 1999, yet he continues to write articles on private prisons and provide evaluations that tout their effectiveness (e.g., Lanza-Kaduce, Parker, and Thomas 1999; see Geis, Mobley, and Shichor 1999).

The most favorable conclusion one can reach after a survey of available evaluations is that private prisons may be comparable to state institutions with low-risk inmates but do not compare favorably with state institutions in cost or security in housing maximum security populations (Bourge 2002).

The major argument against privatization is that government should not delegate what should be a uniquely state function—that is, confining individuals and holding them against their will (Reisig and Pratt 2000). Ordinarily, private persons (or organizations) who hold others involuntarily are guilty of kidnapping. Private prison contractors have the legal authority to do so, however, because the state delegates its authority to the private entity. But what about liability? If the private entity holds prisoners in an unconstitutional manner, is the organization liable or the state? If a prisoner escapes and victimizes a citizen, who is responsible? These legal questions have been hammered out for the most part, creating a delegation of authority, but not liability, so that the state shares responsibility with the private corporation. For instance, prisoners are still able to utilize protections against unconstitutional treatment from state officials under Section 1983 protections. To oversee private institutions, states use monitoring practices similar to those used for state-contracted nursing homes. Some might argue that such monitoring has not prevented abuses in nursing homes, so why should we assume that private prisons would not have similar problems.

Recent incidents are troubling. For instance, in some states, privately run correctional facilities have contracted with faraway states to house offenders, sometimes without informing the home state of the arrangement. Or, in other cases, a home state might be misled concerning the type of inmates held in a private facility. For instance, Texas officials were surprised when they were told by private prison officials that a facility would be for illegal alien detainees, but then 244 sex offenders were brought in from Oregon. The type of prisoners that were being "imported" was discovered only when two multiple rapists escaped and state officials were called in to help recapture them (Shichor and Sechrest 2002, 397).

Scandals over the treatment of inmates and training practices have arisen, such as an incident in 1998, when officers in a privately run jail in Brazoria County, Texas, were videotaped kicking and setting dogs on nonaggressive Missouri inmates (Parenti 1999, 224). It was later discovered that one of the guards participating in the brutality had been fired from the Texas Department of Criminal Justice and served some time in a federal facility for beating a Texas prisoner. Evidently the private company running the facility, Capital Correctional Resources, either did not do a background check or didn't care (Parenti 1999, 224). When the videotape hit the airwaves, Missouri pulled all its prisoners from the facility, but questions remain as to how states can monitor treatment from thousands of miles away and what the responsibility of the home state is in such a situation. When disturbances occur in privately run facilities, state corrections staff are asked to intervene, even when none of the prisoners are from the home state. Some states have started to charge for their services, presenting a bill to the private corporation after the disturbance has been quelled.

The fact is that large numbers of prisoners now spend at least part of their sentence far away from their home state. Shichor and Sechrest (2002) discuss the widespread practice of interstate transfer. The Interstate Corrections Compact creates the mechanism by which an inmate can be legally incarcerated in a different state from the one in which he or she was convicted. Private prisons have substantially increased the number of prisoners who serve time in other states. Viewed as a commodity, prisoners are, in some ways, marketed and moved around as products. More accurately, empty beds are the products and they are brokered by businesses created specifically to locate and/or sell prison bed space.

In 2001, 11,800 prisoners served their sentences in other states (Beck, Karberg, and Harrison 2002, 5). Not all these prisoners are sent to private prisons. Some states also rent beds. Among the states that sent the most prisoners to other states were Wisconsin (4,526), Hawaii (1,225), Alaska (777), and Connecticut (657) (Beck, Karberg, and Harrison 2002, 5). In some ways, this practice makes sense. If a state is experiencing a temporary increase in prisoners, contracting with another state saves money because there is no need to build a new prison. In other ways, however, it is an ominous trend. Prisoners are cut off from their families, they often have fewer program opportunities than similar prisoners who are housed in home-state prisons, they have difficulty pursuing legal issues, and, most important, states have a harder time monitoring conditions from far away. These prisoners, to some extent, have no voice at all unless there is a major scandal—and there have been several.

Ogle (1999) argues that private correctional facilities operate in a Catch-22 situation, where organizational imperatives are contradictory. On the one hand is the corporate imperative of profit, on the other is the public service imperative of "legitimacy." The two conflict when the most profitable way to run a prison conflicts with the perceived "just" or "humane" way to run a prison. When the private corporation is pursuing profit, it uses adaptations such as compromise and avoidance techniques or defiance and manipulation techniques to circumvent governmental mandates for services and contract fulfillment.

A more abstract and subtle criticism of private corrections is that if someone is making money from incarcerating offenders, where is the incentive to correct them? If recidivism were to somehow mysteriously plummet, corporations would show reduced profits and stockholders would lose money. The financial incentive to incarcerate more people for longer periods of time arguably ensures that we will never see a reduction in imprisonment, as long as privatization continues to grow.

One of the biggest concerns of critics is that, unlike with prisons bonds, legislators do not need to seek public approval before committing the state to multiyear multimillion-dollar contracts with private vendors. Before a state can build a prison, there must be a bond election and voters must agree to the state selling bonds to fund the construction. On the other hand, with a private vendor, legislators can simply sign a contract that commits the state to pay a certain per diem rate for a certain number of prisoners for a given number of years. Or they can sign build-and-lease agreements in which the private vendor agrees to build a prison in exchange for a contract to run it for a certain number of years, after which the state is obligated to purchase the facility. Although the money involved can be as much in the long run as a prison construction project, voters do not need to be consulted.

> . . . it's as if the prison expansion is now being funded by way of a credit card issued by the prison-industrial complex—a high-interest credit card that the tax payers have no control over when it comes to spending, but are nonetheless still being required to pay for at the end of the month. (Dyer 2000, 5)

Of course, private corrections officials scoff at the above scenario. They point out that their piece of the "corrections pie" is quite small in comparison to the states' share, that they are closely monitored by staff officials who are unhappy with sharing any amount of resources with them, and that there is plenty of opportunity to expand in other states and even in other countries without somehow conspiring to keep offenders in prison solely for some profit motive.

For whatever reason, as states have backed away from their use of private corrections, the federal government has stepped in to offer contracts. The number of private prison beds utilized by the FBOP increased from 19,252 in 2001 to 20,293 in 2002 (Beck, Karberg, and Harrison 2002, 4). One estimate is that the federal government will spend over $4.6 billion between 2001 and 2011 on private prisons and detention facilities (Greene 2001, 26). Two federal contracts awarded to CCA to provide 3,316 beds in two facilities will pay out $760 million over 10 years and saved CCA from bankruptcy (Greene 2001, 27). Although critics in Congress are attempting to pass laws to disallow the Federal Bureau of Prisons (FBOP) from contracting with private prisons, it is likely that such partnerships will continue, given the close ties between these companies and federal officials. Michael J. Quinlan, CEO of CCA, served as the Federal Bureau of Prisons director under George H.W. Bush, and Norman Carlson, former director of FBOP, is on Wackenhut's board of directors (Greene 2001).

Immigrant prisoners, a rapidly growing group, are increasingly housed in private facilities. Critics argue that these prisoners have virtually no voice. They often do not speak English and have no legal representation or family to stand up for their rights. They languish in detention facilities for years without knowing what is happening to them or when they will get out (Greene 2001). Welch (2002) provides an exhaustive study of the incredible growth of the INS and the number detained in county jails and private facilities under contract with the federal government. Advocates for INS detainees point out that these are not criminals in the typical sense, but they are being housed in prisons. Allegations of brutality, sexual assault, lack of programs, and inhumane conditions are frequent and consistent.

A Modern Alcatraz: The Super-Max

Institutions like Alcatraz and MacNeil Island, Washington, were built to house the "worst of the worst"—prisoners whose violent tendencies or organized crime connections made it impossible to house them in "normal" prisons. Of course, histories of such places point out that they also housed individuals who didn't need to be there, and these prisons seemed to suffer the worst extremes of brutality, corruption, and inhumane conditions. Recently, we have seen the reemergence of such facilities in the "super-max" prisons being built. In 1997, 36 states and the Federal Bureau of Prisons operated 57 super-maximum units (Corrections Alert 1997, 8). More are being built.

[He] has broken down from the stress of his isolation. He has difficulty sleeping and eating and suffers from shakes or tremors . . . he falls into fits of weeping. He's written

> letters to the judge begging for some form of human con-
> tact. . . . The kind of mind it would take to create a place
> like that is beyond me. (a lawyer talking about his client in
> the federal super-max in Florence, Colorado; quoted in
> Annin 1998, 13)

The most notorious of these facilities is Pelican Bay, California. This facility was built in a remote northern region of California to house 2,080 prisoners. It quickly became overcrowded, with over 3,250 prisoners forcing double celling in cells designed for one (Austin and Irwin 2001, 127). Pelican Bay has been the target of court action, television and newspaper journalistic investigations, and American Civil Liberties Union action. For instance, in a recent court case, it was ruled that there was an insufficient number of medical and mental health professionals, excessive force had been used, and policies regarding the use of force were inadequate (Ward 1999, 258). Pelican Bay, like most super-max prisons, confines inmates in their cells 23 or 24 hours a day. That alone is enough to generate some concern, since cell confinement has been found to be detrimental to mental and physical health. Beyond confinement, however, is the practice of limiting and greatly restricting any human contact. In these modern-day Alcatrazes, sophisticated technology is used to open and close cell doors and service the inmates inside the cells. They literally may never touch a human hand for months.

Such practices are regrettable but understandable when used for those inmates who are so violent that it is impossible to trust them not to attack anyone who comes near them, and any contact without a full contingent of specially trained and outfitted officers would be foolish. However, there have been allegations that inmates are sent to such facilities not because of a prediction of extreme violence but rather because they are being punished for demanding rights or for being troublemakers (Parenti 1999, 209). If these allegations are true, there are serious questions as to the right of the state to subject such individuals to such draconian measures.

. . . Pelican Bay's low, windowless, slate-gray exterior gives no hint to outsiders that this is a place where human beings live. But the barrenness of the prison's interior is what is most startling. On each visit to this prison I have been struck by the harsh, visual sameness and monotony of the physical design and the layout of these units. . . . [Y]ou search in vain for humanizing touches or physical traces that human activity takes place here. . . . Prisoners at Pelican Bay are not even permitted to see grass, trees, or shrubbery. . . . (Hanley 2002, 162)

Despite the scrutiny and criticism of Pelican Bay, many state officials have visited the facility and plans are under way in these states to construct their own super-max prisons. For instance, Wisconsin opened its own super-max prison in November 1999. This $47.5 million facility has a capacity of 509. The annual operating budget is expected to be $14.7 million, for an annual per year cost per inmate of $29,400 to $36,750 (Jones 1999). This compares with a national average of $20,000 (in 1996) (Kaplan 1999, 1). Although some legislators boasted of this latest addition to the state's correctional system, others are not so proud. One legislator said that those who open it should "have tears in their eyes" because the "fodder" for such a place is bound to be young black men (Jones 1999).

The Wisconsin prison is much like other super-max facilities. The cells measure six feet by 12 feet. There is a combined stainless steel sink and toilet and a shower in one corner (with a drain in the floor). A six foot by six foot window, high up on the wall, is fogged to prevent any view of the outside. No clock, radio, or television is allowed in the cells. Video cameras can be kept on 24 hours a day. One-hour-a-day exercise is allowed, but the inmate is shackled and guarded by two guards and led to a room not much bigger than the cell itself. Technology includes a "biometric" system that scans hands for security identification, a video visitation system (in place of face-to-face visits), motion detectors and surveillance cameras, and a central command post that uses computers to control movement through every door. Prison officials estimate that inmates may spend one to three years at the facility before being able to return to general population prisons. Critics argue that after such a length of time, the inmates may not be fit to return to any type of freedom, no matter how limited (Jones 1999).

A federal facility in Florence, Colorado, is very similar to the one described above. In Colorado's super-max, prisoners are confined to their cells 23 hours a day; they are allowed one 15-minute phone call every three months. Their windows also are obscured so that they cannot see out. This facility houses 484 inmates (Ward 1999, 258).

In Virginia, twin super-max facilities, opened in 1998 and 1999, have already had three outside investigations stemming from allegations of abuse and inhumane conditions. These facilities were built at a cost of $147 million, and some legislators argue that Virginia does not even have the 2,400 "worst of the worst" inmates to fill the beds. In fact, some of the beds were "rented" to New Mexico until the attorney general of New Mexico asked for an FBI investigation of conditions and pulled all New Mexico inmates out. That investigation still continues. Allegations include the charge that inmates are shocked with stun guns even when shackled and are fired upon by guards (Hammack 2000).

This isn't making the community safe . . . you're just making them the most sickest, most impulse-ridden, most enraged, paranoid, impaired human beings. And then you're just putting them right back into the community. (Dr. Grassian, a psychiatrist opposed to the use of super-max prisons, quoted in Jones 1999, 3)

These facilities concern prisoners' rights groups and those who believe that the United States already lags behind most of Western Europe in meeting standards for humane treatment of prisoners. Critics argue that the super-max prison is psychologically harmful. It is especially so for those who have psychological problems to begin with, and many contend that those who are sent to a super-max for violent acting out are often diagnosed with psychological problems. Symptoms noted include massive free-floating anxiety, hyperresponsiveness to external stimuli, perceptual distortions and hallucinations, a feeling of unreality, difficulty with concentration and memory, acute confusional states, emergence of primitive aggressive fantasies, persecutory ideation, motor excitement, and/or violent destructive or self-mutilatory outbursts (Kupers 1999, 57).

Inmates deprived of any measure of control over their behavior become unnaturally docile and dependent on others, or they irrationally act out to express their own existence, injuring themselves or others in the process. Deprived of any social contact, they may become even more socially withdrawn, avoiding interaction and finding it increasingly difficult to maintain the simplest interchanges with others. Living in a reality that holds nothing but pain, they may retreat into fantasy and lose touch entirely. Deprived of the ability to act like human beings, some become something less than human (Hanley 2002).

Even the cells are eerie. There are no mirrors. The only time you can see yourself is on the little knob in the shower. You shave on your knees looking at the one-inch reflection. There is very little for you to control in your cell. The light switch is a silver bump and no one seems to know how it works. . . . Though the cells are more than 80 square feet, with or without a "cellie" (cellmate), they quickly shrink when you are inside them for 22 hours a day. (Morris 2002, 183)

Riots and Collective Violence

Prison disturbances occur with some regularity. In fact, it is reported that there have been over 1,300 prison riots in this century (Montgomery and Crews 1998, 1). Two well-known prison riots in this country are the Attica (1971) and the Santa Fe (1980) riots . They are interesting in their differences and tell us something about the changing nature of prisons and prisoners. The Attica rioters took over the prison in an attempt to force the governor and prison commissioner to concede to a list of demands. Their "manifesto" was a composite of demands that had been used by California inmates in earlier disturbances and called for such things as better food, more exercise, and programs. By some accounts, after a short period of chaos, organizers (especially Black Muslims) controlled the prison, protected the guard-hostages, and prevented inmate-on-inmate violence.

After several days of negotiations, some of which were televised, state police stormed the prison and regained control but in the process killed many of the hostages. The total count was 43 killed—39 of whom were killed by state police. Abuses occurred after the riot, including making naked prisoners run a gauntlet of officers who beat them with sticks, clubs, and guns. It was years before all court actions against inmates were complete. No officials, despite photographs and eyewitness accounts, were ever convicted of abuse of power. A lawsuit by inmates who had been beaten and tortured after the violent retaking of the facility was finally settled in February of 2000, after 30 years, for $8 million to be divided among all injured inmates—at least those that were still alive (Chen 2000).

> When you explain to your kids and your grandkids what the whole essence of Attica was, you'll be able to tell them that it was to be treated as human beings. . . . (Frank Smith, an ex-Attica inmate testifying at the settlement hearing between New York State and ex-inmates, quoted in Chen 2000)

In contrast to the relative control of prisoners at Attica, the Santa Fe riot was a display of horrific violence by inmates against other inmates. Specifically, protective custody inmates were targeted and subjected to various types of torture before being killed, including being set on fire, hung on cell bars and literally filleted, and thrown off tiers. Other killings took place as roving bands of prisoners took advantage of the chaos. Over 200 inmates were severely injured. Guards were beaten, stabbed, and sodomized. There was no agenda, no political consciousness, and no control. It was a wild killing spree, ending in the death of 33 inmates. While some inmates represented the depth of depravity to which men can descend, others found and protected injured officers, risking their own lives in doing so. They also found and took injured inmates to the front gate to be evacuated for medical treatment (Colvin 1992; Useem and Kimball 1989; Rolland 1997).

Rolland (1997), an inmate who took part in the riot, provides his firsthand description of what happened. According to his account, the riot occurred because of the harassment and abuse inmates experienced at the hands of the guards and the practice of using (and taunting inmates with the use of) informants. What is especially chilling from his account, and others, is how violence is cyclical and related to revenge and counterrevenge. Some inmates hurt victims and were sent to prison, where some guards felt justified in humiliating and brutalizing them because of what they'd done; inmates felt justified in horrifically brutalizing guards when the tables were turned and they briefly had power over them; then, after retaking the prison, some guards felt justified in inflicting their revenge on the inmates; these inmates eventually served their sentences and were released, and may have felt it was their turn again, and so it goes. The story of the New Mexico riot was an ancient passion play in which blood vengeance solved nothing and resulted in nothing but continued violence.

> [the author describes how a group of inmates hunted down and killed another who had been randomly hacking to death anybody he happened upon] . . . I stepped down off the fence to get a better look at this dead madman. The blood from his body had puddled around him from numerous holes and rips. Everything was deathly quiet. . . . "How many did he kill?" Another voice said, "At least eight or ten." . . . [the author then describes how the man is decapitated and his head is put on a shovel handle] . . . This was sick. This wasn't real. . . . Then a much deeper thought whispered in my mind—this was like 'Nam, this was survival. . . . (Rolland 1997, 89)

Those who study riots and prison disturbances destroy the myth that they occur most often in the summer months. According to one study, the months with the most riots and disturbances in descending order of frequency were December, November, August, and July, indicating that Christmas and the holiday season were more powerful predictors than the heat of summer. These same researchers identified a long list of causes and triggering events for riots, including food, racial tension, rules, regulations and policies, mass escape attempts, gangs and other special groups, rumors, security issues, conflict with other inmates, conflict with correctional staff, and alcohol and other drug usage (Montgomery and Crews 1998, 88).

Theories of riots include the powder keg theory, which presumes that the prison is full of violent individuals and that when incidents accumulate, there is an explosion. Another theory is the relative deprivation/rising expectation theory that presumes that when conditions improve, but don't improve fast enough, there is a higher likelihood of a disturbance. Another theory (power vacuum) assumes riots take place when there is no strong authority in control (Montgomery and Crews 1998, 88).

Useem and Reisig (1999) evaluated which factor was more predictive of collective violence in prison: a lack of administrative control, or "oppressive" administrative control that allowed for no input from prisoners. They concluded that the latter factor was more predictive; specifically, the "inmate balance" theory proposes that inmates need to feel some participation in the running of the prison. If they feel totally oppressed, anger and frustration will result in collective violence. One thing seems certain—as long as prisons exist, some prisoners will erupt with fury and violence.

Conclusion

One hundred years ago, and throughout the first half of the twentieth century, prisons were forbidding places in which a few hardened criminals lived under hostile and harsh conditions. The public, for the most part, didn't think about prisons and that was considered a prison management success. Prison wardens ran their prisons like independent fiefdoms. Some were run fairly humanely, and prisoners worked in fields or factories and may even have gained respect for harsh but fair officers. There is no doubt that some officers were brutal, but most inmates survived their visit to "hell." For the most part, officers and inmates understood each other and operated with an understanding that it was best for all if violence was kept to a minimum. And, except for periodic riots, it was.

In the second half of the twentieth century, things changed. Prisons became correctional institutions, prisoners became politicized, states started losing prisoner rights cases, and guards felt the prisons slipping out of their control. All this occurred in the 1970s and early 1980s, and then, before such changes could be accommodated, the prison population literally exploded in the mid-1980s. Partly as a response to rising crime, and partly as an effect of the drug war, states began to double and even quadruple their prison populations. They were literally bursting at the seams. What occurred was a building boom, the likes of which had never been seen before in the world. The need for prisons spawned a whole new industry—private prisons; and crime did pay for those who met the need for more cells.

As the prison populations exploded, prison management became crisis management. Overcrowding has been endemic for over twenty years. In many state systems, no sooner is a facility built than it is filled and another facility is placed on the drawing board. Prisons designed for 500 inmates may hold close to double that number, and inmates are double- or even triple-celled in cells designed for one. Overcrowding is difficult for both inmates and officers. Research indicates that overcrowding can lead to a number of pathologies, including a rise in suicides, deaths from contagious diseases, disciplinary infractions, increases in mental health admissions, and disciplinary infractions (Cox, Paulus, and McCain 1984).

All these changes fragmented the prison world and violence ensued. From the late 1970s through the late 1980s, the level of violence in prisons across the country was unparalleled. By the late 1990s, prison officials seemed to bring the escalating violence under control, but there have been costs involved. Prisoners feel that administrators have received the green light from the public and courts that anything can be done to them in the name of security. For instance, the super-max is considered the ultimate in security and, according to critics, the ultimate in torture.

There are incredible forces, both social and economic, to keep incarceration rates high. Successful management of a prison has been redefined back to the early days, when it simply meant no riots, no escapes, and no headline news. What is most ominous of all, as we will discuss in the next chapter, is the changing demographics of the prison population. The new Bastille is rapidly becoming a racial concentration camp.

Study Questions

1. Describe the types of prisons in this country. What do custody levels mean?
2. Discuss the advantages and criticisms of private prisons.

3. What have evaluations shown regarding the cost-effectiveness of private prisons?
4. What are super-maxes? What are the criticisms of such prisons?
5. What are the theories regarding when prisoners riot? When are riots most likely to occur?

Chapter 4

The Prisoners

We have our rapos (rapists), serial killers, con men, factory workers, pimps, whores, religious groups, wine shops, grocery stores, lenders, laundries, artists, musicians, intellectuals, and people of all political persuasions. You name it, we've got it. We've got the whole world in our can. (an inmate; Martin and Sussman 1993, 73)

Who ends up in prison? Most prisoners are likely to be poor African-Americans with juvenile records and/or multiple crimes, and have histories of drug use. The vast majority of prisoners in the United States are men—about 93 percent. Despite larger "percentage increases" in prison commitment of women in the last 10 years, women still constitute only about 6.7 percent of all prisoners (Harrison and Karberg 2003). Their prison world is so different from that of men's that we must discuss their issues separately in Chapter 8.

One of the first things to understand about prisoners is that they are not all alike. They are not all violent, although many are, and some are forced to be. They are not all drug addicts, although many are. Officers find many inmates to be relatively easy to supervise and even decent human beings. Their crime may have been an aberration. They may have seen the error of their ways and reformed. Maybe they hold conventional social norms. In fact, some were our neighbors and will be again. Placed in the prison environment, however, they do act differently—they must to survive.

I'm a machinist by trade. I live in one of a range of prison cells housing the former owner of an industrial supply business, a truck driver, an apartment manager, a baker, a building contractor, a coordinator of a day center for the developmentally disabled, a scientist who's worked for NASA, a window glazer, an auto-body technician, a radio disc jockey, a professional piano tuner, a house painter, and a cabinet builder. Four of my neighbors have general education diplomas, five graduated from high school and four hold college degrees. Seven of my neighbors are veterans. We've all been married. We all have children who love and miss us, and all but two of us owned homes. (MacLeod 2002, 72)

The Demographics of Prison

Almost 49 percent of prisoners were convicted of violent crimes, 20 percent have been sentenced for property crimes, and 31 percent are in prison for drug or public order crimes (Harrison and Beck 2002, 12). One should be aware of the difference between prisoner population demographics and prison admission demographics. In any prison population, the number of prisoners incarcerated for violent crimes is not the same as the number of those admitted to prison in that year for violent crimes. Violent crimes receive much longer sentences and these prisoners are less likely to receive parole, so they "stack up"; therefore, one cannot use prison population figures to say anything about how many entering prisoners have committed violent crimes.

Authors point out that the largest increases in prison admissions have occurred in nonviolent crime categories, accounting for 77 percent of the growth (Greene and Schiraldi 2002, 4). Nonviolent crimes include drug crimes involving no weapons and property crimes. Some argue that there are at least 1 million people incarcerated in this country who, because of the nonviolent nature of their crimes, might be punished by other methods with no increased risk to public safety (Greene and Schiraldi 2002, 5).

Contrary to public opinion that our system is "soft on crime," many offenders receive prison sentences for first offenses. For instance, about 95 percent of those convicted of homicide receive a prison sentence; but so do about 73 percent of all drug offenders and 71 percent of all burglars (cited in Austin and Irwin 2001, 21). In one Texas study, it was found that 53 percent of all drug offenders who were sentenced to prison were convicted for possession of one gram or less of the illegal substance (cited in Austin and Irwin 2001, 21). What also seems to be driving the prison population increase is that sentences are getting longer and parolees and probationers are more likely to experience revocation and end up back in prison. The minimum time served has been getting longer and is now 43 months (Gilliard and Beck 1998, 12).

About 37.7 percent of inmates are recidivists, returning to prison on new charges or parole violations (Camp and Camp 1997, 46). Actually, other studies report that the number may be somewhat higher. In a large national study of prisoners released in 1994 and followed for three years, it was reported that 68 percent were rearrested sometime during that three-year period. Further, about 47 percent were reconvicted and 52 percent were back in prison, although only about one-quarter on new charges. Those most likely to be rearrested included those who had been in prison for robbery, burglary, larceny, motor vehicle theft, or possessing/selling stolen property (Langan and Levin 2002).

Prisoners returned to prison for parole violations increased from 17 percent in 1980 to almost 30.7 percent of all admissions in 1997 (Harrison 1999, 6). Parole violations may occur because of failed drug tests, even if no other crime has been committed. In one state (Texas), it was reported that nearly two out of every three prisoners are being returned on parole or probation violations (Kaplan, Schiraldi, and Ziedenberg 2000).

Table 4.1 Characteristics of Prisoners in State Prisons

	Characteristics (%)	
	1991	**1997**
Number of prisoners	704,203	1,059,607
Male	94.6	93.7
Female	5.4	6.3
Race/Ethnicity		
White	35.4	33.3
Black	45.6	46.5
Hispanic	16.6	17.0

Continued next page

Table 4.1 Characteristics of Prisoners in State Prisons Continued

	Characteristics (%)	
	1991	1997
Other	2.4	3.2
Age		
17 and younger	.6	.5
18–24	21.3	19.3
25–34	45.7	38.1
35–44	22.7	29.4
45–54	6.5	9.8
55–64	2.4	2.2
65+	.7	.7
Median age	30	32
Marital Status		
Married	18.2	16.6
Widowed	1.9	1.9
Separated	6.2	5.8
Divorced	18.5	18.6
Never married	55.3	57.1
Education		
8th grade or less	14.3	14.2
Some high school	26.9	28.9
GED	24.6	25.1
High-school graduate	19.4	18.5
Some college	12.2	10.7
College graduate+	2.7	2.7
Some college	12.2	10.7
College graduate +	2.7	2.7

Adapted from Bureau of Justice Statistics *Correctional Populations in the United States 1997* (Washington, D.C.: Department of Justice, 2000).

Table 4.2 Prison and Jail Inmates—2002

	Male				Female			
Age	Total	White	Black	Hispanic	Total	White	Black	Hispanic
	1,848,700	630,700	818,900	342,500	165,800	68,800	65,600	25,400
18–24	418,700	120,100	195,500	89,300	26,300	11,400	9,000	5,400
25–34	670,000	210,600	303,900	137,600	62,500	24,500	25,000	10,200
35–44	508,000	192,100	223,000	7,900	56,400	23,400	23,900	7,000
45+	234,500	104,100	87,200	34,300	19,200	9,200	7,100	2,600

Adapted from P. Harrison and J. Karberg, *BJS Bulletin: Prison and Jail Inmates at Mid-Year 2002* (Washington, D.C.: Department of Justice, 2003), 11.

Tables 4.1 and 4.2 provide some information on the nation's prisons. Table 4.1 presents demographic information for the prisoner population in 1997, the last date available for this type of information. Most prisoners are under age 35, belong to a minority group, and are single. The majority have not completed high school. Table 4.2 provides more current information but includes jail inmates, so it is not strictly comparable. However, one can see the size of the different age and ethnic groups in prison.

This system is now filled with non-criminals! Mostly behind crack or some spur of the moment crime to get money for crack. Then it's who can make a deal first to get off the lightest. The percentage of [homosexuality and drug use] have been steadily declining over the years. I have been in prison for 17½ years, and before AIDS, the percentages were way higher. Security has also gotten tougher because of lawsuits and investigations into the D.O.C. making it harder to get drugs into the system. . . . (a prisoner responding to a questionnaire, quoted by Krebs 2002, 41)

While the public may have the perception that prison houses only violent and recidivistic criminals, the reality is that many thousands of individuals in prison have committed relatively minor crimes. The following profile is taken from a representative sample described by Austin and Irwin (2001, 27): Edmond was a 50-year-old white carpenter who worked in Florida in the winter and Seattle in the summer. He had been arrested once 22 years before for receiving stolen property. He was passing through Las Vegas on his way to Seattle and said he found a billfold with $100 on a bar where he was drinking and gambling. The owner, who suspected him of taking it, turned him in. He was charged with grand larceny and received three years. When proponents of prison use argue that we need to lock up criminals for our safety, one suspects they are not thinking of people like Edmond.

Race

The huge spike in incarceration that occurred in the 1980s and 1990s affected minority men more severely than white men. In

1990, about 50 percent of the male prisoner population was white, but by 2002 that percentage had dropped to 34 percent (Harrison and Karberg 2003, 11). The incarceration rate for African-American men was 2,234 per 100,000 in 1990 but rose to 4,810 in 2002 (compared with 338 and 649, respectively, for white men) (Harrison and Karberg 2003, 11). Hispanic men were incarcerated at a rate of 1,016 in 1990, and 1,740 in 2002 (Harrison and Karberg 2003, 11). What bears repeating is that in the space of less than 100 years, African-Americans and Hispanics went from being about 30 percent of the prison population to about 70 percent.

Prisons are disproportionately populated by young minority men. It is an inescapable fact that can only be partially explained by crime rates, seriousness of crime, or other factors. In Ohio, for instance, there are about 23,200 young African-American men in prison, but only 20,074 are enrolled in colleges and universities (Collins 2002).

A recently reported statistic is that there are now more black men in prison than in higher education (Justice Policy Institute 2002). The source of that statistic has been criticized because the authors used a total age range for black males 18 to 67, rather than only college-age years. Using just the traditional college-age population, there are more African-American men in college than in prison, but not by much. In the 18-to-24 age-group the ratio of college to prison attendees is 2.6:1; for white men in this age-group the ratio is 28:1 (Hocker 2002, 1).

Whitehead (2001) discusses how an entire generation of young black men is being socialized to become prison inmates. In some communities, everywhere they look and every experience they have leads them to the conclusion that they are likely to end up in prison. Rap music and movies glorify or endorse the cultural legend of the black male criminal. The author noted that residents of low-income housing communities commented that the high-security fences that were put up to protect the community were really intended to prepare their children for Lorton (the District of Columbia prison complex).

Kupers (1999) describes how whites are disproportionately represented in the mental health units of prisons, while African-Americans are represented in the solitary confinement and secure housing units. What may be interpreted as a mental health problem with a white inmate will more likely be viewed as a behavior problem with an African-American inmate.

Many African-Americans in prison perceive that the institution is a place of oppression and torture and the only way to survive it is to band together and, perhaps, attack first. Thus, the cycle of violence continues. A statistic that should give one pause is that although about two-thirds of the drug treatment beds in California prisons go to whites, about 70 percent of those sentenced to California prisons for drugs are African-Americans (cited in Kupers 1999, 111).

To what extent does disproportional crime have to do with the disproportional incarceration of African-American men? According to some studies, quite a bit. Mauer (1999, 127) reports on several studies by Alfred Blumstein that show that arrest rates "explain" about three quarters of the race differential. However, that leaves one-quarter to be explained by racial discrimination or other factors. Further, arrest figures are themselves the product of the system and cannot necessarily be used as a purely objective measure of criminality. It is true, however, that African-Americans tend to be more involved in street crimes, such as robbery and auto theft, and these crimes are more likely to receive prison sentences than white-collar crimes. What research also shows is that drug sentencing has a greater amount of difference unexplained by any factor related to the crime itself. It seems clear that it is in this area that a great deal of racial disparity exists (Mauer 1999, 127).

... the bottom line is not crime, the bottom line is the racial tensions in our large urban areas, and there's no escaping that. We may, in fact, have an impact upon crime, disorder, and fear, but if in the course of doing that, we substantially increase tensions in the community, we've made matters worse. (Herman Goldstein, cited in Mauer 1999, 98)

Young and Old Prisoners

There were fewer inmates under 18 in 2001 than in 2000 (Beck, Karberg, and Harrison 2002, 6). However, the problem of juveniles in prison is a troubling one. Waivers to adult court and subsequent incarceration in adult facilities are a fate awaiting some juveniles who commit serious crimes such as murder. These young people are highly vulnerable in prison, where weakness is exploited and there are precious few altruistic defenders of children. Nathanial Abraham, for instance, was charged with murder at the age of 11. But not all children who end up in prison commit murder. A significant number (about 40 percent) have committed only property or drug crimes (Austin and Irwin 2001, 56).

Even though prisons are largely populated by young men, the average age of prisoners seems to be increasing. One effect of longer sentences and a higher incarceration rate has been the increasing number of elderly prisoners. The strange reality is that in most prison systems there is now a geriatric wing. Here walkers and wheelchairs are as much a part of prison life as bars and uniformed guards. These prisoners are highly vulnerable and must be protected from other prisoners. Just as do the elderly on the outside, they experience failing eyesight, decreased mobility, loss of mental acuity, loneliness, and disorientation. Unique to prisoners, however, is the fear of release, which often holds nothing for them, since family and friends all may be dead and the inmate has nowhere to go. Such inmates have even been known to refuse parole, preferring the familiar world of the prison to the unfamiliar world outside.

Related to the issue of geriatric prisoners is that of prisoners with extremely long sentences. Most of them will be in the geriatric population before they've served their sentences. The prisoners who face 10, 20, or 30 years or more in prison pose different programming needs and security issues than young offenders, who usually have shorter sentences. Custodial staff will usually describe long-termers as better behaved than short-termers, but that is after a period of adjustment in which they are likely to experience rage and frustration over their fate. Further, they can be very uncontrollable because they know that the prison staff cannot do much to affect the sentence length—losing a year of good time doesn't mean much when you are facing 30 (Flanagan 1995).

One study indicates that at least 52 percent of elderly prisoners are incarcerated for nonviolent crimes (National Center on Institutions and Alternatives 1998). At least one state (Virginia) has passed legislation allowing compassionate release for geriatric prisoners (Greene and Schiraldi 2002, 15). One of the most consistent findings in criminology is called the "maturation effect"; this is the pattern whereby criminals older than 35 years of age seem to substantially lower their criminal activity. Unfortunately, by that time, many have accumulated enough convictions so that they are facing 25-year sentences and won't leave prison until retirement age. What is driving their desistance seems to be a general disgust and tiredness with the excitement that they had lived before; many prisoners want fairly simple things upon release. The sad reality is that, for many without skills and without resources, even these simple goals are unlikely to be met.

I did want a lot, but now my ambition's shrunk. I used to be kind of wild, but now I'm realistic—just a nice home, two cars, a wife and kids . . . my goal is just to be middle class. . . . (a prisoner, quoted by Lin 2000, 144)

Education and Employment Histories

Most prisoners are young and have less than a high-school education; therefore, high school and basic literacy education is extremely important. Although there are vociferous critics who oppose providing college educations to prisoners, the number of prisoners who can take advantage of such programs, even if they exist, is very small. The majority of inmates are either functionally illiterate or have yet to achieve a high-school diploma or its equivalent. Thus, the largest education programs in prison are basic education (literacy) and GED certification.

According to most studies, about two-thirds of prisoners were working prior to their imprisonment (Lin 2000, 147). The idea that criminals commit crime full-time is a myth; most offenders commit crime sporadically and often have legitimate jobs, pay rent, and support families. Drug offenders, especially, may be surprisingly "middle class." Of course, their jobs may be unskilled and pay very little. As we will see in a subsequent chapter, vocational programs in prison can influence recidivism if they lead to a job upon release.

Family

Prisoners are very likely to have parents or other relatives who have spent time in prison. Justice Department figures indicate that 47 percent of inmates in state prisons have a parent or other close relative who has been previously incarcerated. Half of all juveniles in custody have a father, mother, or other close relative in jail or prison. This intergenerational history of incarceration is expensive. An Oregon prison staff person estimated that five members of the same family who were currently incarcerated were costing the state $5 million a year. That estimate did not even count the expenses of court costs or community supervision—just prison (Butterfield 2002b). It is not unusual to have multigenerations within the same prison; for instance, a grandmother, mother, and daughter in the same prison.

My family keeps telling me, "You're just going to end up like your father," and they're right. I didn't have anyone teach me to be a man. All the men in my family, they're either dead, locked up in jail, or on their way, but I'm trying to be the first to make it to graduation. (an inner-city youth whose father is in prison, quoted in Kleiner 2002, 48)

The other commonality among prisoners is domestic violence. To recognize the fact that many people in prison come from abusive and/or neglectful backgrounds does not excuse the fact that they victimized others or violated the law. However, it does help to explain why they commit such crimes. There are large differences between male and female inmates in their reporting of abuse. Whereas 57 percent of state female prisoners reported "ever" having been abused, 16 percent of male prisoners did. About 38 percent of the women said they had been abused before the age of 18, whereas 14 percent of male prisoners reported early abuse. About a quarter of women reported both physical abuse and sexual abuse, while about 12 percent of men reported physical abuse and only 5 percent reported sexual abuse. Of course, it is possible that men might have underreported their abuse and been more likely to do so than women. These numbers do not tell us what percentage of men lived in families where they saw either parent being abused (Harlow 1999).

> Understanding that some thieving, conniving son-of-a-bitch behaves the way he does because he's black and his mother was a whore and he never knew his father and he had to steal to eat—understanding that—is important, but it don't alter the fact the son-of-a-bitch is still a son-of-a-bitch. (a guard, quoted in Webb and Morris 2002, 77)

Abuse of men was likely to be by family members, whereas abuse of women was likely to be by family members or intimates. Those who reported abuse were more likely to have been raised in foster care if their parents or caregivers were heavy users of drugs or alcohol and/or if either parent or caregiver spent time in prison. Further, abuse seemed to be linked to violent crime, especially for men. Those who reported abuse were more likely to be abusers of drugs (Harlow 1999). Although a common retort is that a bad childhood does not give one the right to commit crime, it seems obvious that there is some connection between childhood abuse and the choices one makes as an adult. The tragedy is that prisoners are also parents, and if they do not understand the forces that influenced them, they will have a difficult time helping their children avoid the same path.

> My father died of tuberculosis when I was twelve. For the next two years, my mother beat me every night upon her return from her second-shift job, except one night when my sister hid my father's leather belt, my mom's weapon of choice. . . . I entered adulthood with no self-respect, no concrete values and enough hatred to have fueled a world war. I felt like an intruder in a world belonging to other people. (an inmate sentenced to 20 to 40 years for repeatedly seriously injuring his wife, MacLeod 2002, 73)

When more and more people are incarcerated, more and more children are affected. Sometimes, it is a good thing that an abusive or drug-abusing parent is out of their lives. More often, it is psychologically traumatizing. The sad reality is that children with a parent in prison are six times more likely to end up in jail themselves. In 2000, more than 1.5 million children had a parent in prison. These children are at higher risk for emotional problems, school difficulties, and delinquency.

Many prisoners want to be good parents, but the distance between the prison and family and restrictions on visitation and telephoning make keeping in touch difficult. There are programs, especially in women's prisons, that help prisoners improve their parenting skills, but these programs are not found in every prison and often they cannot do much to improve the visitation opportunities.

Prisoners: Yesterday and Today

One of the early pieces of research on prisons developed a prisoner typology. In fact, there were several, but one of the earliest and best-known typologies describes the "con politician," the "outlaw," the "square john," and the "right guy." The con politician was an inmate who was articulate and interacted with the administration. Although he might participate in prison programs, he was, at heart, a con and furthered his own interests. The outlaw was a prisoner who would use violence to get what he wanted. The square john was the middle-class guy who committed a crime but did not have a criminal outlook or lifestyle. He was vulnerable in prison and was not trusted. The right guy was the king of kings in prison. He was respected for his toughness but also for his strict adherence to the inmate code, which included the precept "don't exploit inmates." He was likely to be in prison for a serious crime like mob activity or bank robbery. But he was perceived as honest. He was the hero of the prison subculture (Schrag 1961).

Although this typology was developed 40 years ago, it still has some validity today. Of course, there are differences. Irwin and Cressey (1962) added some additional types connected with the drug culture. Also, many inmates never fit neatly into a type at all. Still, the idea of the right guy continues in prison today; if only by prisoners noting that no right guys exist any longer. Older prisoners bemoan the "good old days," when convicts followed a code. They may be accurately perceiving differences in the type of inmate and how they behave in prison, but some evidence indicates that the right guy role is still in existence. For instance,

Winfree, Newbold, and Tubb (2002) described inmates in a New Mexico penitentiary and a New Zealand one. The authors found that inmates, when asked what qualities they respect in other inmates, listed most frequently the qualities of honesty, how they treat others, intelligence, attitude, and reservedness (2002, 223). These characteristics closely represent the right guy role of years past.

If the right guy has the highest status in prisons, the child molester and rapist are on the lowest rungs of the ladder. In fact, crimes do carry some weight in assigning status in the prison world. The highest status criminals are robbers, drug offenders, murderers, burglars, assaultive offenders, and thieves; while the lowest are murderer-rapists, rapists, incest offenders, and pedophiles (Winfree, Newbold, and Tubb 2002).

> No one knows what motivates the new breed of convicts. Their values are few, and they refuse to adopt the traditional rules and customs of prison life. I can't explain modern prisoners because I understand them less than anyone. The most glaring difference between the new and the old is that today's prisoners are more apt to plead guilty and to inform on their associates. . . . (an older ex-inmate; Martin and Sussman 1993, 213)

Recently there have been other descriptions of prison typologies. Richards (2003) describes some types of prisoners found in federal prisons, including smugglers, pilots and boat crew members, Latino and Hispanic drug soldiers, members of the Mafia, bikers, and white supremacists. Sabo, Kupers, and London (2001, 9) also describe types of prisoners and rank them in order of status in the prison: the highest ranking prisoners are the "tough guys" (Mafia members) and prisoners with resources (gang members, merchants). Then there are marginalized prisoners who do not truly belong to the subculture (college kids, program participants, prisoners who do their own time). Finally, there are the weak and victimized (snitches, homosexuals, child abusers, "punks") Thus, it appears that some things have not changed at all—punks and child molesters are still the untouchables in prison.

Prisoners in Prison

Walking through a prison, one is likely to see a bodybuilder in the yard (in the states that still allow weights). He single-mindedly works out in any kind of weather, pushing himself to the limits of his physical capacity. He does this because he knows that the appearance of strength is sometimes enough to forestall any threat of victimization. He runs the risk, though, of encouraging challenges.

In segregation, one is likely to find a "cutter." This is an inmate covered in self-inflicted scars. He or she might slice the skin with razor blades. If she can't get a razor blade, she will use a broken glass, scissors, a pen or pencil, an edge of an electrical plate, or a piece of a metal bed. Her ingenuity is matched only by her pain. Cutters inflict injury on themselves evidently as a way to feel. Their mental trauma is so great and so protracted that their minds often retreat into a numbness where the world and the people around them don't seem real. Cutting is a way to reconnect to the living. The physical pain and the attention assuage, at least for a time, the utter loneliness and despair that they feel. In the world, this behavior would clearly be seen as a cry for help and a need for immediate mental health intervention. In the prison, it is viewed quite often as a disciplinary issue. It is against the rules.

In segregation, one might also find individuals who exhibit their mental health problems in other ways. Throwing urine and feces on guards and other inmates has long been a way of showing contempt and one of the only ways inmates locked in isolation cells can get revenge. Other inmates smear feces on themselves; they may be in segregation because of an incidence of violence— either against another inmate or a guard. Once they are locked up in an isolation cell for 23 hours a day, their mental health deteriorates so much that they may be in active psychosis most of the time. They literally may not know who they are or where they are. Often, if some attention is paid to them, it takes the form of Thorazine or other antipsychotic drugs.

In southern prisons, prisoners used to act as "dog boys." These prisoners would help train the tracking dogs used to find escaping inmates. Tracking dogs, in order to train, must receive the scent of and chase a human. So these inmates would be given a running start and then the dogs would be loosed upon them. In most cases, the handlers reached the dogs before they attacked the dog boys. But not always. Today, although inmates are still used to help train, the dogs do not attack—most of the time (Bergner 1998).

Another inmate may be a "programmer." Many inmates take full advantage of correctional programs. A typical day for one of these inmates might be: Rise at 5:30 to work in the kitchen until 10; go to school from 10 until 4; back in the cell for count, dinner at 5; evening programs might be group therapy, Jaycees, or a volunteer group that makes toys for kids; lights out at 11. The inmate might also be working on a correspondence course or filing an appeal *pro se.*

Another inmate may be on a prison work crew. He may have worked with the same correctional officer (CO) for years. Usually on these work crews, the guard is chosen partly for his knowledge of carpentry or plumbing skills. The relationship between guard and prisoner is more boss-to-worker than CO-to-inmate. Although it is always clear who is in charge, the CO may give the prisoner a great deal of latitude in his schedule, or how he plans to prioritize jobs, or even the right way to do the job. When an inmate gets into this kind of groove, it is unusual for him to disrupt it by becoming involved in activities that could get him disciplined.

Bergner (1998) described a tattoo artist in prison. Tattoos are sometimes extremely crude in prison, but not always. Some prisoners take tattooing to fine art status. One particular artist created his tattoos by completing the following steps: He burned plastic and caught the burning colored soot on paper. He then mixed the soot with toothpaste and water to make an ink. He had threaded a steel guitar string through an empty pen shaft and attached it to a tiny motor from a cassette player. With this handmade instrument, the steel string was jabbed thousands and thousands of times into the skin to deposit the ink according to the design the tattoo artist had sketched on the skin (Bergner 1998, 109).

There are many other prisoner profiles that can be drawn from the 2 million individuals incarcerated in prisons and jails in this country. The point is that prisoners are not a monolithic group composed of violent, antisocial characters, although those people do exist. There are also those for whom the prison experience has been the trigger to a mental breakdown, and they descend to active psychosis or extreme personality disorder, sometimes resulting in violence to themselves and others. There are those who are far more victimized in prison than the injury they inflicted on their victim—if indeed there even was one—on the outside. There are those, too, who actually use the prison experience to improve themselves—earning a college degree or at least credit hours, learning to control their anger, and/or overcoming their addictions.

Prisons are emotional zoos filled with paranoids, manic-depressives, aggressive homosexuals, schizophrenics, and assorted fruits and vegetables without labels that explode at various times. Living in a prison is not only a matter of physical survival; emotional survival is at issue, too. So you regularly check your feelings, reactions, and disposition. . . . Whatever anger, whatever agony, whatever desperation you feel, you cry without a tear and you scream in silence. For you cannot show weakness to others who will take advantage of it. (an inmate, Patrick, in Johnson and Toch 2000, 141)

The Will to Change

One of the most interesting questions is why some prisoners, on their own, decide to change their lives and stop committing crimes and/or using drugs. The will to change is a mystery regardless of what type of change effort is targeted. The general thought, certainly among officers, is that prisoners will never change. Probably the most common salutation an inmate upon release hears is "you'll be back." And in many cases, that is all too true. But some inmates objectively evaluate their lives and they don't like what they see. Some of them are able to change, despite the subculture. Whether their new persona survives release is a different question.

I'm sitting there . . . and it's like I had an out-of-body experience, man, it's like I could see myself from the back, squatting down, playing with these fucking turds, mashing this fucking turd up, souping it up and I'm watching myself, and I said, Man, that's a fucking shame, fucking disgusting animal savage that I've turned into. Savage. And

> I'm looking at myself, and I started thinking, I don't know
> nothing, I don't read, I'm caught up in this bullshit. I knew
> then that I had to turn around. . . . From that day on I tried
> to enlighten myself. But I still went and did what I had to
> do. Because I don't want to be no fucking victim. (an in-
> mate in Angola Prison who described himself preparing a
> "feces cocktail" to throw at another inmate; Bergner
> 1998, 6)

There are prisoners, both men and women, who earnestly take advantage of programs. They devour education and self-help programs, work and earn what little money is available, join volunteer groups, and otherwise act as good citizens would in the community. Why many of these good prisoners fail on the outside is an extremely important issue. It is usually connected to a return to old friends and old temptations; the inability to get a job, or at least a job that pays enough to live on; and the stress of re-entry that then leads to using drugs or alcohol as a coping mechanism. Of course, a return to an addictive lifestyle is not only a violation of parole, but also leads to new crimes.

Conclusion

John Conrad (1981) has argued that prisoners have several fundamental rights as a function of having their liberty taken away. In other words, society has a right to incarcerate, but if we do, then prisoners deserve

1. The right to personal safety
2. The right to [appropriate] care
3. The right to personal dignity
4. The right to work
5. The right to self-improvement
6. The right to a future

These are rights that every person deserves regardless of what he or she has done. They are rights that prisoners may not enjoy in some prisons, or at least to the extent that Conrad intended. To provide less denies them basic humanity and degrades our own.

One of the most important realizations learned by visiting prisons is that they are full of people who are not monsters. Visitors to prisons inevitably ruefully, sheepishly, or innocently say, "They are not like I thought they'd be." Even those men who are covered with prison tattoos and talk the talk of the prison yard might be studying sociology in a college class or learning computer programming. Women in prison will show visitors pictures of their children and proudly display their artwork on the walls of their cells. Clearly, there are dangerous, violent people locked up, but there are also many who are not dangerous. How do they survive the prison world? In the next chapter, we will see how prisoners learn to live in the prison subculture.

Study Questions

1. Describe the demographic profile of prisoners, both men and women.
2. Explain the role of childhood abuse for men and women in prison.
3. What are the figures regarding minority representation in prisons.
4. Discuss the growing problem of the elderly in prisons.
5. Provide a typology of prisoners.

Chapter 5

Living in Prison

Wasted Lives and Broken Dreams

Secretly, we all like it here. This place welcomes a man who is full of rage and violence. Here he is not abnormal or perceived as different. Here rage is nothing new, and for men scarred by child abuse and violent lives, the prison is an extension of inner life. (Masters 2001, 205)

What is it like to live in a prison? Descriptions of prison life have been offered by screenwriters in movies such as *The Shawshank Redemption* and television series such as the HBO series *Oz.* Academic researchers have also given us book-length descriptions, such as James Jacob's *Statesville* (1977) and Gresham Sykes' *Society of Captives* (1958). Other books, written by convicts or ex-convicts, provide a firsthand account of prison life, including Jack Abbot's *In the Belly of the Beast* (1981), Vic Hassine's *Life Without Parole: Living in Prison*, or Dannie Martin's *Committing Journalism* (1993). Some correctional professionals present their views in books as well. Journal articles and books apply social science analysis to the world of the prison; for instance, the controversy over whether the prisoner subculture is a product of the deprivations of prison or imported from outside subcultures continues to be debated 30 years after its initial presentation.

One thing that all these sources have in common is that they paint a prison world that is very different from the outside. There is more violence, more tension, and more hate. Especially for men, an individual who successfully navigates the treacherous waters of the prison world is that much less able to reintegrate successfully to the outside world. He has learned, if he did not know before, how to ignore human suffering, preemptively strike so that he is not victimized, mind his own business when he sees others victimized, and submerge any perceived weaknesses including kindness or tolerance, and, more than anything else, he has probably learned how to hate if he didn't before.

Prisoner Subculture Research

Before we delve further into what it is like to live in prison today, a brief exploration of past studies would be helpful. This discussion can be found in other sources, so it will not be exhaustive. Some of the earliest studies of prison were by early sociologists who worked in prisons. These researchers started to sketch out the parameters of the social world of prisoners. Their work included typologies (types of prisoners differentiated by behaviors, values, and pre-prison experiences) and the "inmate code."

Some of the earliest prison research portrayed the prison as a world complete with its own culture. Inmates were socialized to that culture; in other words, they were "prisonized," which meant that they behaved differently and even believed differently in an accommodation to their new world. The earliest documented descriptions of this culture include Hans Reimer's (1937) observation of a Kansas penitentiary and Hayner and Ash's (1940) study of Washington State Reformatory. Donald Clemmer (1940) more fully described the inmate code, which included such tenets as:

Be cool.

Don't interfere with inmate interests.

Don't weaken.

Be sharp.

Play it cool and do your own time (Sykes and Messinger 1960, 6–9).

Sykes (1958) explained that the culture one found in a prison was a direct result of the deprivations of the prison world. Thus, homosexuality occurred because of the deprivation of the opposite sex; the black market developed because of the deprivation of autonomy and goods and services; and so on. Later research tested and enlarged these original ideas. For instance, it was hypothesized and proven that maximum security institutions had a stronger prison culture because it was less permeable, had more deprivations, but also, probably, because the most "criminalized" criminals were sent there.

Irwin and Cressey (1962), Schrag (1961), and Irwin (1970) all presented evidence that the prison culture was not purely a creation of deprivation. Rather, many aspects of the culture came from the street. Irwin, especially, pointed out how the newly emerging drug culture was finding its way into prison, both in types of prisoners and in changing values. Thus was born the long-standing debate—whether the deprivations of prison created the subculture or whether the subculture was simply imported from street culture. The literature on this question is quite extensive.

Later researchers came to the commonsense conclusion that both theories helped explain the subculture one found in prison. The theories are still being tested today and used to study a range of issues, including cross-cultural comparisons, the impact of crowding, homophobia, predictions of violence, rule violations, high-risk behaviors for HIV transmission, and the like (for a review, see Pollock 1997b; Krebs 2002; or Winfree, Newbold, and Tubb 2002). Most studies find that a combination of both theories has the greatest explanatory power (e.g., Akers, Hayner, and Grunninger 1977). It is obvious that a minimum-security camp is not going to have the same type of prison culture as a maximum-security institution. Further, there may not be much of a culture at all in the super-max prisons because inmates are, for the most part, isolated and constrained from any interaction with each other. In fact, that is probably one of the greatest deprivations of that type of prison—the inability to be a part of any social world.

Hans Toch is one of the most well-known contributors to the "prison ecology" literature. With a number of student-colleagues, he has studied the patterns of coping and the adaptation of prisoners for several decades. His contributions include the "ecological dimensions" of coping: activity, privacy, safety, emotional feedback, support, structure, and freedom. His research indicates that different ethnic groups and men and women experience prison differently, due to their different needs along these dimensions. For instance, Hispanics and women more acutely feel the absence of "support" and "emotional feedback"; freedom resonates more strongly in samples of African-American men. Certain groups of prisoners have such high needs for certain dimensions that the prison pushes them into crisis—this research is helpful for understanding mental breakdowns in prison (Johnson and Toch 1982; Toch and Adams 1989). Prison staff should care to know how to recognize and respond to prisoners' differential needs, if only to prevent violence (Toch 1975, 1977, 1980b, 1982).

The Prison World: 1900s–1960s

We have very few descriptions of the prison world in the early part of this century. Johnson (1997, 2002) provides some historical context, as does Rothman (1971). Life for those in early penitentiaries was harsh. Conditions were, for the most part, abysmal, and there was pervasive brutality and racism. Inmates tended to be older, with long criminal careers. There weren't very many of them, however, and prisons were not massive as they are today. There was a large gulf between guards and inmates that neither side breached. Each knew their place and both sides valued predictability and order.

Descriptions from the 1940s through the early 1960s painted a somewhat idealized view of prison life, where "right guys" were looked up to and lived by an honor code that included such principles as "don't snitch" and "don't exploit other inmates." Other principles of the code included "be cool," "do your own time," "be tough," and, above all else, "never talk to a screw [guard]" (Sykes and Messinger 1960). Later researchers argued that most prisoners, when asked, knew very few right guys, the type of prisoner who upheld all the principles of the prisoner code. However, the descriptions are fairly consistent of a prison where convicts created their own world, complete with politicians, outlaws, and commerce. Prison administrators left inmates alone as long as things were quiet and prisoners could fashion a life that was, if not comfortable, at least livable. Irwin (1980; also see Austin and Irwin 2001) explains that the changes that began in the 1960s have fragmented the prison social world. By the 1960s, even the idealized code was changing with the entry of drug offenders and a younger prisoner population. Three elements converged to create a completely different prison world from any that had come before: racial politics, drugs, and a massive influx of much younger criminals.

The 1960s—Change in the Prison World

In the 1960s, there was the growing political consciousness of some prisoners, especially African-Americans. The number of African-Americans and other minorities in prisons was growing. As they became a more powerful force in the prison world, and especially as some redefined themselves as political prisoners, racial strain developed. The racial strain often broke out in race riots or individual acts of violence. Prisoners alleged that officers incited and encouraged racial unrest in order to control prisoners, but in truth prisoners probably did not need much help to justify acts of aggression.

Groups that began as political entities with political agendas quickly turned to prison rackets (drugs, gambling, and other contraband sold and bartered as a black market). Gangs were powerful competitors because of the number and loyalty of members. Gangs such as the Mexican Mafia, the Texas Syndicate, the La Nuestra Familia, and Black Guerrilla Family rapidly took over prison drug markets and forced inmates to join or be victimized by the gang. The Chicano gang now known as the Mexican Mafia began with a group of Los Angeles Chicanos locked up in juvenile institutions. As they graduated to Chino and other prisons, they preyed upon northern Chicanos. Eventually Chicanos from northern California formed their own gang for protection—this gang became known as La Nuestra Familia.

The Black Guerrilla Family started as a black nationalist group stemming from the Black Panthers. Today, the political agenda has been completely supplanted by criminal objectives. Two other African-American gangs—the "Crips" and the "Bloods"—have also arrived on the scene; these gangs are more closely tied to neighborhood allegiances and tend to engage in conflict with each other rather than with other races (Parenti 1999; Hunt et al. 1993).

Whites responded to the threat of gang victimization by forming gangs of their own, usually with some neo-Nazi element, such as the Aryan Brotherhood and, more recently, the Nazi Lowriders. Whites are still less likely to belong to any gang than minority pris-

oners, however, which leaves them more vulnerable to victimization (Trout 1992; Pelz, Marquart, and Pelz 1991; Parenti 1999). The
threat of victimization and the need for protection were cited by
defense attorneys as a reason for John King's membership in a neo-
Nazi prison group in a Texas prison. King was one of the men who
participated in the dragging death of James Byrd in Jasper, Texas.
Defense attorneys, in their plea to avoid the death penalty, argued
that prison turned King into a racist. However, it should be noted
that racial war takes a backseat to profit, and the Aryan Brotherhood has been known to partner with La Eme (Mexican Mafia) for
profitable smuggling or distribution schemes.

Drugs have influenced the prisoner subculture in a number of
ways. First, drugs led to a breakdown of the so-called "inmate
code." Often drug offenders did not have entrenched criminal
identities, nor were they socialized through the criminal street culture. Also, the drug culture was an entity unto itself and principles
such as "don't snitch" were replaced with more egocentric concerns. Drugs led to increased prison violence in several ways.
Some drugs themselves tended to create irrationally violent
behavior (e.g., PCP). Also, violence is sometimes used by drug
dealers in prison to enforce a contract or punish a debtor. Finally,
dealers will use violence or the threat of violence to coerce other
inmates and their families to participate in drug smuggling. Today,
drugs continue to be a management issue for prisons. Because
most prisons are so large (many house over 5,000 prisoners), it is
extremely difficult to control all contraband coming into the
prison. In fact, a certain percentage of drugs are smuggled in by
officers who are seduced by large financial compensation or
coerced by intimidation and blackmail to take the risk.

Another element that has changed the prisoner subculture has
been the increase in young offenders. Prison populations in the
1950s were composed of older inmates, and although certainly not
upstanding citizens, they tended to be stable, taking care of their
own problems and desiring little interaction with guards. Drug
offenders tend to be younger and this influx of younger offenders,
especially through the mid-1980s and 1990s, led to increased disturbances and violent incidents. In an effort to control younger
inmates, some systems mixed older and younger inmates together,
but usually all this did was make prison life miserable for the old

cons, who could not control and were not respected by the Young Turks. Housing all younger inmates in one facility created havoc for officers since the frequency of fighting and other incidents went up dramatically.

> They have nothing but younger guys in prison now. And . . . it has just changed . . . since there are so many children and kids in prison it is hard to do time now. It is not like it used to be where you can wake up one morning and know what to expect. But now you wake up and . . . anything might happen. . . . (an older inmate, cited in Hunt et al. 1993, 407)

Throughout the 1960s and 1970s, inmates were given new ground rules. To be a good prisoner not only meant staying out of trouble, or at least not getting caught; it also meant the person had to "program." The inmate subcultural rule to "never talk to a screw" was difficult to adhere to when a guard was running a group therapy session that the inmate had to attend. Officers, too, were confused, since their task was expanded to not only guard but also to be an influence on the offender. They greeted the changes with a considerable amount of cynicism. From their perspective, prisoners were gaining more freedom and that made their job more difficult and dangerous. A few inmates and a few guards welcomed the changes and embraced the correctional philosophy; others manipulated the system; and many bemoaned the good old days, when guards and inmates knew their place. Old norms against inmate-guard interaction have broken down but have not entirely dissipated.

Court decisions arguably changed the balance of power in prisons by giving prisoners some early victories. They are also pointed to as the reason for an explosion of violence in prisons as each prison accommodated change. For instance, between 1972 and 1975 there were 40 inmate murders and 360 stabbings in Angola Prison in Louisiana (Bergner 1998, 64). In Texas, the dismantling of the "builder tender system," wherein inmates basically guarded other inmates, led to a vacuum of power taken over by gangs and cliques that exploited weaker inmates (Crouch and Marquart 1989). Killings were common. Prison homicides went from 16 in the period 1970–1978 to 52 in 1984–1985, some argue as a direct result of Judge Justice's ruling in *Ruiz v. Estelle* (1982). In this case, the Texas prison system was placed under a court-appointed monitor to ensure compliance with a number of court-ordered changes. Texas has only recently been released from this monitoring condition.

Change was afoot in other prisons as well. In Massachusetts, Walpole Prison was described as a hellhole where excrement littered the hallways and officers rarely ventured into inmate living areas (Kauffman 1988). Carroll (1998) paints a similar picture in Rhode Island and Hassine (1999) provides a firsthand account of his experience in Pennsylvania's Graterford prison during turbulent times.

> These were violent and deadly times at Graterford; times of random violence, murders, cell fires, paranoia, and knife carrying. According to the Department of Corrections' Monthly Morbidity Report in 1986–87, Graterford accounted for the highest rate of assaults out of Pennsylvania's 12 state prisons: 392 assaults by inmates against inmates and 47 by inmates against staff.... While it seemed like total anarchy, it really wasn't. This was mob rule with a purpose, a throwback to a time long before civilized man developed modern social institutions. By now I began to realize how fragile civilization was and how easily modern man could be reduced to the savagery of his prehistoric ancestors. (Hassine 1999, 28)

Others have also described the mammoth changes and turmoil that gripped prisons in the wake of court-mandated changes, prison population changes, and societal changes (Irwin 1980). It is interesting that prison violence may have reached its peak at the same time as did criminal violence on the street. By some accounts, it has also followed the downward trend of violent street crime, but prison has never been, and probably will never be, a place free of fear.

> If you clearly didn't care, if you could convince inmates and guards that you had absolutely nothing to lose and

that your countermeasures to even the most trivial provocation would be totally unrestrained and pursued to the utmost of your abilities—then you were given respect and a wide berth, and people looked to you for leadership and advice. "He's crazy," they'd say admiringly, even longingly, when the name came up. "He's just totally, completely insane." (Early 1992)

The Prison World Today

Today's prison is quite different from the prison world described by early researchers. There are some elements of the subculture that have remained, but other things are quite different.

The Inmate Code

The inmate code that Sykes and Messinger (1960) described may have been somewhat idealized but, in general, it probably represented the values of most inmates. Inmates were supposed to be tough and avoid guards, and mind their own business, but not exploit other prisoners. The vast changes that occurred led to younger inmates with different street values, and the clash between the old and the new might have undergirded some of the violence that occurred in the 1980s. Many old-time cons saw that younger prisoners did not respect them and cared nothing for their values.

To the Old Heads, prison life today lacked the honor, quiet solitude, and routine that had once made incarceration more noble. Now the greatest threat to an inmate had become other inmates, particularly the "young bucks" who had infested the general population. (Hassine 1999, 31)

Hassine (1999) provides a fascinating account of one inmate's experience through the 1980s and, if it is representative at all, it illustrates how the prison culture itself adapted and stabilized, gaining control over roving predators and the violence of the drug trade. The inmate code he describes is quite different from the earlier version: "Don't gamble, don't mess with drugs, don't mess with homosexuals, don't steal, don't borrow or lend, and you might survive" (Hassine 1999, 42). His words are supported by current ethnographies that describe how a large percentage of inmates today stay in their cells whenever possible and avoid the yard.

Winfree, Newbold, and Tubb (2002) compared a New Zealand prisoner sample with a New Mexico prisoner sample and found some interesting differences between the two groups in their adherence to principles of the code. The New Mexico group exhibited attitudes and values that were quite a bit more positive toward guards than the New Zealand group. The authors explain this difference by the relatively longer criminal histories of prisoners in New Zealand. A substantially larger percentage of the New Mexico group were first-time offenders. Also, the New Zealand group were high-security offenders, while a good portion of the New Mexico group were in protective custody.

Lerner (2002), a middle-class guy who was sent to prison for voluntary manslaughter, recently described the prison from the perspective of a prison "fish." Once in prison, he became a "lawdog," since he had a college education and could help other inmates interpret court papers. Soon his vocabulary absorbed the prison slang, including descriptions of prisoners such as dawgs (friends, associates, acquaintances), queens (homosexual men who dress like women), punks (the sexually victimized or anyone who is taken advantage of), fish (new inmates), woods (from "peckerwoods," a name for whites), toads (also a derogatory name for whites), shotcallers (prisoners who had some power), wiggers (whites who associated with blacks), fishcops (new COs), and old heads (older cons who liked to talk about the old days in prison).

In Lerner's (2002) description of prison, queens were obvious. They wore the state-issued denims cut off about two inches below their crotch, with the prison shirt cut short to show the midriff. Mascara was blue pool-cue chalk and cherry Kool-Aid served as lipstick. Much of the violence revolved around sex and relationships. Shotcallers were those with power. They could "fix" anything, including securing a cell assignment, obtaining drugs, and ordering a hit on another prisoner. Although their power might come from gang affiliation, it was not necessarily mandatory.

He learned that every newcomer to prison would face a "heartcheck" and must show a willingness to fight; otherwise, he would become a punk or a yard trick (one who carried contraband and did menial labor for others). He discovered that there was a daily yard toll, a cell or bunk rental fee, and if the fish had resources he might end up paying a life insurance policy of $500 a week. If an inmate didn't fight, didn't have friends, or couldn't pay, he would be victimized. Other newcomers were greeted warmly. He explains that those with "full sleeves" (many tattoos) were not vulnerable to extortion, especially if they sported a swastika or a teardrop (said to denote someone who has murdered a police officer).

He also explained why the requests prisoners fill out to see a counselor or go to sick call are called kites: "clear to anyone who has ever been advised to go fly a fucking kite" (Lerner 2002, 67). Lerner's description paints a prison world where the guards, in a sense, become prisonized and even adopt the prisoner language. *You've Got Nothing Coming* was the title of his book and the mantra of the prison staff, according to Lerner. Cruelty by guards wasn't necessarily extreme; rather, it was banal and pointless.

Richards (2003), Ross and Richards (2003), and Sabo, Kupers, and London (2001) are all recent sources containing information about prisons. The prison world is, in some ways, different from 30 years ago and, in some ways, very much the same. For instance, the black market has always characterized prison life.

The Black Market

One of the most enduring elements of the prisoner subculture is the black market one can find in any prison of any size. Inmates are truly ingenious in acquiring and utilizing contraband. One can literally "buy" anything in prison. Prisoners operate fairly freely with some degree of tolerance by prison officials, except for drugs, weapons, and violence. Once the black market began to provide drugs, they became more popular than prison "hooch" and much easier to hide. Today, while drugs have not been completely eliminated, some prisons have taken aggressive steps to curtail the drug trade, including random drug tests on prisoners and prosecuting guards who are caught smuggling. The other elements of the black market are more resistant to enforcement and there is some question as to whether or not prison officials even desire to curtail all aspects of it. Some guards may believe that a satisfied inmate (whether his needs are for alcohol, drugs, sex, or sandwiches at night) is less likely to cause trouble.

I had at my disposal the eager services of swag men [contraband food], laundry men, ice men (for summer ice cubes), barbers (to cut my hair in my cell), and phone men (to make sure I got signed up for phone calls). I could even have a cell cleaner, though I felt there were certain things a man should do for himself. All in all, Graterford had become a predatory institution where nothing worked right and everything was for sale. (Hassine 1999, 37)

Racial Tension

In the 1970s, the era of court activism over prisons, some court decisions mandated that prisons become racially integrated in cell and program assignments. Prison officials, convinced that judges had no business telling them how to run prisons, used this ruling as an example of how outsiders did not know what prisons were like. Racial segregation in prison was (and is) practiced by the prisoners themselves. In some prisons, the dayrooms have chairs allocated to Hispanics, African-Americans, and whites, and the person who accidentally sits in the wrong chair is in trouble. The yard is balkanized into racial groupings, and an inmate will rarely, if ever, sit with someone of another race in the dining hall if allowed to select a seat.

Prison officials predicted a bloodbath if forced to integrate, and there is some evidence that indicates at least some officials tried to instigate prisoner unrest (Trulson and Marquart 2002a). Actually, according to some research, the predicted violence due to racial integration did not occur to the degree feared, although racial violence has continued to plague prisons (Trulson and Marquart 2002b).

Today, racial unrest continues and, especially in some prisons, accounts for quite a bit of the violence, although Trulson and Marquart (2002b) show that at least in the Texas prison system, intraracial and interracial violence occur at about the same rate. Much of the violence in prison is related to racial gangs. The California Department of Corrections estimates that nearly 7,000 gang members reside in their state prisons (cited in Parenti 1999, 194). In addition to the older gangs described above, new gangs have formed, including new forms of the split between northern and southern California Chicanos—the Nortenos and the Surenos, and the "border brothers" (Hunt et al. 1993). The Crips and Bloods are now joined by the 415s (named for the 415 area code in San Francisco). Some argue that because there are many more gangs today than in the past, they are looser and do not have the power over prisoners they once did (Hunt et al. 1993). However, it may also be true that the shifting allegiances and loyalties between these gangs make it more difficult to stay safe today in prisons. Also, inmates form less formal, semi-organized groups that utilize racial and geographic categories. These cliques draw individuals together for defense, support, and trade in the prison black market.

It should be understood that tension between racial gangs today has as much to do with financial interests as it does racial prejudice. Since gangs control most, if not all, of the black market, violence between gangs is often attributed to business and gang members protecting their market. Prisoners still maintain that prison guards incite racial violence. The most notorious stories come from Corcoran Prison in California. Numerous allegations of guards setting up gladiator fights and otherwise pitting racial gang members against each other have surfaced and have even been the object of litigation (1999).

Gang management policies are a mix of control (identifying and separating gang leaders), enriching program offerings (to keep inmates busy), and practicing good management (eliminating procedures and locations in a prison that are vulnerable to violence) (Fleisher and Rison 1999, 237). There are continuing allegations that guards encourage racial violence to keep inmates from organizing together against the guards (Hunt et al. 1993). Allegations of officers participating in or at least allowing gang warfare to occur continue. Overt or covert racial guard organizations exist (such as the "Society for the Prevention of Niggers Getting Everything" and the "European American Officers Association") and provide support to neo-Nazi inmate gangs (Parenti 1999, 206).

African-American inmates may account for a disproportionate share of prison violence. Harer and Steffensmeier (1996) review previous findings regarding the correlation between race and prison violence. Some studies found a relationship, others did not. In Harer and Steffensmeier's study of 58 federal prisons for men and misconduct reports for July 1988 through December 1989, the authors were able to control for structural variables and community background variables, and found that violence was correlated with race. African-American men were more likely to be disciplined for violent infractions. Of course, since the study depends on official identifications of violence, there may be some bias introduced to the relative total number of incidents reported for African-American versus white inmates. They also found that whites were more likely than African-Americans to be disciplined for alcohol or drug violations.

Prison Violence

More than anything else, the prison world is associated with violence. One author characterizes the types of violence occurring in prison as the following: intrapersonal (self-mutilation, suicide attempts, etc.), interpersonal (sexual, physical, or psychological), group (gang activity or loose associations), organized (riots or organized attacks on officers), and institutional (beatings or other physical or emotional harm inflicted by officers) (Braswell, Montgomery, and Lombardo 1994). The most extreme forms of violence found in prison, of course, are homicide and rape. Rape and the threat of rape are used as a device of intimidation. Rapes, along with beatings, are used to humiliate, control, punish, and/or exploit. While no one is exempt, those who are not affiliated with some group or powerful individual are most often victimized.

Prison rape. One study found that 22 percent of male prisoner respondents had been raped or forced into sex while incarcerated. Only 29 percent had reported their rape to authorities (Struckman-Johnson et al. 1996). Other studies have reported rates of rape between 1 and 25 percent (Krebs 2002, 21), but another researcher notes that these figures do not count those who consent to sex after being threatened with homosexual rape (Kupers 2001). Human Rights Watch (2001), reporting on the problem, also concludes that it occurs much more often than reported figures indicate. One victim of sexual assault in prison, Stephen Donaldson, was a Quaker peace activist. He was jailed when he refused to post a ten-dollar bond. In a Washington, D.C., jail he was raped over 50 times. He died of AIDS, contracted from one of his assailants (Man and Cronan 2001, 127).

> The sexual activity is rampant and encouraged by guards. Guards believe that the sex will provide release for sexual tension; this is faulty logic though, as more tension is produced from the dislike of homosexuals, the bartering of homosexuals, and the protection of gays by other prisoners. I sincerely believe that the promiscuous sexual activity here is encouraged to alleviate the tension here. The authorities it is my belief don't give a damn if we kill each other; so what, they say, he is a fag or they are just inmates. (an inmate responding to a questionnaire, quoted by Krebs 2002, 38)

This type of prison violence has been chronicled since the early 1900s. Officers sometimes ignore it, pretend it doesn't exist, or actively encourage and support rape and sexual predation of the strong against the weak. Observers note that officers obtain some benefit from the forced emasculation and prostitution of young men. Gilligan (2002) reviews the literature and utilizes his own experiences as a prison doctor to conclude that officers benefit by allowing some inmates to brutalize others. Some believe that a predator becomes more manageable and calm if he has a "wife," a man forced into sexual submission.

> [Staff members] used to perform prison marriages in which the convict and his galboy-wife would leap over the broomstick together in a mock ceremony. (Wilbert Rideau, an inmate in Angola State Penitentiary in Louisiana, in Rideau and Wikberg 1992, 90)

It is interesting that the aggressors do not consider themselves to be homosexual. While it does not impact one's masculinity to be the aggressor (in fact, in a way, it enhances it), the "catcher" or "receiver" is considered less than a man. Once made into a punk, whore, or sex slave, the man is emasculated and is, in the sense of social relations, a different gender. Sex slaves are bartered, traded, and sold in prison. They are forced to do service labor, including laundry, cleaning, and food preparation for their husbands or whoever their husbands sell them to. The punk acts as wife in all senses of the word in some relationships, providing emotional support as well as services. In most relationships, however, the "man's" relationship with the punk doesn't stop him from lending him out for sexual services.

Observers note that prisoners engaged in homosexual dyads, just as heterosexual couples, have varied relationships: "The men tend to treat their catchers much as they habitually did their female companions, so a wide range of relationships, ranging from ruthless exploitation to romantic love, exists" (Donaldson 2001, 121). In some relationships, the "daddy" becomes emotionally attached to his "wife" or "kid."

Rape is devastating and victims suffer a range of medical and psychological effects. There is virtually no professional intervention for victims of rape within a prison. Men who suffer rape are released bearing psychic scars that last a lifetime, and that may lead to the victim becoming a sexual offender (Dumond 2000). Human Rights Watch (2001) reports that victims commonly report nightmares, depression, shame, loss of self-esteem, self-hatred, and suicidal thoughts.

Inmates rape each other partly as an outlet for sex but also as a means of ensuring their masculinity. In a prison world, to be a man is reduced down to the very basic element of power. For some, power is experienced as the power to abuse and enslave another. It is instructive to note that most men in prison feel powerless in their lives; in fact, quite a bit of the incentive for crime includes the feeling of power that comes with taking control of a victim, even if it is only over property.

_____

It's fixed where if you're raped, the only way you [can escape further abuse is if] you rape someone else. Yes I know that's fully screwed, but that's how your head is twisted. After it's over you may be disgusted with yourself, but you realize you're not powerless and that you can deliver as well as receive pain. Then it's up to you to

> decide whether you enjoy it or not. Most do, I don't. (an
> inmate, cited in Mariner 2001, 128)

If inmate victims sue, the test used by the court to determine whether or not officers or administrators are liable is the "deliberate indifference" test. Basically, this means that the inmate victim has to prove that the prison officials knew there was a risk and consciously disregarded it and that their disregard was instrumental in the victimization. This test is a difficult one to meet, since the argument could be that there is no way to prevent all rapes in prison (Man and Cronan 2001).

Non-coercive sex. It should be noted that not all sex in men's prisons is obtained through rape or even coercion. Hensley, Struckman-Johnson, and Eigenberg (2000) provide a comprehensive review of research that focuses on prison sex. They note that most of the research has focused on prison rape and coerced sex and, therefore, we know very little about noncoercive sex in men's prisons. Their review also covers sexual relationships and coercion in women's prisons. The majority of researchers have concluded that there is less coerced sex in prisons for women, although it is present to some small extent.

'Official' Violence

"Official" violence is that inflicted on inmates by officers. Obviously, force is necessary at times; however, illegal use of force occurs when the violence is gratuitous, unnecessary, and used as an extra-legal means of punishment. There are numerous reports of inappropriate and illegal uses of violence by correctional officers—most incidents probably go unreported. There is also no doubt that inmates are an extremely challenging group of people to supervise. Individuals who would never inflict gratuitous violence in the real world may become inured to it in the strange world of the prison.

> For fun and games they like to save paper cups and fill
> them with grits and urine, which they lined up and stored
> on the top bunks. When they had collected enough am-
> munition, they would summon the guard they hated the

> most, and then pummel him with this disgusting brew.
> The "screw" would blow his whistle, and the rest of the
> "good old boys" would "come a running" armed with
> clubs. . . . When the door opened it was "off to the ro-
> deo," with the prisoners, led by the youngest, surging for-
> ward to battle the guards with fists and food trays. When
> it was over, the guards would handcuff the worst offend-
> ers and tie them to the bars to be beaten some more
> with truncheons. (Richards 2003, 132)

Some research indicates that the state of California has disproportional rates of inmate shootings. From 1989 to 1998, 219 inmates
were shot by California prison guards and 39 died. No other state
comes close to those numbers. In all other states combined, only six
inmates were shot by guards between 1994 and 1998, and those were
during incidents of escape. Only one inmate was shot and killed in
Texas between 1994 and 1998 (Parenti 1999, 171).

What accounts for this huge disparity? Probably the difference
is that, except for California, very few states allow shots to be fired
to break up fights. Added to this is the practice of some California
guards (evidently) to set the stage for a fight by releasing rival
gang members into the same yard and sitting back to watch what
happens (Parenti 1999, 171).

> Just a fistfight, I sighed with relief. No way the guard will
> shoot unless one man goes down and the other refused
> to back off and starts kicking the downed man in the
> head. . . . my eyes went up to the catwalk and spied the
> twenty-something-year-old blonde badge racing till he
> stood directly above the combatants. Swinging the barrel
> of his rifle down, he fired, re-aimed in less than a single
> second, and two more flat cracks spat. One prisoner
> dived away, the other limply toppled over, his head
> cracked open from one or more bullets rudely introduc-
> ing themselves. A crimson mist filled the air; big red
> drops rained onto a corpse. . . . Guards burst out of East
> Block, ran to yard six with a bright orange stretcher, and
> the sergeant leading the pack yelled at the only breathing

prisoner, "Get up! Get to the gate!" . . . I don't imagine too many citizens are too terribly concerned about the prisoners I've seen shot/killed and the many more shot/ maimed. The blonde guard and his few psychotic brethren sprinkled among the professional correctional officers manning gun posts don't imagine anyone will care and they feel absolutely free to pull a trigger . . . , bloody a body, and publicly chuckle about it later. (an inmate, Hunter in Johnson and Toch 2000, 195–196)

Allegations of beatings and shootings by California officers working at Corcoran Prison, even of one inmate in his cell, have spurred investigations by the FBI, the Justice Department, and California investigative bodies. Parenti (1999) and others have summarized the news reports and court records that indicate that many Corcoran officers were out of control, and that the California Department of Corrections attempted to cover up the scandal rather than deal with it. About the same time that the Corcoran investigation was under way, a federal judge handed down a decision in a civil rights claim by a Pelican Bay inmate that detailed a horrifying array of brutality by guards against inmates in Pelican Bay, including beating, leaving inmates chained in their own excrement, submerging them in boiling water, and keeping them in telephone booth size cages (1999).

I get attacks, My heart starts pounding like it's going to break out of my chest, I can't breathe, I start to see lights, I get to where I feel like I'm gonna faint. I can't tell when it's going to happen. . . . I'm just always scared the cops [guards] are going to jack me up for something. There's no telling when they're gonna beat you, or even kill you. They beat up a cellie of mine so bad he's been in a wheelchair ever since. I'm just trying to do my time peacefully so I can get home in one piece. (an inmate, quoted in Kupers 1999, 103)

Another form of guard brutality is using other inmates to inflict pain and suffering. Again, Corcoran Prison figures prominently in a case that illustrates how this form of violence works. Officers sometimes put targeted inmates into cells with known rapists. In most cases, the expected occurs and the inmate is brutally raped and beaten. Officers have clean hands and they innocently argue that they didn't know it would happen. In the Corcoran case, the aggressor was known as the "Booty Bandit." An officer who questioned the transfer was told that Eddie Dillard, the victim, was a troublemaker who kicked a female guard. For the next several days the Booty Bandit raped, tortured, and beat Dillard, and his screaming and begging for someone to help echoed throughout the tier (Arax 1999a, 1999b). No officers have been convicted of anything as a result of this incident. Some argue that officers encourage and perpetuate prison rape because it serves their purposes. It is used as a threat against prisoner troublemakers and keeps other, powerful prisoners happy by providing an outlet for sexual release (Parenti 1999, 189).

Can prison violence be reduced? In a research study that looked at a variety of measures of individual and collective violence in prison, it was found that poor prison management was a predictor of both inmate-on-guard and guard-on-inmate assaults (McCorkle, Miethe, and Drass 1995). It seems to be the case that there is a range in the level of violence among prisons. Certainly part of the difference has to do with the type of prisoners housed in the institution, but it is probably also true that prison management bears some responsibility for both the level of "official" violence and inmate-on-inmate violence. It is also probable that the two are, in some ways, related to each other.

There, at two a.m. one night, Terry woke to see a man sliding a pair of sneakers from beneath another's cot. While the second inmate slept under the soft blue of the security lights, the man pulled the high-tops onto his feet, laced them snugly, tied them, and, fully dressed now, walked up the aisle to his own bed. He removed the padlock from his box. Holding it, he returned to the sleeping inmate, knelt on top of him, and pinned his head to the pillow with one hand. Terry guessed he was about to deal

out a whipping with the padlock, then saw he carried a
razor in addition. . . . Now he carved with the razor. He
sliced deep from temple to jaw. Then he dealt out the
lock-whipping. And then the guard's backup arrived.
(Bergner 1998, 226)

Changes in Prison Violence

Prison has been described as an "unstable and violent social jungle" (Johnson 1996, 133), and inmates describe a world of unrelenting fear. Indeed, because of drugs, gangs, and increased freedom of movement, prisoners probably have more reason to fear each other in today's prisons, even if they encounter less violence from guards. The explosion of violence in prisons in the mid-1980s was said to be related to court decisions that gave prisoners greater freedom of movement within the prison. Prison officials allege that their control was reduced by court actions and the result was an increase in assaults and killings by inmates. It is argued, for instance, that eliminating the "building tenders," inmates who helped keep order in the prison, created a vacuum of power that was soon filled by warring gangs. This certainly is supported by the unprecedented number of killings that took place in 1984–1985, after the building tenders (BTs) were abolished by the order in *Ruiz v. Estelle.* No less than 52 killings took place, along with 600 stabbings; this compares with the 16 killings recorded in eight years between 1970 and 1978 (Ekland-Olson 1986).

If I made eye contact with a stranger, I would feel threatened. An unexpected smile could mean trouble. A man in uniform was not a friend. Being kind was a weakness. Viciousness and recklessness were to be respected and admired. (Hassine 1999, 13)

It should also be noted, however, that Crouch and Marquart (1990) point out that in a survey of inmates, Texas prisoners reported feeling less secure in prisons before the ruling than after, and in fact in the early 1980s, when there were high rates of homicides recorded, prisoners did not report elevated levels of fear. This could be due to the fact that the violence was centralized to certain parts of the prison and to certain groups. After 1985 there was a dramatic shift and prisoners reported feeling substantially safer than ever before. This period was marked by a reduction in gang wars and prison system officials who had given up fighting Judge Justice's orders in *Ruiz v. Estelle* and began to comply. They also discovered through their survey that African-Americans felt less safe than whites in the 1970s and early 1980s, but that after court-mandated reforms, whites felt less secure than African-Americans.

> Getting rid of the BTs, turnkeys, and countboys was a very good thing because in the old days it was a simple matter for them to "cross out" somebody they didn't like. They did that shit all the time. . . . Most people were tense all the time. (a Texas inmate quoted in Crouch and Marquart 1990, 119)

Creating a 'Home'

Prison is home to inmates. For some, it is home for decades. Whereas many "rip and roar" and engage heavily in the inmate subculture, others try to find some semblance of safety by choosing job assignments that take them away from the mainstream and avoid the mess hall and yard and any other place where they may get involved in trouble. Zamble and Porporino (1988) describe long-termers who sought a structured, safe, and orderly life. These inmates stayed in their cells during free time, they developed only a few relationships with other prisoners, and they avoided commerce in the black market. They, in effect, created a world within a world, moving through the chaotic and trouble-plagued social world of the prison, but not a part of it.

Others also describe inmates, perhaps a growing number of inmates, who try to avoid the prison subculture. Owen (1998), too, describes how most of the women she talked to avoided the yard and stayed away from "the mix." Irwin (1980) describes how many prisoners minimize their interactions with the black market and avoid the violent gangs and cliques, spending most of their time either at work or in their cell. Johnson (2002) describes how prisoners seek "niches" that provide safety and psychological support.

Sheehan (1978) describes in detail the life of one prisoner, George Malinow, who seems atypically comfortable because he has systematically constructed his day-to-day activities in a way that reduces his chance to be exposed to danger or trouble. For these inmates, successful living in prison is dreary boredom.

So I'll get up this morning, like every other morning, and I'll go through the routine, because the routine is what saves me. The days are all the same . . . and looking back a year ago when I got this jolt, it seems like only yesterday because yesterday was just like it was a year ago. (Manocchio and Dunn 1982, 188)

Conclusion

One of the first things to note in summarizing the changes that have taken place in the prison world is that we have less ethnographic research today than we did in previous decades. We get glimpses of the prison world through the eyes of prisoner writers, and try to put together puzzle pieces of it with survey results; but the rich, detailed work of the early ethnographers are decades out of date. That being said, it seems clear that prisons today are more heterogeneous and therefore the subculture is not as monolithic. Many competing groups and gangs struggle for power. In the mid-1980s this evidently resulted in spikes of violence in some state systems. Also, the increasing presence of drugs led to violence. Today, the violence seems to have abated, partly because of prison officials controlling gangs and reducing the prevalence of drugs by testing and tighter security. However, given the constant stream of new prisoners, the increasing numbers of prisoners facing very long sentences, and the increasingly laissez-faire attitudes of courts toward official abuses of prisoners, one might predict violence will continue in some form.

The subculture of prisons is a changing, dynamic entity partly formed by the elements of prison living and partly by those we send there. There are interesting similarities between prisoners of today and those of years past. For one thing, prisoners still seem to yearn for right guys—even though outlaws seem to have taken over.

Study Questions

1. Describe the inmate code.
2. Describe how drugs have affected the prisoner subculture.
3. What types of violence exist in the prison?
4. What percentage of prisoners have been sexually assaulted? What are the effects of sexual assault on the victims? How does the subculture view prison rape?
5. Describe "official" violence in prison. How can prison management reduce its occurrence?

Chapter 6

Programs, Education, and Health Care

Earl also mutilates himself by cutting. I ask him why he cuts and he describes very poignantly how, after he has been confined to a cell for awhile, his anxiety level rises to an unbearable degree and he feels compelled to cut himself. He thinks the cutting is the only way to alleviate the anxiety. Eventually he discovered that each time he cut himself, across the wrist or across the abdomen, he would be removed from his cell and sent to the infirmary for stitches. (Kupers, a prison doctor, 1999, 37)

It is an overstatement to declare that prisoners today receive no education, training, mental health treatment, or personal improvement programs. Virtually every prison offers some type of basic education and at least a few vocational programs. All prisons offer some level of health care. The problem is that there are more prisoners than program slots and services available. For instance, although most prison administrators will profess that their prisoners all have work assignments, many of these assignments are make-work, such as sweeping one hallway for four hours. In reality, many prisoners are idle not because they choose to be, but because there are not enough program slots or work assignments for everyone.

In this chapter, the formal activities of the prison will be discussed. These include all treatment programs, education, recreation, and work; but first, we will also explore issues related to health care.

Medical Services

Medical budgets for state prison systems are expanding exponentially, partially due to lawsuits, partially because of the increasing number of geriatric prisoners, but also because of the continuing plague of AIDS. The number of HIV-positive inmates is frightening—by some accounts, it is five to seven times higher than in the general population (Altman 1999; Keeton and Swanson 1998). In 1997, an estimated 8,900 inmates had AIDS and another 35,000 to 47,000 were HIV positive. In that same year, 907 inmates in prison died from AIDS, representing 29 percent of all institutional deaths (Altman 1999; Welch 2000). Because of sexual practices, intravenous drug use, and the widespread practice of tattooing, inmates who enter prison without the disease may contract it there. Some prisons have gone so far as to defy public opinion and offer condoms to stem the contagion. Almost all prisons offer counseling and education on AIDS. However, according to a recent report, only 10 percent of state and federal prisons and 5 percent of city and county jails offer comprehensive HIV prevention programs (Altman 1999).

Back in the early days of "The Game, [homosexuality]" nobody gave a damn about AIDS. Hell, we weren't exactly sure what it was. We knew from reading the newspapers or watching television that a whole lot of people were afraid of whatever it was. We might have been, too, if we thought that it had something to do with us. Back then, only gays got AIDS. I never considered myself gay until some years later. (Gilbreath and Rogers in Johnson and Toch 2000, 188)

Offenders, because of their sexual practices and drug use, are already a high-risk group. Court decisions have made it difficult but not impossible for institutions to segregate HIV-positive inmates. Inmates argue that segregation exposes them to stigma and harassment by other prisoners and staff (Welch 2000). On the other hand, a lack of segregation and confidentiality creates the situation where an infected prisoner may spread the disease to his sex partners or drug partners without their knowledge. If a prisoner develops a full-blown case of AIDS, the medical costs are astronomical and this expense is multiplied by the large numbers of prisoners suffering from HIV/AIDS. If the problem is not contained, it has the potential to bankrupt state systems and pull resources away from every other program and service offered.

Some states have tried to resolve the issue by releasing sick offenders, but this practice is legally questionable and arguably does not remove the state's responsibility in providing care. In reality, most prisoners with AIDS do not receive state-of-the-art care. In fact, there are allegations that AZT and other drugs are withheld from prisoners as punishment or through incompetence. Not receiving the drug according to its required dosage is obviously less effective, so correctional officers and medical care providers can literally kill an inmate by neglect (Welch 2000; Hemmons and Marquart 1998).

Other diseases also pose problems in prison. In the early 1990s, several dozen prison inmates died of a strain of tuberculosis resistant to all available medications. One correctional officer died as well (May 2001, 133). Overcrowding probably hastened the spread of this disease, as did poor ventilation and the practice of moving prisoners from one facility to a central medical facility without proper precautions taken for infectious diseases. Outbreaks of pneumococcal pneumonia and meningitis have occurred in jails and prisons around the country.

Obviously, the costs involved in meeting the needs of the elderly in prison are not insubstantial. One estimate is that they cost about three times as much to house as a younger prisoner because of increased health needs ($69,000 per year compared with $22,000: National Center on Institutions and Alternatives 1998). Brown (2002) reports that a Pennsylvania study estimated that an average inmate's health care cost $3,809 per year, but that figure rises to $11,427 for older inmates. Because of the increasing use of three strikes laws and life without parole sentences, the number of geriatrics in prison can only increase. This will mean that prison management will increasingly have to consider issues regarding housing the elderly, including expanded health care and special diets. Several states have established hospice units for terminally ill patients.

There are widespread allegations of medical neglect. It can be argued that inmates may misuse and manipulate the medical treatment system for special privileges or drugs. Further, the state could not possibly undo years of living in which the inmates themselves did not care for their health and abused drugs, practiced poor nutrition, smoked, abused alcohol, did not take care of their teeth, and/or did not seek medical care when sick. However, the extent and consistency of allegations in some state systems are evidence that the medical care system is often inadequate, either because of a lack of resources or because of staff who do not care. After years in the system, staff burnout is understandable, but medical personnel who do not listen to inmates' complaints or overlook serious conditions create a type of torture for truly sick individuals wherein they suffer and can do nothing to help themselves get relief. Medical problems are more common among older inmates and range from cancer to dental problems.

In addition to serious illness, inmates require medical treatment for injuries that occur either through assaults or on a prison work assignment. In 1997, about one-quarter of all inmates in state and federal prisons reported injuries. Injuries are more likely to happen the longer the inmate remains in prison. Inadequate care may result in an inmate needlessly losing a limb or even dying.

There is a truism in corrections that female inmates demand much more medical attention than men. In a national survey of incarcerated men and women, about 25 percent of women and 20 percent of men reported some type of medical condition, but the percentages reversed when asked about injury, where 29 percent of the men and 21 percent of the women reported being injured (Maruschak and Beck 2001).

The medical staff is the worst of the lot. If they weren't taking away the meds or changing and mixing them, they were overdosing us. . . . Drug withdrawals were tough to see, but we had all witnessed them. Women couldn't breathe because inhalers had been taken away from them. Seizures would grab a girl at any unexpected moment; then she was told she was faking it or that they had given her her drugs wrong or that they didn't know. A girl died earlier this year because the medical staff didn't

know what they were doing. She wasn't the only death
this year. . . . (an inmate; Redifer in Johnson and Toch
2000, 145)

Vaughn and Smith (1999) document cases of medical abuse in
jails, but many of the same issues apply to prisons as well. Their list
of abuses include using medical care to humiliate inmates, withholding medical care from AIDS patients and other patients with
problems as severe as broken bones or miscarriages, exposing prisoners to extremes in temperature and sleep deprivation, using dental care as an instrument of ill treatment or withholding dental care,
and falsifying medical records. The authors looked at inmate letters
that described abuses such as a Vietnam veteran who suffered from
posttraumatic stress disorder and was prevented from continuing
his free-world prescribed Xanax; thus, he suffered hallucinations
and anxiety. Also described were a woman who went through DTs
with no medical care and suffered delusions and psychotic behavior, a woman who experienced a miscarriage and bled for several
hours before receiving any medical attention, a male inmate who
had a broken jaw swollen to several times its normal size and was
denied medical assistance, and so on. Their findings represented a
systematic pattern of mistreatment through the denial or misuse of
medical care.

California recently agreed to spend $21 million in 2002 and
$122 million a year in subsequent years to settle a lawsuit filed on
behalf of inmates. The lawsuit alleged that the prison system was
primarily responsible for the deaths of several inmates because of
inadequate or delayed medical care. Included in the deaths was a
young man with a two-year drug sentence who died from tongue
cancer diagnosed three months before he had any treatment. Eight
women's deaths were chronicled in the lawsuit, including one
who died after having an asthma attack. Inmates testified that
medical care did not come for three hours after they alerted officers
that the woman had collapsed in her cell. Along with extra money
for more doctors and medical staff, new procedures were also part
of the settlement agreement. Inmates who are transferred now
must have their medical charts transfer with them to ensure conti-
nuity of treatment. Further, inmates will be seen, when feasible, by

a primary care physician rather than by rotating doctors or nurses. There will be a team of auditors and a panel of outside medical experts who will review the medical care for prisoners (Warren 2001, 2002).

My son was a drug addict, but he was not a bad person. I never dreamed something like this could happen in American prisons. Unless you have a loved one in the system, you have no idea what goes on. (a mother whose son died in prison of a curable form of cancer, Warren 2001, 3)

In other states there are also allegations of poor medical care. The Austin newspaper published a multipart series on the prison health care system in Texas. The series chronicled the same type of allegations that led to the California class action suit, including interruption of prescribed medicines, neglect of diagnosed conditions, and nonmedical staff making "gateway" decisions (deciding who was sick enough to see the doctor). The series spurred some legislators to call for a special inquiry. The University of Texas, the contractor for all health care in Texas prisons, denied the allegations but subsequently has called for an external audit to quiet the critics (Ward 2002).

Mentally Ill and Mentally Retarded Inmates

Some estimate that about 10 to 20 percent of the prison population suffer from either mental illness or some form of mental handicap (Johnson 1999, 107). Roughly 210,000 prisoners in state or federal prisons and jails have some form of mental illness. In comparison, there are only about 70,000 beds in mental health facilities in this country. Thus, over twice as many mentally ill are in our nation's prisons and jails as are in mental facilities (Kondo 2001, 255). In one study of a jail population, for instance, a rigorous evaluation of jail admittees uncovered the fact that fully two-thirds met the criteria of being psychiatrically disturbed and in need of specific mental health treatment service and 34 percent possessed identifiable symptoms of psychopathology (Guy et al. 1985). Of course, not all these jail inmates end up in prison, but many do.

Unfortunately, jails and prisons are the largest providers of mental health services in the nation and the least trained, the least equipped, and the most under-resourced. This must change (from a report chronicling services to the mentally ill in prison in Maine, quoted in Hench 2002).

Inmates may be especially vulnerable to mental illness because of their past lives. A large percentage of inmates have been exposed to violence, sometimes starting very early in their childhood. They may have been victims of physical and/or sexual abuse themselves or witnessed abuse. It is not uncommon at all for inmates to relate experiences in which they have seen people die violently, sometimes loved ones, when they were quite young. It is probable that many individuals who grew up in impoverished, high-crime areas and experienced violence suffer from untreated posttraumatic stress disorder. These individuals may then become involved in the criminal justice system and undergo even more extreme stress and sometimes abuse. Rape is all too common in prison, as was discussed in a previous chapter, and the mentally ill are especially vulnerable to victimization. Overcrowding stresses even the most even-tempered and mentally healthy inmate. For those who suffer from mental illness, extreme overcrowding, as it occurs in some of this nation's prisons and jails, may be the trigger for a psychotic breakdown (Kupers 1999).

. . . he ate dirt, dust balls, pieces of trash, with the voraciousness of a billy goat. We knew that Dirt Man understood what he was doing wasn't right because he would do it on the sly. His favorites were the old mop strings that got caught and broke off beneath the legs of the tables in the chow hall. . . . (Stratton 1999, 84)

The mentally ill are not an easy group to manage. They are more likely to be violent offenders (53 percent versus 46 percent of other inmates) and recidivists (about 75 percent have already been in prison or on probation). Only 60 percent of those diagnosed as mentally ill reported that they have ever had any treatment. Those with diagnosed mental problems are seven and one-half times more likely to get disciplinary reports than the greater population (Ditton 1999). In fact, it is probably true that the greatest majority of officer assaults and repetitive acting-out behavior is performed by those who have chronic mental health problems.

Toch and Adams (1989) explored and analyzed breakdowns in prison by sampling prisoners with disciplinary records. Those whose mental illness manifests itself in assaultive or acting-out behavior are obviously difficult to handle—correctional staff want them transferred to mental facilities because they are irrational; mental health staff don't want them in such settings because they are violent.

. . . it's kind of like kicking and beating a dog and keeping it in a cage until it gets as crazy and vicious and wild as it can possibly get, and then one day you take it out into the middle of the streets of San Francisco or Boston and you open the cage and you run away. (a prison doctor, cited in Weinstein 2002, 121)

Inmates in these groups are especially vulnerable to victimization and manipulation. The prison experience, stressful as it is, may serve to exacerbate mental problems. Some inmates taunt and torment those with mental illnesses. Officers may be unable to differentiate between an inmate who is unwilling to follow an order from an inmate who is experiencing a psychotic episode or may be psychologically unable to conform their behavior to what is ordered. Management is concerned that sometimes these inmates are irrationally violent (for instance, an inmate with paranoid delusions may suddenly and unpredictably attack another standing behind him in line because of some delusion). Those who are mentally handicapped may be manipulated and intimidated by other inmates.

Court cases have established these inmates' rights to some form of treatment if witholding treatment constitutes "deliberate indifference"; however, more often than not, they are housed with the general population and get minimal special attention, unless they commit some act that attracts the attention of custodial officials. Treatment consists more often than not of stabilizing the inmate through the use of antipsychotic drugs and then sending the person back into the general population. Psychiatric counseling is widely considered a joke, partly because so many of the state-employed psychiatrists are foreign-born doctors and prisoners literally cannot understand them because of their accents (Johnson 2002, 252; Martin and Sussman 1993). The most common form of treatment seems to be medication.

> It was common practice for a third of a unit's inmate population to be walking around under the influence of Thorazine or some equally powerful psychotropic drug. . . . After taking the drug for a while, convicts tended to get a yellow, jaundiced look about them. The blank stare and the short, stuttering steps referred to as "the Thorazine shuffle," made them look like zombies as they slowly marched down the hallway. Their speech became slurred and their mental reactions slowed; a previously loud, disruptive convict would adopt a meek and mild manner. (a retired warden, Glenn 2001, 271–272)

The use of psychotropic drugs may be increasing. In one study, it was found that 9 percent of a sample of men in prison and 16 percent of females were receiving psychotropic medication (Morash, Har, and Rucker 1994, 200). Some object to the use of psychotropic medications because they can be easily abused. They may be used as simply behavior controls, they may not be accompanied by any professional therapy, and they may be given to an inmate for long periods of time, leading to a range of side effects. Perhaps the most troubling element of the use of psychotropics is that inmates may have their medications stopped abruptly upon release.

In one review of the treatment of the mentally ill in prison, Hartstone et al. (1999) concluded with a list of "findings." Some of their findings are as follows:

1. Department of corrections staff perceive about 6 percent of offenders as suffering from a serious psychotic mental disorder and another 38 percent as requiring some type of psychological treatment.

2. Different states operate with different philosophies regarding who should provide mental health treatment: i.e., the prison system or the mental health system.

3. Almost always, a transfer recommendation by the prison psychiatrist is followed.

4. Usually it is behavioral management concerns that instigate identification of an inmate as needing psychiatric care; thus, many who "suffer in silence" are missed.

5. A sizable number of staff feel more inmates should be transferred to mental health facilities.

6. Most staff members felt the transfer procedures worked well; but prison staff were less satisfied than those in central office positions or in the mental health units.

You didn't have to work the galleries long to realize that a large proportion of inmates were mentally ill. The symptoms ranged from the fairly mild—talking to oneself, neglecting to bathe—to the severe: men who didn't know where they were, men who set fire to their own cells, men so depressed they slashed their wrists or tried to hang themselves. (Conover 2000, 138)

Suicide. Suicide happens with depressing regularity in jails and prisons, despite mandated suicide diagnosis and watch programs. Suicide, natural causes, and AIDS are the most common causes of death in prisons. Rates of suicide vary depending on the study, ranging from 18 per 100,000 inmates to 53 (Hayes 1996, 88).

Suicide accounts for at least half of all deaths in prison. The suicide rate in prison is about twice that of the general population, but it varies dramatically from state to state. For instance, Florida's and Georgia's rates are less than half those of Texas and California (Kupers 1999, 177). Suicide in jails is even more commonplace than in prison (Haycock 1991; Kennedy and Homant 1988; Bonner and Rich 1990).

Reasons for suicide include finding out one has AIDS, despair over long sentences, anxiety about release, being denied parole, being raped, missing loved ones, finding out that loved ones have divorced or disowned the inmate, fear over being in prison, and a number of other triggers.

> . . . a 23 year old inmate, who was incarcerated since he was 17, and prior to that was a youthful offender. He came into the system as a result of an armed robbery; also, an outside charge for arson, for setting fire to an adjacent cell with somebody in it, about a year after he was in the system. . . . His primary problem is extreme acting out . . . threats, self-mutilation by cutting, swallowing, hanging himself. He swallowed pens, toothpaste tubes, bed springs . . . and these appear to be an expression of rage at the system. He hates the system, particularly whenever any kind of disciplinary action occurs—when he's not getting what he wants. His most extreme acts have occurred as a result of discipline. (notes from the mental breakdown in prison study, Toch and Adams 1989, 255)

In a truly bizarre example of our "corrections" system, Kupers (1999) reports that sometimes prisoners who fail in a suicide attempt are punished for it, because it is considered a prison infraction, and are put in solitary confinement, where their precarious mental health decomposes even more rapidly.

A recent report was issued in Maine prompted by the deaths of 17 inmates in the last five years. The deaths are at least partially attributed to the dearth of mental health services. The recommendations include adding forensic beds to the new state mental health hospital, training judges in how to divert the mentally ill from the corrections system, requiring treatment of those who act out in prison because of mental illness, and conducting independent reviews of all mental health services in prisons and jails (Hench 2002). In *Ruiz v. Estelle,* the Texas prisoner's rights case mentioned in a previous chapter, Judge Justice enumerated the minimal necessary elements for a mental health system in prison:

1. A systematic screening procedure;
2. Treatment that entails more than segregation and supervision;

3. Treatment that involves a sufficient number of mental health professionals to adequately provide services to all prisoners suffering from serious mental disorders;
4. Maintenance of adequate and confidential clinical records;
5. A program for identifying and treating suicidal inmates; and
6. A ban on prescribing potentially dangerous medications without adequate monitoring.

There is no doubt that the massive deinstitutionalization of the mentally ill in the 1970s, the closing of mental health facilities, and underfunding of community health centers has led to large numbers of the mentally ill in jails and prisons. Most receive virtually no care other than medication. Many are victimized in prison and/or they victimize others through unpredictable violence. If medicated, they shuffle through their prison sentence, and, upon release, for the most part are left to fend for themselves. It is no surprise that so many of them come back, and it is tragic that some ensure that they don't by killing themselves.

Programs and Programming

As noted in the first chapter, prisons began as institutions of change. The philosophy of change, however, has been altered over several eras. Originally, penitentiaries were places where a religious transformation was to take place—the sinner would be transformed when he sought repentance. Later, in the reformatory era, secular views of change supplanted religion and young, amenable offenders were educated and given vocational skills along with a strong dose of discipline. Constant monitoring, discipline, and education were believed to be the way to reform offenders. The "rehabilitative era" was a time during the 1970s and early 1980s when the vision of the correctional institution was at its strongest. Prison systems had "diagnostic centers" and the medical model or treatment ethic was the philosophy of change—specifically, that crime was a result of an underlying pathology that could be treated. At the height of the rehabilitative era a variety of treatment programs—including behavior modification, transcendental meditation, and even psychodrama therapy—could be found in some prisons. Most of these types of programs have been abandoned as irrelevant, ineffective, or inconsistent with the mission of the prison, which changed to retribution and punishment rather than rehabilitation and correction (Cole 1999). Other program offerings evidently were victims of disinterest or the changing fads of treatment professionals. Transactional analysis and reality therapy were popular programs in the 1970s, but it is difficult to find any current programs that identify themselves with these approaches, although many eclectic programs use some elements of each program in their curriculum (Pollock 1997c).

The decline of rehabilitative programs in prisons was due to a coalition between conservatives and liberals. Both groups thought the medical model (or treatment model) was inappropriate for criminal offenders. Liberals contested the model because there was disparity in sentencing (individuals with similar sentences might serve vastly different amounts of time because of perceived treatment needs), and because individuals were at the mercy of parole boards and other decision makers as to the actual amount of time served in prison. Conservatives were against the perceived "coddling" that treatment implied. Punishment was the priority and purpose of prison, and, thus, anything else was more than the prisoner deserved.

While rehabilitative or personal growth programs are harder to find, the most common are "anger management" programs, "survivors groups" (especially in women's prisons these groups are for victims of incest and abuse), and "life skills" programs (which are an amalgam of practical and personal content courses). Also, drug treatment programs exist in almost all prisons. Most prisons have at least Alcoholics Anonymous or Narcotics Anonymous, but in general, drug treatment programs are woefully inadequate to meet the need of prisoners, as was discussed in Chapter 2. Virtually all prisons also have some type of basic education. Most prisons also have at least a couple of vocational programs, even though more popular programs may have a waiting list.

Treatment programs include psychotherapy, behavior modification, group therapy, family therapy, therapeutic communities, AA, and a wide range of eclectic programs. Therapeutic communities are those programs that attempt to create an isolated world within the prison. Inmates are separated as much as possible from the general population and learn to live together in their community. Daily meetings and interactions form the basis of the therapy with an emphasis on personal responsibility and self-awareness

(Toch 1980a). Most analysts see the failure of prison programs in their inability to individualize treatment options for inmates. There is a tendency to offer a one-size-fits-all treatment program to all inmates and, because inmates are different, this approach is bound to fail.

Recently, religious programs have become popular again. Charles Colson, of Watergate fame, has promoted the use of one particular religion-based program, Prison Fellowship Ministries, and has convinced several states to implement the program in prisons. This is an ironic return to the early years of the penitentiary when the prisoner was encouraged to seek forgiveness and expiation through religious reformation. At least for these programs, religion has once again replaced psychology. Governmental support is growing, especially with the support of President George W. Bush and his concept of faith-based social programs. Critics allege that such programs violate the First Amendment by subtly coercing participation. It should be remembered, however, that chaplains and other religious leaders have been involved in prison ministry since the earliest prisons and have been successful in getting a certain number of inmates to change their lives (Marks 2001).

There are sincerely religious inmates in prison. Karla Faye Tucker, the Texas inmate who was executed despite worldwide pleas for clemency, was one such inmate who became deeply religious in prison. By all accounts, her spiritual awakening was real and lasting. Those who argued for executive clemency from then-Governor George Bush asked an important question: if executive clemency is available, and it is not given to someone who has truly reformed and become, in effect, a new person, then who is it reserved for?

Education

Education in prison is largely ABE (Adult Basic Education), which is primarily literacy training or programs of study that lead to either a GED or high school diploma. It is reported that one in three inmates score at the lowest level of literacy (Jenkins 1999). About 68 percent of prisoners had not received a high school diploma in 1997. About 40 percent had not received either a high school diploma or a GED, compared with only 18 percent of the general population (Harlow 2003). Harlow's (2003) national study found that only about 11 percent of state prisoners and 24 percent of federal prisoners had some college (compared with 48 percent of the general population). While over half of the sample reported that they participated in educational programs in prison, only about 10 percent of prisoners participated in college, a decline from 14 percent in 1991.

In the national study, it was found that women in prison were more likely than men to have graduated from high school (30 percent compared with 25 percent), and to have had some college. The author reported that white, black, and Hispanic men in prison were "markedly" less educated than their counterparts in the general population (Harlow 2003, 6). Another important finding was that those inmates without a high school diploma or a GED were more likely to be recidivists (Harlow 2003, 10).

Some state systems have quite large educational systems and offer a range of educational programs from basic literacy to college classes. There is some controversy over whether or not education is correlated with a reduction in recidivism (Stone 1997). However, no one can deny that education can help to make the inmate's time in prison productive and improve his or her life upon release. Welsh (2002) and Messemer (2003) report on studies that show that a college education does reduce recidivism among prisoners.

Other studies have also found education to be positively related to success after release. For instance, the Texas Criminal Justice Policy Council released a report in 2000 that tracked almost 26,000 inmates who had been released from prison in 1997 and 1998. They found that young property criminals were 37 percent less likely to recidivate if they learned to read while in prison. It was also found that education seemed to have a greater impact on younger inmates than older inmates (Susswein 2000).

Just because there is an education program on paper does not necessarily mean that the program is helpful; inappropriate resources, lethargic teachers, and hostile or unaccommodating security staff can sabotage a program. This makes large-scale evaluations of education problematic; it may be that recidivism is not affected because no real education takes place.

With the alphabet marching in cursive script around the walls and the date written on an otherwise pristine blackboard, about twenty functionally illiterate men sit

> facing their teacher. The men range in age from 20 to 55;
> some have the knitted caps of Black Muslims, others a
> host of religious medals dangling around their necks. . . .
> Six or seven of the men are sitting, heads in hands, staring
> at workbooks; the rest are sleeping, talking, or doodling.
> The teacher reads a newspaper at her desk in front, look-
> ing up once in awhile to restore order or answer a ques-
> tion when someone approaches her. Given the amount
> of sleeping and staring in the classroom, the occasions
> requiring her intervention are few. (Lin 2000, 15)

Lin (2000) describes a number of prisons, some where educational programs were vibrant and inmates and teachers were invested in the process; others where the program existed but nothing
much happened in the classrooms. In general, she found that any
evaluations of rehabilitation programs were problematic because
some on paper did not have commitment on the part of the institutional staff, and, since they were merely "walking through the motions," the evaluation of such a program would be misleading.

In 1994 federal Pell grants, which had been used to fund prisoners' college since 1994, were taken away by an amendment to the
1994 crime bill. The Pell program contributed to 43 states offering
Associate degrees and 31 states offering Baccalaureate degrees.
Nine states even offered Master's degrees. In a 1997 survey, most
states reported that the elimination of Pell grants resulted in a
drastic curtailment or elimination of their college education program (Welsh 2002). Parenti (1999, 181) reported that degree-grant-
ing programs in over 30 prisons ended and by 1998, only eight
states still offered any degree granting at all. However, another
study reported that 25 states offered college classes, with 15 offering Bachelor's degree programs (Messemer 2003). The discrepancy may be that only nine states have a program in which the
prisoner is able to complete a degree, or perhaps there have been
more states able to revive their college programs in recent years.
Alternative funding comes from other grants or private sources.

"Spector grants" (otherwise known as Youthful Offender
Grants) were added to the crime bill as an amendment and provide
up to $1,500 for inmates under 25, convicted of a nonviolent crime,

and with less than five years remaining on their sentence until release. It is reported, however, that the program is woefully under-funded and not used at all for its intended purpose by some states (Treaga 2003).

Welsh (2002) looked at the effect of eliminating the Pell grants by surveying directors of education in prison systems across the country. She found that they perceived a significant decrease in the access, quality, and success of college programs after the Pell Grants were discontinued. Messemer (2003) found that some states were able to use other grant-making programs, such as the Carl Perkins Vocational and Applied Technology Education Act of 1998, to fund college classes, many educational programs appealed to private funding sources, and in many cases, the prisoner was obligated to pay for the college class either directly or reimburse the state at some future time.

The complaint that prisoners get college educations while honest people have to pay for them seems to be, by and large, an empty one since very few inmates are in college programs, and those few that are, are most likely paying for the privilege. Arguing against basic education for prisoners makes no sense at all since if they are to obtain and retain a job upon release, they are going to have to have the skills to do so. It is in everyone's best interest to make sure inmates possess the basic qualifications for working.

Vocational Training and Industry

Vocational training programs should be distinguished from prison labor. While "hard labor" has been associated with confinement facilities since their inception, vocational training programs have a shorter history. In the 1960s and 1970s, prisons were able to access federal money from several sources to provide vocational training programs. Programs such as typewriter repair, auto mechanics, data processing, electricians' apprentice, and commercial cleaning, among many others, were begun. By the 1980s, overcrowding and budget shortfalls threatened the existence of many programs. Despite the numbers that indicate all prisons have one or more vocational programs, nationally only about 9 percent of inmates were enrolled in the early 1990s (National Institute of Justice 1993). Austin and Irwin (2001, 104) report that only 24 percent of inmates are officially "idle" but also report that only 7 percent are employed in prison industries, 5 percent in prison farms, and 9 percent in prison vocational training or education. That leaves about half of inmates "employed," but such employment may be sweeping the tier or being on a yard detail.

As mentioned, in 1994, the new federal crime bill prohibited inmates from receiving Pell grants. This legislation blocked the opportunity for many inmates who were pursuing or wanted to pursue a college degree, but it also closed many vocational programs dependent on these federal funds (Stone 1997). Still, one might find programs such as computer repair, simple programming, carpentry, commercial cleaning, heavy equipment operation, and food service in prison. Some are more likely to lead to jobs upon release than others.

The best vocational model might be one that combines prison labor with job training. In this way, a product is produced that can offset the cost of the training. Some private businesses have entered prisons or prisons have created industries and use prisoner labor to produce goods sold on the open market. Industry in prison can include vocational training that might lead to finding a job on the outside, or it may simply be menial labor that at least allows the inmate to earn some money while inside. Whatever the model, there are proponents and opponents of private industry partnering with prisons.

During the depression, several federal laws were passed that restricted prison-made goods from competing with the private market. These laws protected civilian workers by limiting prison-made goods to state-use only and included other restrictions designed to curtail competition with civilian labor. The result was that it was not economically feasible for private companies to use inmate labor.

This situation changed with the passage of the Federal Prison Industries Enhancement Act of 1979 (P.I.E.). This law allowed prison-made goods to be sold on the open market with certain restrictions. The prison must certify that the prison industry pays the same wages, consults with representatives of private industry, does not displace civilian workers, collects funds for a victim assistance program, provides inmates with benefits in the event of injury, ensures that inmate participation is voluntary, and provides a substantial role for the private sector. The inmate is allowed to keep up to 20 percent of his or her wages, but the rest can be taken to meet legal judgments or pay restitution, child support, and room and board. If all these conditions are met, then the goods can compete on the open market. However, it is difficult to meet all conditions, evidenced by the fact that as of 1998, only 2,539 prisoners, nationwide, worked for private firms (Parenti 1999, 231), and as of 2000, the number was still only 3,826 (cited in Johnson 2002, 304). This is a very small number considering that the number incarcerated in state and federal prisons is well over a million.

One example of a combination of prison labor and vocational programming is found in the federal system. UNICOR is the prison industry program in the Federal Bureau of Prisons. It employs about 27 percent of all federal prisoners and produces in excess of $200 million worth of goods annually (Stone 1997, 123). UNICOR makes over 150 different products—from safety goggles to road signs. Selling only to governmental agencies, UNICOR is criticized by some as producing an inferior product for an inflated price (Parenti 1999, 232), but others tout it as an unqualified success. Studies indicate that federal prisons involved in UNICOR or other vocational training were less likely to break prison rules, more likely to get jobs upon release, and less likely to recidivate (Saylor and Gaes 1994, 538).

Iowa has a number of examples of prisoners working for private companies. Inmates have worked at a chicken farm, a boat factory, a telemarketing firm, and a food packaging company. Even with all these placements, however, there were only 225 of Iowa's 7,800 inmates working for private companies in 2001. Since Iowa requires companies to try to hire inmates once paroled, it is a promising model, but one that has met resistance from unions such as the AFL-CIO (Wall Street Journal 2001).

Despite the P.I.E. program and governmental markets, only 5 percent of all inmates are employed in any prison industry at all, and proportionally, fewer prisoners work today than in 1980 (Parenti 1999, 231). Why do outside industries avoid prison partnerships? One reason is that certification under the P.I.E. program is difficult; it is hard to show how civilian labor is not displaced if there is any amount of unemployment in the area of the prison. Second, prisons are simply not built with the needs of private industry in mind. There is a lack of space and, often, an inability to accommodate the requirements of a private industry. Third, stringent prison rules and regulations clearly show that custody concerns will always eclipse profit concerns. Fourth, the prison labor force is largely unskilled and uneducated. Even apprentice programs require at least a high school reading level and many prisoners do not have such skills. Finally, the prison labor pool, while they may be there on time, are not necessarily the most committed and energetic group of employees. Parenti (1999, 234) also mentions that some employers are afraid of negative publicity if the public found out they use convict labor. They also fear lawsuits. These are some of the reasons industries have not formed prison partnerships. If there was stronger support from state officials and prison staff, many of these problems might be resolved.

What is the effect of vocational training on recidivism? Studies seem to show that the training is less important than what happens to the offender after release. A Texas study, for instance, found that those inmates who completed a vocational training program, but did not get a job upon release, were not significantly less likely to recidivate than controls. Further, those inmates who did get a job, but one which paid less than $10,000 a year, were also no more likely than controls to stay out of trouble. It is clear from this study that education or vocational training must lead to employment upon release in order for recidivism to be affected (Susswein 2000).

Recreation

Perhaps no issue of prison life receives more negative publicity than recreation programs. Prisoners lifting weights or playing ball are inevitably the topic of those who argue against making prisons "hotels" instead of "hard labor camps." Yet, prison officials are sometimes the biggest supporters of such programs. Why? Officials largely support recreation because it is, usually, a prosocial use of time, and it tends to direct energy away from more deviant pursuits. To be sure, at times recreation programs can be the impetus for violence. Fights will break out on the basketball court or on the softball field. Betting takes place over games that can then lead to violence when losers must pay. Further, many states have banned weight lifting equipment in prison because it is felt that the state should not be paying for equipment that will assist in creating a stronger prisoner who may assault officers.

In general, male prisoners tend to be more active participants in recreation than female prisoners. Virtually every prison has a yard and, in some part of the yard, there is probably a basketball court and an area for softball. In some states, prisoner teams play against community teams or even guard teams. Some prisons also have a gymnasium, although many of these were converted to dormitories during the 1980s in reaction to overcrowding. It is also true that many prisons today are in lockdown so much of the time, that inmates have less opportunity for yard time or exercise than in past years.

Other avenues for recreation exist in hobbies. Many prisons have a candle-making shop, leather working, or perhaps a stained glass shop. Prisoners may create beautiful artwork that is sold to the public in the prison administration building or, perhaps, given to friends or relatives as gifts. Most often, the supplies for such crafts must be purchased by the inmate. Women in prison often engage in needlework projects that are also charity works since they make stuffed animals or quilts that are then distributed by agencies in the community. When asked why they participate in such activities they answer much like anyone would; usually some version of wanting to help others or giving back to the community.

Prison clubs (not gangs) also sometimes have charity works as their primary activity. Good works, such as preparing tapes for the blind, are often done under the auspices of a "lifer's club" or even a Jaycees chapter in the prison. Club meetings and activities take place in the evening when all prisoners are allowed to go to the yard.

While there is no evidence that recreation programs in prison have any effect on recidivism, it may be that they at least have the potential to improve behavior in prison. Any type of sports is a healthy addition to one's life and can help the inmate avoid, perhaps, some temptation to use drugs or engage in less positive pursuits. Other types of recreation keep inmates busy, if nothing else, and some activities are clearly helpful to the community.

Prison Treatment Programs

As stated earlier, there are fewer programs in prison today than there were in years past. Drug treatment is common and has been discussed previously, in Chapter 2. Other treatment programs in prison may focus on anger management, life skills, or group therapy for incest/rape survivors. Sex offender treatment programs are present in a few prisons. According to some ex-inmates, "programmers" in prison are looked down upon by those who actively participate in the subculture. That may be, but there are many inmates who do take advantage of programs and who may even obtain some measure of enlightenment by going through the experience. The all-important question, of course, is whether or not any of the programs lead to a reduction in recidivism.

Evaluating prison programs. As noted in the first chapter, the end of the rehabilitative era was helped along by Robert Martinson's (1974) meta-analysis of a large number of treatment programs. His conclusion that nothing worked fueled reformers' efforts to eliminate indeterminate sentencing and reduce funding for treatment programs. Researchers who followed, and even Martinson himself, concluded more optimistically that some success could be found in prison treatment programs. Gendreau and Ross (1979, 1980) and Palmer (1994) have published numerous studies, as have others (Cullen 1982; Harland 1996), all showing some measure of success in prison programming.

Evaluations of prison programming do find success and they even are able to describe the elements of successful programs. For instance, Andrews et al. (1990) pointed out in their meta-analysis of a number of evaluations that the impact of treatment upon recidivism was influenced by the extent to which service was appropriate according to the risk of the offender, the need of the offender, and the responsiveness of the offender. They estimate that appropriate treatment may cut recidivism by as much as 50 percent.

Others list the following elements as important when weighing the effectiveness of correctional programming: the program should include the inmate in program planning; successful programs address strengthening prosocial behaviors rather than targeting antisocial behaviors; and successful programs are able to neutralize the antisocial peer group or turn it to support prosocial values (cited in Johnson 2002, 298). Gendreau (1996) further describes successful programs as those that are intensive (occupying 40 to 70 percent of the inmate's time), utilizing behavioral strategies, with therapists matched to offenders. Wilson et al. (1999) conducted a meta-analysis of 33 evaluations of educational, vocational, or other rehabilitative programs in prison. Their findings indicated that modest improvements in recidivism existed across all program types. Gerber and Fritsch (1995) also provide findings from their study that indicate educational and vocational programming can reduce recidivism and increase the likelihood of post-prison employment.

Current research indicates that the most effective types of programs are those that utilize a cognitive-behavioral approach. For instance, Pearson et al. (2002) presented the findings of a meta-analysis of 69 research studies on prison programming between 1968 and 1999. Their review of the literature indicated that cognitive programs were often correlated with lowered recidivism. Cognitive-behavioral programs include behavioral programs that utilize token economies and other forms of behavior modification. One such program is "contingency contracting," in which the inmate enters into a contract for desirable behaviors that then earn rewards. "Cognitive-behavioral" programs emphasize thought and emotional processes. Social skills training, role play, problem solving, rational emotive therapy, and cognitive skills programs (sometimes known as the "Reasoning and Rehabilitation" program) are some of the types of programs categorized under the cognitive-behavioral label. Pearson and his colleagues found that cognitive-behavioral treatment approaches did reduce recidivism by "significant amounts" (Pearson et al. 2002, 490). Further, the programs within the category that showed these effects were those that employed cognitive skills training and social skills development training, not the token economies or the standard behavior modification programs (Pearson et al. 2002, 491).

Evaluations of prison programming have been bedeviled by difficulties. Follow-up time periods are usually short and attrition is high. Furthermore, despite program descriptions, the actual policies, procedures, and curriculum of each program are often very different, making comparison of similar types of programs impossible. Recidivism is not uniformly defined so while one program may count an arrest as a failure, another program may count only a return to prison as failure. Crow (2001, 46) also mentions that reconviction is not necessarily re-offending; in fact, errors occur in two ways. First, the offender may be re-offending but not get caught; or, second, the offender may be arrested and convicted of offenses that had taken place before the treatment intervention.

Crow (2001, 49) points out that a meta-analysis, an evaluation that collapses several studies into one data set, may present some problems. First, it may mix "apples and oranges"; different measures for different things may be collapsed into one meaning. Second, poor-quality research may be included. Third, meta-analyses depend on published research and, so, miss some efforts. Fourth, because researchers are using one data set, multiple results may not be independent of each other.

Despite these difficulties, meta-analyses, even Martinson's 1970 study, have found that some programs, most notably cognitive and behaviorally based programs, show some degree of success (Palmer 1994; Glaser 1994). But others insist that even cognitive programs won't rehabilitate without also offering the inmate some chance at learning a skill that can earn the individual a living wage (Austin 1999, 293).

As mentioned before, one of the problems of evaluation is that a program may not consistently contain the same content. Programs are heavily dependent on staff characteristics; thus, a fully participating, enthusiastic staff is probably going to show more program success than a bored or burned-out staff, regardless of the modality in which they operate. Lin (2000) fully explores the problems of programs "on paper" that do not display anywhere near the type of rehabilitation in real life as one would expect when reading the institutional description of offerings. Treatment staff that must constantly fight against a custodial staff may simply give up and become bureaucrats. Custodial officers often feel oppressed because treatment needs strain staffing resources. If there are not enough officers to patrol the living units, the need to have officers assigned to a recreation program, for instance, is resented (Lin 2000, 59).

They don't like us helping the inmates. They think they should make an inmate's life as miserable as they can. Custody's attitude is, get out of my way because you got nothin' comin'. . . . When I was in custody, I guess I had the same feeling, but I had to change when I got to education

because you can't degrade people if you're going to do this
job. . . . (vo-tech instructor, quoted by Lin 2000, 67)

The most obvious problem of all evaluations of treatment programs in prison is that they cannot control for all the many influences that each offender experiences once he or she leaves prison. If
two offenders participate in the same drug program and, also, a vocational training program, they may still end up differently because
of situational elements upon release. Perhaps one individual is able
to find work and start a new life with helpful friends, but the other
may not be able to find work, has to live at home with drug-using
parents and siblings, and is drawn inexorably back into the drug
world, because of desperation and loneliness.

Therapeutic communities. A therapeutic community is a self-
enclosed community within a prison that attempts to shield the
prisoner from the negative effects of the general population. In the
living unit, inmates are given increasing responsibility concomitant with their exhibiting responsible behavior. Most of all, the pervasive message and culture of such communities is support and
trust, which, in itself, is a much different living situation than what
prisoners in the general population are exposed to.

Singer (1996), a director of a therapeutic community, describes
important elements of a successful program. He includes the following:
1. Isolation from the general population. As much as possible,
   treatment inmates should be removed and isolated from the
   negative subcultural elements of the general population.
2. A healthy partnership between custodial and treatment staff.
   If custodial staff continually undercut and sabotage treatment initiatives, the program is doomed to failure. Custodial
   staff are an integral part of a therapeutic community and
   must be invested in the success of the program.
3. A referral system that provides appropriate inmates for re-
   cruitment. There should be a careful screening and selection
   process as well.
4. A program director who can work well within the correctional environment, can mediate staff conflicts, and is sensitive to burnout.

5. Substance abuse counselors who are committed and consistent, and who have good decision-making skills. The presence of recovering addicts and/or successful ex-inmates is helpful. Treatment staff should be diverse and reflect the population of clients.
6. Clients should not have mental health problems and they should be motivated. They should have time to complete the program.
7. An atmosphere where the clients are free to trust, take risks, challenge themselves and each other.

Some participants of such programs, especially women, eloquently describe how the program may have saved their life. They explain how they have never felt support or caring from anyone before, even their families, and so they never respected themselves. They are able to get the degree of positive reinforcement that they need in order to explore the reasons they abuse themselves and others and find the will to change. It is actually very sad to think that they are perfectly serious when they say that the best time of their lives has been in prison. Therapeutic communities, combined with cognitive-behavioral approaches, and practical skill acquisition (i.e., education or vocational training), probably offers the highest probability for success in prison programming. If nothing else, therapeutic communities tend to counteract some of the negativity of the prison experience.

[Without the prison program] I think I would have been dead . . . I didn't go in there looking for a change. I went in there looking to get off the work crew . . . I probably would have been back out there and either dead or back on the streets doing what I do best. . . . What this class gave me, you know, was not some magic potion that I could walk out those gates and that life was going to be okay, because it wasn't. What this class gave me was the desire and the willingness to make things okay. (a prison inmate, quoted in Pollock 1998a, 120)

The Will to Change

Can prisoners change? There is no doubt that they can. How many do is another question. It is a mistake to assume that there will ever be one prison program that will be the "cure-all" for the myriad of reasons why offenders commit crime. What prison programs can do is provide opportunities and remove barriers to success. If an inmate can't get a job when he is released, he is that much more likely to commit another crime, but a prison program might give him the skill to get a job. If a prisoner has abused drugs most of her adult life, and, in prison, she is able to figure out how to avoid addiction upon release, then that is one less challenge to overcome in the quest to stay out of trouble.

It is true that not all inmates want to stay out of trouble. Some are so twisted and warped in their views of what they deserve, and so unable to feel empathy or care for others, that they should be locked up until they pose no danger to society because of age or incapacitation. It is very important to understand, though, that these are the minority in prison, not the majority. There are many weak people in prison. There are many who have had terrible lives and have not had any role model for a moral lifestyle. There are also those in prison who, with help, could control their behavior. Finally, whether the public believes it or not, there are many in prisons who are not necessarily bad people; they just made bad choices. Some of their choices are perhaps no worse than the choices of individuals' on the outside who have had the fortune to escape detection.

What is very interesting and needs to be explored in much more detail is the "spontaneous remission" of some inmates. There are individuals who, without any prompting or outside influence, suddenly decide to completely change their lives. They can quickly change from being a troublesome, recalcitrant prisoner to one who utilizes every opportunity open to them. They stop looking for trouble and begin to try and avoid it. Why this change of heart happens is a mystery, even to those who experience it. If we could identify the process, it would greatly assist in designing rehabilitative efforts. In the meantime, the goal of those involved in program services is to make sure that such opportunities are available for those individuals who decide to use them. It is clear that prison can't make people "go straight." However, it can help them do so or make it harder for them to do so, depending on the programs available. What is truly ironic is that instead of using incarceration to improve oneself, many prisoners end up coming out of prison with more problems than when they went in. Some may have a drug addiction they didn't have before. Some may be the victim of violence and bear psychic as well as physical scars. Some may have become violent themselves as a reaction to their environment. While some prisoners have experienced transformation in a good way, the result of prison is all too often not greater enlightenment and improvement of skills to survive in the "real" world, but, rather, greater bitterness, anger, and despair. It doesn't have to be this way.

> I am not a vicious dog or any other type of violent animal. I am a prisoner. I live in a world many of you believe I deserve . . . a prisoner's world is beyond a non-prisoner's comprehension. Any human can become an animal in prison. (an ex-prisoner, Arriens 1991, 46)

Conclusion

In this chapter the range of programs in prison was described. Prisons today do have more programs than they did fifty years ago, but fewer than they did 30 years ago. Prisoners who desire to change themselves have the opportunity to do so to a point. The biggest barrier to change is that there are not enough program slots for all the people in prison, and the number of programs that are "on paper" only. Just because a program exists and is staffed, doesn't mean that there is any real heart to the program. A good staff member is better than a good program with no good people working in it. Prisoners today can at least take advantage of education programs and some type of life skills program. They may have access to a vocational program or even accumulate some savings from a prison-industry partnership. The problem is that there are never enough of these programs to meet the ever-increasing numbers of prisoners being sent to prison, nor are many programs able to counteract the incredibly negative stigma of a prison sentence, so that, upon release, prisoners have almost insurmountable barriers to a productive and law-abiding life.

Study Questions

1. What are some problems with health care in prison?
2. What are Pell grants and what has happened to them and college programs in prison?
3. What does research show regarding prison education and recidivism?
4. What other types of treatment programs are there in prison?
5. What seems to be the most effective type of treatment program in prison?

Chapter 7

Prisoners' Rights

Now You See Them, Now You Don't

In essence, TDC [Texas Department of Corrections] has failed to furnish minimal safeguards for the personal safety of the inmates. Primarily because the civilian security force is insufficient in number and poorly deployed, inmates are constantly in danger of physical assaults from their fellow prisoners. . . . Simply put, inmates live in a climate of fear and apprehension by reason of constant threat of violence. (Ruiz v. Estelle 1980, 26)

Introduction and History

Once an individual has been found guilty and sentenced to prison, many people assume that he or she has (or should have) no rights. Up until the 1960s this was, to some extent, true. Federal and state courts refused to hear "prisoners' rights" cases or decided such cases in a way that made it clear that prisoners had few, if any, of the rights of free people. This era was called the "hands-off" era, meaning that the federal courts rarely became involved in prisoners' rights cases.

In *Ruffin v. Commonwealth* (1871), for example, the Virginia Supreme Court stated that the inmate was a "slave of the state," with only those rights given to him by the state. In contrast, the later opinion that prisoners have not lost all of their constitutional rights was voiced by the U.S. Supreme Court in *Wolff v. McDonnell* (1974, 539): "There is no iron curtain drawn between the Constitution and the prisons of this country."

It should be noted that careful historical legal research by Wallace (2001) indicates that the "slave of the state" approach was never monolithic, and many early court decisions in the late 1800s and early 1900s condemned inhumane treatment, but there were no effective procedures to secure prisoners' rights. Tort remedies, habeas corpus relief, mandamus actions, and injunctive relief were not very effective means to enforce the courts' will.

During the so-called Warren Court era (1953–1969), named after Chief Justice Earl Warren, the Supreme Court published a number of opinions that expanded the civil rights of several groups of people, including students, the mentally ill, racial minorities, criminal defendants, and prisoners. This time period became known as the "activist era." The Court utilized the Fourteenth Amendment to expand the protections enumerated in the Bill of Rights. Most of the cases establishing prisoners' rights were first decided during this time period. For instance, some cases recognized prisoners' rights to practice religion in ways that did not interfere with the security of the institution. Other cases granted due process before prisoners were deprived of good time or placed in segregation. Still others granted the right to be free from corporal punishment.

One of the first prisoners' rights cases was *Cooper v. Pate* (1964). In this case, the Supreme Court held that Muslims in prison did have standing to challenge religious discrimination on the part of prison officials under Section 1983 of the Civil Rights Act of 1871. This recognition of prisoners' rights was a trumpet call for prisoners to demand court intervention in a number of other areas where, before, prison administrators had operated with almost no oversight whatsoever.

Despite some people's belief that the courts still favor prisoners' rights, one could see increasingly restricted views of these rights as early as the late 1970s. In *Meachum v. Fano* (1976), for example, the Supreme Court held that a prisoner had no due process rights before being transferred to a harsher prison. In their words, the prison administration could transfer for "good" reasons, "bad" reasons, or "no" reasons. In *Bell v. Wolfish* (1979), the Court held that pretrial detainees held in jails had no more rights than those convicted and that only those rights "consistent" with their confinement would be recognized. During the 1980s and

1990s, prisoners lost more cases than they won and the court took increasingly more restricted views regarding prisoners' rights.

Then, in 1996, Congress passed the Prisoner Litigation Reform Act. This legislation was supposed to curtail "frivolous" lawsuits by prisoners. It requires early dismissal of frivolous suits, more thorough screening of cases, and exhaustion of administrative and state remedies before filing federal claims. Recent cases solidify the opinion that today courts, including the Supreme Court, follow a "due deference" model. Most prisoners' rights cases are decided in favor of prison administrators because courts give due deference to prison administrators' expertise in running the prison as long as there is the merest rational relationship between the challenged rule, procedure, or activity and prison safety or security.

Causes of Action and Sources of Rights

In every case involving prisoners' rights, there is a decision to be made between the alleged right of the prisoner and the state interest to run a safe, secure, and orderly prison. Issues such as the prisoner's right to practice his or her religious beliefs, the right to correspond without censorship, the right to adequate medical care, and the right to have some type of hearing before being punished are only some of the issues that have been litigated. Prisoners' rights come from, in most cases, either the federal or state constitutions. For instance, the right to practice one's religion freely comes from the First Amendment; the right to be free from excessive brutality comes from the Eighth Amendment; and so on. In some cases, specific state legislation or interpretations of the state constitution may give prisoners rights beyond those recognized as coming from the federal Constitution.

In many cases, the test used by the court will determine whether the state wins or the inmate wins. In general, if the court uses a strict scrutiny test, the state must prove an overriding state interest, a close relationship between the rule or procedure at issue and the safety or security of the institution, and that no less intrusive means are available to reach the goal of safety and security. If, on the other hand, the court applies a rational relationship test, then prison administrators must simply prove a state interest and some relationship between that interest and the rule or procedure in question.

One of the more frequently used legal mechanisms for suing is found under 42 U.S.C. Section 1983. This act strips officials of immunities enjoyed by governmental entities. This is the reason that many prisoners' rights suits are filed against the director of corrections or the warden. In effect, the suit is against the official in his or her individual capacity. The prisoner must show that there has been a constitutional deprivation or violation by the governmental official acting under color of law. Under Section 1983, the prisoner is entitled to actual and punitive damages and injunctive relief if successful.

As stated before, a prisoner must identify a source for the right at issue. Most often, prisoners look to the Bill of Rights and the Fourteenth Amendment. It should be understood that the protections enumerated in the Bill of Rights applied only to individuals as citizens of the United States. They protect us from intrusive actions by the federal government. Before any of the protections could be applied against actions by state officials (i.e., prison administrators of state prisons), that right had to be "incorporated" into one's rights as a state citizen. This is done by case law through an application of the Due Process Clause of the Fourteenth Amendment. For any particular prisoner's case that utilized a right specified in the Bill of Rights, the Supreme Court determined whether the right was important enough that a violation of it by a state actor would violate "fundamental fairness." If it did, then the right was granted.

In addition to the federal Bill of Rights, prisoners might also have rights recognized under their own state constitution. In fact, today, there are probably more court-recognized rights coming from state sources than federal constitutional rights. Rights might also be created by state statute. For instance, if a state statute specifies that each prisoner "must" have a parole hearing every year, then the statute has created that right. It does not exist in either a state or federal constitution. Of course, what is created by statute can be taken away by rewriting the statute. In this chapter some of the cases that have been litigated using the Bill of Rights will be discussed: specifically, the First, Fourth, Eighth, and Fourteenth Amendments of the Constitution of the United States.

The First Amendment

The First Amendment: Congress shall make no law respecting an establishment of religion, or prohibiting the free exercise thereof; or abridging the freedom of speech, or of the press; or the right of the people peaceably to assemble, and to petition the government for a redress of grievances.

The First Amendment challenges to prison practices cover such areas as religious practices (diet, hair, clothing, rituals), censorship (both incoming and outgoing and prison newspapers), association (visiting, labor unions), media access to prisoners, and others.

It is a mistake to believe that anyone's First Amendment rights are absolute. Although we have a great deal of freedom to say what we want, some types of speech are restricted and can be punished. Examples include speech defined as obscenity and speech that poses an immediate threat (yelling "fire" in a crowded theater). Nor does one have complete freedom to practice religion in any way one sees fit. If one's religious practices violate some law, then the behavior will be punished. Our freedom to associate is similarly circumscribed. The state can regulate associations (i.e., demonstrations) that pose a clear and present danger to the public. Thus, even free people do not have completely untrammeled rights under the First Amendment; however, before the government can infringe on these rights, they must show a "clear and present danger." Obviously, prisoners have more First Amendment restrictions than free people. The test the Supreme Court has used to evaluate whether or not governmental restrictions on prisoners' rights under the First Amendment are legitimate has changed over the years from "strict scrutiny" to the "rational relationship" test. As we will see, the test used has everything to do with who is likely to win the case.

Freedom of Religion

The first point to note is that these cases concern religious practices as opposed to beliefs. It is only when the prisoner desires to undertake some practice to further his or her beliefs that controversy arises. Some of the practices that have been litigated include wearing religious jewelry, that is, a crucifix (Christian); wearing hair in dreadlocks (Rastafarian); refusing to take a shower in front of others (Islam); demanding the prison allow a sweat lodge to be built (Native American); wearing a head covering (Islam and Judaism); demanding the prison provide a pork-free diet (Islam and Judaism); and demanding the space and time for religious ceremonies (all religions).

The arguments for restricting religious practices in prison usually involve security. If the government makes a good case that the practice interferes with the security of the institution, then the courts always decide in their favor. If the practice has no security implications, and the state's only concern is convenience, then the courts have sometimes upheld the prisoners' rights to practice.

Another question, however, is whether the prisoner's religion is a religion at all. This question has forced the court to deal with some very fundamental issues, such as "What is a religion?" Obviously, when the prisoner practices an established, recognized religion such as Islam, Christianity, or Judaism, this is not an issue. However, some prisoners' rights cases dealt with unrecognized and/or newer religions (arguably cults or made-up religions). For instance, several cases concerned a group of inmates who had created the "Church of the New Song" (CONS). They argued that in order to practice this religion, they must eat steak and drink cream sherry. In *Theriault v. A Religious Office* (1990), it was clear that the court was not amused. Eventually this so-called religion was practiced in several different states and spawned a number of court cases. Interestingly, some courts recognized it as a religion and others did not, but they couldn't convince any court of their need to drink Harvey's Bristol Cream as part of their religious doctrine (see also *Theriault v. Silbur* 1977).

. . . a religion addresses fundamental and ultimate questions having to do with deep and imponderable matters . . . a religion is comprehensive in nature, [consisting] of a belief system as opposed to an isolated teaching . . . religion can often be recognized by the presence of certain formal and external signs. . . . (*Africa v. Commonwealth of Pennsylvania* (1981, 1032)

Typically, courts have held that in order to be considered a religion, a system of belief must be shown to address fundamental questions such as right and wrong and good and evil, and to provide guidance in morals. Another issue that has arisen is the inmate's sincerity in practicing the religion. Courts have routinely refused to consider this issue with the reasonable argument that no one can stand in judgment of another in this regard. The analysis, therefore, hinges on the balancing test between the right in question and the state's security or order interest.

The early cases balancing religious rights against institutional security tended to be brought by Black Muslims who were denied the opportunity to meet for religious purposes, access religious leaders, wear religious emblems, and so on. Prison officials in the 1960s and 1970s believed that the Muslim faith included beliefs that were contrary and threatening to the security of the institution, so consequently Muslims were usually treated differently from those who practiced other faiths. For instance, religious leaders were barred from the prison and the Muslim prisoners were not allowed to gather for religious ceremonies. Although some lower courts agreed at times that there was a compelling security interest, many more cases were decided in favor of the inmates' rights, especially when their argument also included an equal protection challenge.

One of the only Supreme Court cases dealing with religious freedoms and equal protection was *Cruz v. Beto* (1972). This was a Texas case concerning prison officials' decision to restrict and prohibit a prisoner who desired to practice his Buddhist faith. The Court held that inmates cannot be denied the opportunity to practice an unconventional American religion (Buddhism) when other inmates are given the chance to pursue conventional faiths.

When the state's argument is merely convenience or economic considerations, courts are sometimes more protective of religious freedoms. However, courts have been more willing to accept economic rationales. For instance, in *Gittlemacker v. Prasse* (1970), a Jewish prisoner wanted the prison to provide him with a rabbi at state expense. Because of the small number of Jewish prisoners in the prison, the Third Circuit did not require the state to provide one. In *Walker v. Blackwell* (1969), the Court upheld the state's right to deny Muslims special meals during Ramadan, a religious holiday, because they asked for the meals at special times, with special foods, for 30 days. The Second Circuit decided much the same thing when they determined that the prison was not obligated to provide Jewish prisoners with kosher foods in *Kahane v. Carlson* (1975).

In the myriad of lower court cases, confusion reigned. Some federal courts used a fairly stringent test to determine whether or not prison regulations passed constitutional muster; others used the rational relationship test, which was more likely to result in the upholding of prison regulations. Some courts held that prison officials could not deny entry to Muslim religious leaders (due to their criminal records); some courts held that such prohibitions were justified by security concerns. Most courts held that the state did not need to provide a pork-free diet or pork alternative for Muslims, but a few courts said that the state could provide a pork substitute with low-cost protein, such as peanut butter. While some courts held that prison officials could not prohibit religious publications or materials, other courts held that as long as there was some opportunity to practice religion, those materials that might be misconstrued or inflammatory could be denied.

The Supreme Court finally accepted a religious freedom case in 1987. By this time, the Court had adopted a due deference position, with greater weight given to prison authorities' arguments that the practice in question compromised the safe, secure, and orderly running of the prison. In *O'Lone v. Shabazz* (1987), Muslim prisoners in New Jersey on an outside work squad argued that their religious freedom was being compromised. Their challenge concerned a prison regulation that prohibited all inmates from returning to the prison during the day, which prevented them from attending the Jumu'ah, a weekly religious ceremony held during the middle of the day on Fridays. The prison argued that it was a security breach to allow inmates back into the facility during the day and that it was operationally inconvenient, since if one member of the work detail needed to return to the institution, the whole work detail, supervised by only one guard, must return.

The Court, in a 5 to 4 decision, adopted the "rational" or "reasonable" relationship test. This test determined that as long as prison authorities showed a legitimate governmental interest, and the regulation or restriction in question bore some rational or reasonable relationship to the governmental interest, then the prison authorities would win, even if the restriction compromised or abrogated the prisoners' right to exercise their religious beliefs. Because the rational relationship test was used, the prisoners lost.

> To ensure that courts afford appropriate deference to prison officials, we have determined that prison regulations alleged to infringe constitutional rights are judged under a "reasonableness" test less restrictive than that ordinarily applied to alleged infringements of fundamental constitutional rights [for citizens in society]. . . . (*O'Lone v. Shabazz* 1987, 343)

The dissent argued bitterly that the rational relationship test used was ineffective in protecting constitutional rights. The dissenting justices argued that even under the rational relationship standard, there was nothing in the inmates' request that would compromise security and convenience sufficiently that it was necessary to deny individual religious freedoms. After *O'Lone v. Shabazz*, lower courts have typically followed the Supreme Court's lead and deferred to prison officials' arguments in conflicts between prison policies and inmates' rights to exercise their religion.

In 1993, Congress passed the Religious Freedom Restoration Act (42 U.S.C. Section 2000b(b)(1)). Congress was attempting to bolster protection for religious convictions against governmental actions because the Supreme Court had begun to use the rational relationship test in all controversies when religious practices conflicted with state laws, which meant, of course, that individuals almost always lost. Prisons and jails were not expressly excluded from the protection of the act; thus, it appeared that the act would drastically limit the state's ability to restrict or prohibit religious practices even in prison.

Under the Religious Freedom Restoration Act (RFRA), if the state restriction constituted a "substantial burden" on one's ability to practice his or her religion, then the government must show that the restriction "is in furtherance of a compelling governmental interest" and that it is the "least restrictive means" of furthering that interest. When prisoners first started to employ the RFRA to challenge prison regulations, most courts looked to legislative intent to determine whether or not the act was meant to apply to prisoners. Since legislative history indicates that discussions occurred regarding prisoners and there was an explicit rejection of a suggestion to exempt prisons from the reach of the new law, courts were forced to apply it to prisoner suits.

Most lower courts agreed that the prison's interest in security was a "compelling" governmental interest, but disagreed on what was considered to be a "substantial burden." Ordinarily, in order to be defined as a substantial burden on one's ability to practice one's religion, the state regulation must compel someone to do something that is directly contrary to his or her beliefs, or to force that person to refrain from doing something required by their religion. Also, the use of the term "least restrictive alternative" has been an issue in such cases. This area of law is still unsettled. The Supreme Court in *City of Boerne v. Flores* (1997) declared the RFRA to be unconstitutional, at least as a federal law. The Court held that Congress did not have the authority to pass such a law, although state legislators might be able to do so. The state legislation that has followed the *Boerne* case decision has usually specifically excluded prisoners from its protection.

The "establishment" clause of the First Amendment refers to the prohibition on "state religion" in this country. That is, our government is prohibited from forcing us to practice any specific religion, nor can it give legitimacy to any given religion or favor one religion over others in entitlement programs. Religion has been present in prisons for a long time and early court cases approved of the practice of the state paying for chaplains for prisoners. However, some states have recently been experimenting with faith-based rehabilitative programming, and this raises some concerns.

There have been a few cases concerning prisoners' challenges to requirements that they attend Alcoholic Anonymous (AA) meetings. Since AA refers to a higher power and does have religion as one of its core values, some courts have forbid states to require AA attendance. The Court of Appeals of New York in *Griffin v. Coughlin* (1996) and the Seventh Circuit Court of Appeals in *Kerr v. Farrey* (1996) held that privileges given to those inmates involved in Alcoholics Anonymous and Narcotics Anonymous violated the First Amendment. This is because these programs are based on a belief in a supreme being. Thus far, no higher level court holding exists regarding any challenges to the new faith-based religious programs.

Freedom of Speech and Press

In addition to religious freedoms, the First Amendment also protects an individual's rights of speech. Freedom of speech, as applied to prisoners, has typically dealt with censorship of both incoming and outgoing mail and publications. The interests of the media have been a special category of First Amendment rights. Again, we have seen a sequence of shifts in approach that dramatically changed the way these cases are decided.

The prisoner's right to receive mail and publications is balanced against the prison's right to protect safety and security. So, for instance, a prisoner has no right to a publication that describes, in detail, how to make a bomb out of kitchen ingredients, nor does he have a right to receive a letter detailing an escape attempt, nor a publication that advocates the overthrow of all prison regimes. The prison also has a right to address "order" concerns, so that they are usually free to restrict the number of pieces of outgoing and incoming mail (in order to manage it).

Some of the issues that are raised concerning the First Amendment and prison regulations include the following:

- communication with the news media (generally courts have upheld prisoners' right to contact the media through letters, although they have rejected the media's rights to interview or visit inmates);

- communicating with public officials (this type of mail is generally considered to be legal mail and deserving of legal mail privileges);

- communicating with other inmates;

- receipt of inflammatory or pornographic material;

- use of mail lists that restrict inmates to "approved" individuals are generally upheld when inmates can add individuals to the list and there is a valid reason for denying a request;

- receipt of books and packages are usually allowed, but prisons may specify prohibited items and may have a "publisher only" rule that limits books only to those sent directly from publishers (these regulations have generally been upheld as rationally related to prison security).

One of the early cases concerning censorship of mail was *Procunier v. Martinez* (1974). This Supreme Court case dealt with a challenge to California prison rules regarding outgoing mail. Not unlike other states at this time, prison officials in California routinely read outgoing mail and censored or refused to mail letters that were critical of the prison administration or made political statements. The regulations at issue in *Procunier* prohibited inmates from "unduly complaining" or "magnifying grievances," or "expressing inflammatory political, racial, religious or other views or beliefs." Another regulation prohibited letters that were lewd, obscene, defamatory, or contained foreign matter or were "otherwise inappropriate."

In the case holding, the Supreme Court switched the analysis from a consideration of prisoner rights to one where the First Amendment rights of the free person receiving the letter were considered. In *Procunier,* the Court seemed to use the highest level of scrutiny to judge whether the prison regulation was acceptable. In this so-called "strict scrutiny" test, the state must show a "compelling" governmental interest, the regulation must be strictly tailored to that interest, and the regulation must be the "least restrictive alternative." Furthermore, the suppression must be unrelated to the expression—meaning that prison officials could not suppress inmates' views because of their content (unless such content was directly related to a security threat).

After *Procunier v. Martinez,* state officials had to show that there was a legitimate governmental interest at stake, and that they were using the least restrictive means necessary to meet that interest. Ordinarily, this meant that inmates' letters were read but only at random, unless there was some reason for suspicion, such as an inmates involvement in escape plans or contraband smuggling.

In 1987, the Supreme Court dramatically changed the balancing test to one where prison officials only had to show a reasonable or rational relationship between the restriction or regulation and a state interest. In *Turner v. Safley* (1987), the Court upheld a ban on mail between inmates in two different prisons because it could be justified by "legitimate penological interests." Missouri prison officials argued that such mail might be used for such things as communicating about escapes, fostering gang activity, and arranging to assault other inmates. Rather than employ a "least restrictive alternative test," which might have allowed such mail but subjected it to censorship or required that the prison show cause before denying the right to such mail to any individual prisoner, they applied the rational relationship test. In this test, the prison official must show only that:

1. There is a rational connection between the prison regulation and the legitimate governmental interest put forward to justify it;
2. There are alternative means of exercising the right in spite of the regulation;
3. Accommodating the asserted right would be burdensome and affect guards, other inmates, and prison resources; and
4. There are no ready alternatives to the prison regulation available and the regulation is not an "exaggerated response" to the problem.

The state won, although the Supreme Court left open the question of mail to and from those outside prison.

Two years later, in *Thornburgh v. Abbott* (1989), the Court dealt with regulations in federal prisons regarding what type of outside publications prisoners could receive. Not surprisingly, the Court explicitly rejected the more stringent requirements of *Procunier* in favor of allowing broad deference to prison administrators' judgments. Prison administrators merely needed to have a "reasonable" relationship between the ban or rejection of a publication and institutional security. Nor did they require prison administrators to search for the "least restrictive" alternative such as, banning only certain issues of a publications rather than a blanket prohibition. Thus, it seems that the Court is saying that prison administrators can reject inmates' incoming publications if, in their judgment, the publications are detrimental to the order, discipline, and security of the institution; and it can also reject incoming correspondence from private parties, even non-prisoners, for the same reasons.

Despite *Turner v. Safley* and *Thornburgh v. Abbott*, there is no clear Supreme Court holding regarding whether or not prison officials can read all inmates' mail. Some lower courts have ruled that the mail may be read routinely; others have held that there must be cause. There is also the question as to whether or not a prisoner's right to receive or send mail may be suspended. At least some lower court decisions have upheld temporary suspensions of mail privileges. Legal mail (mail addressed to or from an attorney, court, or legislator) is a special category and receives special protections. It is protected by the Fourteenth Amendment and cannot be read, restricted, or otherwise interfered with by prison officials.

A special case of First Amendment rights concerns the media's right of access. In early and more recent cases, media representatives and prisoners have argued that the First Amendment guarantees the media's right to access prisons, specifically to interview certain inmates and "tell their story" to the world. In *Pell v. Procunier* (1974), prisoners challenged a California prison regulation that denied inmates personal interviews with members of the media. The state's position was that individual interviews were contributing to the "celebrity" of inmates who undermined the authority of the institution. In this decision, the Court made it clear that newsmen enjoyed no special rights of access over and above the general public; thus, the case could not be decided on the basis of the media's right of access. The Court accepted the governmental objective of preventing the creation of celebrity inmates and made note that there were alternative ways the inmate could reach the public, including writing letters and having visits with a family member who, in turn, could be interviewed by the media. The media could participate in public tours and speak to inmates during these tours, so there was no absolute ban on media access.

Saxbe v. Washington Post Co. (1974) was a companion case to *Pell*. The Court dealt with a case concerning the newspaper's denied request to interview particular inmates. As in *Pell v. Procunier*, the Court denied the media's request for "special" access. These decisions were reaffirmed again in *Houchins v. KQED* (1978). In this case, the right of a sheriff to deny jail access to a television station after an inmate suicide was challenged. Again, the Court held that the media had no greater right of access to prisons or jails than did the public, and whether or not to allow such interviews was a policy decision that infringed upon no constitutional right of the media. For instance, the Fifth Circuit denied any special right of the media to access and televise executions in *Garrett v. Estelle* (1977).

Rights of Association

The First Amendment has also been used to address prisoners' rights to associate and assemble. In *Jones v. North Carolina Prisoners' Union* (1977), the Court dealt with North Carolina's restrictions of the activities of a growing prisoner union. This case was argued under both the First Amendment rights of speech as well as the right to associate. The prisoners' union, modeled after such prisoner unions in some Scandinavian countries, had reached a membership of 2,000 by 1975. The state, in an effort to restrict and discourage membership, did not prohibit individuals from joining but did prohibit solicitation, meetings, and bulk mailings. The Supreme Court upheld these regulations, despite inmates' allegations that the regulations violated their First and Fourteenth Amendment rights (they argued that barring them from soliciting members violated equal protection, since other groups could do so freely). The state won again.

Maintaining contact with family has long been held to be an important part of reintegration for inmates. Despite the importance of visitation, the Supreme Court has never identified visitation as a liberty interest that must be protected by the Due Process Clause. This area of law is still somewhat unsettled, since the Court has never dealt with an absolute ban on visitation.

In *Kentucky v. Thompson* (1989), the Supreme Court held that the prison was not required to provide due process protections before denying an individual inmate a visit with certain individuals on his visiting list. The case dealt with two inmates who were denied visitation from specific visitors. In one case, the mother of an inmate was denied entry because she brought another person who had previously been caught bringing contraband into the facility. In another case, a mother and female friend were denied visitation for a short time because the inmate was caught carrying contraband after one of their visits. Neither inmate was prevented from seeing other visitors. In both cases, and in other situations, the duty officer and/or a higher official made the decision without any hearing or other due process protection.

In its holding, the Supreme Court first pointed out that there was no liberty interest in "unfettered visitation" to be found in the Due Process Clause itself. Then, it looked to whether the policies and procedures of the prison created the right. The Court concluded that even though there appeared to be mandatory language in some of the policies regarding visitation, the overall implication was not worded in such a way that an inmate could "reasonably expect" to receive visits. Thus, according to the Court, there was no liberty interest or right of the inmate to visitation. The Supreme Court accepted a Michigan case for review in its 2002 term that was a challenge to Michigan's stringent visitation rules. In 1995, Michigan enacted some of the most strict visitation rules in the country, mandating non-contact visits for a wide range of offenders and barring some offenders from receiving visits at all. The case, *Overton v. Bazzetta* (2003), has not been decided yet. When it is, we will find out the Court's current views on the extent of prisoners' right to visitation.

Conjugal visitation is that which allows "marital relations" between inmates and their spouses. Although a few states allow conjugal visits, or "family" visits, no court has ruled that inmates have a right to them. Contact visitation is that in which the visitor and inmate are not separated by a glass or mesh screen. There may still be rules regarding touching: for example, inmates in some states are allowed only one kiss and/or hug at the beginning of the visit. Again, no court has ruled that inmates have a right to contact visits. In *Block v. Rutherford* (1984), for instance, the Court held that pre-trial detainees can be denied contact visits due to security concerns. Obviously, if pre-trial detainees can be denied contact visits, it is certain that the Court would not extend such a right to convicted felons.

Interestingly, in *Turner v. Safley* (1987), the same case in which the Court upheld an absolute ban on inmate-to-inmate correspondence, the majority rejected a prison ban on marriages between inmates. Although the right to marry might be supported by the First Amendment, there is a broader basis of support in Supreme Court case law. The "penumbra" of privacy rights has been created through a succession of cases dealing with such things as zoning regulations, contraception, state interference in medical decisions, abortion rights, and other cases wherein the state seeks to control an individual's decision over a private, individual matter, such as who to live with and/or marry and whether or not to have children. Although space does not permit an exhaustive review of such cases, suffice it to say that in these opinions the majority have come to recognize rights of privacy that, while not specifically stated in the Constitution, were nevertheless intended by the framers.

Of course, just because a free person has a right to decide who to marry or whether or not to have a legal abortion does not necessarily mean such a right exists for a prisoner, especially under the current analysis, where prison regulations must merely meet the rational relationship test. However, in *Turner v. Safley*, the majority did recognize the essential right of a prisoner to marry whomever he or she chooses, even if that happens to be another prisoner. The state regulation in question denied the right to marry, unless it was approved by the warden, and even then, approval could only be given for "compelling reasons." The state's argument was that prisoners did not have the same rights as free people, and that the ban was "rationally related" to security and rehabilitation concerns. The Court disagreed. The *Turner v. Safley* holding has been criticized as being logically inconsistent. It certainly does seem strange that the Court upheld a restriction on inmate-to-inmate correspondence but rejected the regulation banning inmate-to-inmate marriage. This means that inmates may marry, but after the marriage, they cannot write to each other.

The Court seemingly used the rational or reasonable relationship test to arrive at both parts of the holding, but this illustrates the somewhat arbitrary nature of how the test might be applied. Obviously, both sections of Missouri's regulations were related to the stated objectives of security and rehabilitation. It is hard to see why one was considered "reasonable" and the other not.

Other issues that fall under the general rubric of privacy rights include the imprisoned parent's rights regarding his or her children. While no state allows imprisonment itself to be a sufficient cause to terminate parental rights, it is given great weight in such proceedings, especially if the parent has not made every effort to stay involved in the child's life. An imprisoned mother who gives birth evidently has no constitutional right to be with her newborn. While a few states have special provisions allowing bonding between mothers and infants, there has been no Supreme Court ruling that determines what rights, if any, the mother or child might have in such expanded visitation.

The Fourth Amendment

The Fourth Amendment: . . . the right of the people to be secure in their persons, houses, papers, and effects, against unreasonable searches and seizures, shall not be violated, and no warrants shall issue but upon probable cause, supported by oath or affirmation, and particularly describing the place to be searched, and the persons or things to be seized.

The Fourth Amendment protects our right to be free from unreasonable search and seizure by governmental officials. Inmates basically have no Fourth Amendment rights in prison. There is simply no such thing as an "unreasonable" search of a prisoner, up to and including full body cavity searches.

Two cases illustrate the Supreme Court's views on this issue. In *Bell v. Wolfish* (1979), the Court ruled that inmates had no right to be present during searches of their cells and also ruled that strip searches (including body cavity searches) are reasonable for purposes of contraband control and do not require probable cause. In *Hudson v. Palmer* (1984), a Virginia inmate sued for violation of his Fourth Amendment rights after prison officials conducted what the inmate saw as an unreasonable search of his cell. The Supreme Court declared that since prison officials must look for contraband and maintain sanitary conditions, the Fourth Amendment has no applicability to a prison cell. In effect, they said that the Fourth Amendment was "fundamentally incompatible" with prison security and order. The only time a court might reject a search as unreasonable or unconstitutional is when it is done conclusively for purposes of harassment, in which case the source of the right comes from the Eighth Amendment's protections against cruel and unusual punishment, not the Fourth Amendment.

There have been cases of prisoners protesting body cavity searches by opposite-sex guards. In some lower court opinions, privacy rights have been recognized, especially for female inmates who protest searches by male officers, although there is no consistency in this opinion and there are conflicting decisions among the lower courts (see Pollock 2002, 166–167).

The Eighth Amendment

The Eighth Amendment: . . . excessive bail shall not be required, nor excessive fines imposed, nor cruel and unusual punishments inflicted.

The Eighth Amendment protects us from cruel and unusual punishment. It has been used in the past to invalidate corporal punishment (i.e., whipping) practices (*Jackson v. Bishop* 1968). It has also been used to challenge inadequate medical care and inadequate or nonexistent rehabilitative treatment. On the other hand, it has also been used to challenge forced or coerced rehabilitative treatment. Finally, the more recent approach under the Eighth Amendment has been called "the totality of circumstances" approach. In these cases, an argument is made that the combination of conditions creates a total experience that is unconstitutional.

Medical Care and Rehabilitation

In *Estelle v. Gamble* (1976), the Supreme Court held that to be "deliberately indifferent" to the medical needs of an inmate would cause needless pain, unrelated to the goals of incarceration. As such, it would constitute cruel and unusual punishment and violate the individual's constitutional rights. The standard to be met, however, is higher than simple or even gross negligence. As long as the prisoner has "some" medical attention, evidently it is not "deliberate indifference." Medical care or, more accurately, the lack of medical care has been the topic of many court cases. *Madrid v. Gomez* (1999) is probably the best-known recent case where allegations of neglect and malfeasance were substantiated and became the basis for a court order and consent decree. In this case, inmates proved that the California Department of Correction was deliberately indifferent to the medical needs of prisoners in its staffing patterns and in having non-medical staff make decisions about who could see the doctor. Further, the practice of transferring inmates without their charts or prescription drugs and the delay in providing medical care for sick or injured inmates was found to be undue interference in the right of the inmate to have reasonable medical care. The case resulted in a consent decree whereby the state of California agreed to pay millions of dollars in improvements in its medical care delivery system.

Although prisoners may deserve medical attention for injuries or illnesses, no such right exists for rehabilitative treatment, such as for drug abuse. For instance, in *Marshall v. U.S.* (1974), the Supreme Court held that a prisoner did not have a constitutional right to drug treatment. However, mental health treatment is more akin to medical treatment than "rehabilitative" treatment; thus, the absence of any psychiatric or psychological treatment has been ruled unconstitutional (*Bowring v. Godwin* 1977).

No court has held that lack of rehabilitative programs constitutes a violation of the Eighth Amendment, except perhaps as part of a "totality of the circumstances" case. The only other way a "right to rehabilitation" might exist is if there is a sentencing statute that increases or changes the sentencing of an individual for the purpose of treatment (i.e., special sex offender sentencing).

The Eighth Amendment has also been used to challenge being required to participate in treatment programs and/or be subjected to involuntary injection of psychotropic drugs. In *Knecht v. Gillman* (1973), it was decided that prisoners could not be forced to stay in a behavior modification program that was defined as experimental. However, in *Washington v. Harper* (1990), the Supreme Court held that prisoners could be injected with antipsychotic drugs against their will if prison and medical staff felt the inmate posed a continuing danger to self or others.

Excessive Use of Force

They would make you lie down on your stomach and whip you with a bull hide. I got whipped the first day I was on the hoe squad. . . . It was like being backed up against a heating stove all day long. At night, you couldn't pull your shorts off. You had to take a shower and shake them loose. (an inmate describing the Cummins Prison Farm before prison reform, quoted in Nelson 2002, 2)

In *Jackson v. Bishop* (1968), a lower federal court held that whipping was cruel and unusual punishment. Since the Supreme Court denied certiorari, and has subsequently cited the case with approval, it has become accepted law that physical punishment—that is, beatings, whippings, and so on—is unconstitutional. More recent cases concern issues over "excessive force." Two cases illustrate the Supreme Court's view on what is permissible under the Constitution.

In *Whitley v. Albers* (1986), the Supreme Court held that an Oregon inmate who had been shot in the leg during a prison hostage situation needed to demonstrate "unnecessary and wanton infliction of pain" to prove that the state had violated his Eighth Amendment rights. The Court concluded that the shooting took place in a good-faith effort to restore prison order rather than for malicious or sadistic purposes. It was clear from the Court's holding that they were willing to grant state officials great latitude in determining the proper course of action in such situations.

However, in *Hudson v. McMillian* (1992), the prisoner did win his claim that he had been the victim of excessive force. In this case, the prisoner had been hit in the face after being handcuffed and shackled. The state attorneys deemed his injury "minor" and undeserving of Eighth Amendment protection. The Supreme Court ruled that an excessive use of force against an inmate need not cause a significant degree of injury to constitute cruel and unusual punishment. Even relatively mild injury (minor bruising to the face) might offend standards of decency if imposed in a manner that was unnecessary and wanton, and in this case, since the inmate was already subdued, the injury was deemed wanton and in violation of the Eighth Amendment.

Totality of Circumstances

The more recent cases involving the Eighth Amendment propose a "totality of the circumstances" argument. In these cases, no one condition or procedure is isolated, but rather the argument is that the combination of violence, lack of staffing, sanitation deficiencies, lack of rehabilitative programs, and other issues create living conditions that constitute cruel and unusual punishment. The remedy in many of these cases has been to appoint prison monitors to track the progress of prison systems in meeting many court-ordered conditions; sometimes these monitors oversee prison systems for years.

In fact, the *Ruiz v. Estelle* case only recently concluded after 20 years. In 2001, the Fifth U.S. Circuit Court of Appeals handed down a decision that said that unless the U.S. District Court Justice could show serious abuses still present, the court monitoring would end; however, Judge Justice, who appointed the court monitor 20 years ago, responded that there were still areas of concern, including conditions of confinement in administrative segregation, the failure to provide reasonable safety to inmates against assault and abuse, and the excessive use of force by correctional officers. He did, however, relinquish control over medical services and staffing. Then in June 2002, the case finally came to an end and the state of Texas was released from court monitoring (Moritz 2001; Timms 2001; *Austin American Statesman* 2002).

The Supreme Court has made it much more difficult for an inmate to win a "totality of circumstance" case. In *Wilson v. Seiter* (1991), an inmate alleged a totality of circumstance argument whereby the total conditions of the prison, including overcrowding, sanitation, programs, and violence, created conditions that violated the Eighth Amendment. In a reversal of past analyses, the Court held that the inmate had to prove "deliberate indifference," not just a pattern of deficits. Thus, inmates would have to prove that the prison administration knew and deliberately disregarded all the elements that constituted the claim of unconstitutional conditions. What sort of evidence an inmate could use to prove such a claim is not clear.

The Fourteenth Amendment

The Fourteenth Amendment: Section I: All persons born or naturalized in the United States, and subject to the jurisdiction thereof, are citizens of the United States and of the State wherein they reside. No State shall make or enforce any law which shall abridge the privileges or immunities of the citizens of the United States; nor shall any State deprive any person of life, liberty, or property,

without due process of law, nor deny to any person
within its jurisdiction the equal protection of the laws.

The Fourteenth Amendment includes both the Equal Protection
Clause and the Due Process Clause. Both have been utilized in prisoners' rights suits. The Due Process Clause dictates that every individual facing a possible deprivation of a "liberty interest" by a
governmental entity be entitled to certain due process procedures
designed to prevent or minimize error in the decision. So, for instance, when the government seeks to take away one's life, liberty,
or property, or any other liberty interest, it must first allow certain
fact-finding procedures namely, notice, neutral hearing, the right to
be present and present evidence, the right to cross-examine, counsel, and the right of appeal. Not all elements are deemed to be necessary for all deprivations. Generally, the greater the deprivation, the
more extensive are the due process elements. Note that the Due Process Clause does not protect individuals against these deprivations
by the state; the purpose is only to prevent arbitrary and capricious
state action or deprivations through error.

Substantive due process is slightly different from *procedural* due
process. A substantive due process issue is whether or not the right
exists at all. Is there a right to practice one's religious beliefs by
having a sunrise service? Do prisoners have the right to stay in a
minimum-security prison? Do prisoners have a right to visitation?
Is there a right to be free from solitary confinement? Procedural
due process identifies what protections would need to be in place
before such a right was abrogated by a federal or state authority.

The Fourteenth Amendment is the source of prisoners' rights
either directly (if the right is determined to be of a fundamental
nature) or indirectly (if it is a state-created right, because then procedural protections attach). The Fourteenth Amendment covers
issues such as access to courts, prison discipline, parole and probation revocation hearings, mental health/transfer hearings, and
perhaps protections for such things as visitation, a healthy environment, treatment, and so on.

Access to Courts

It is not an overstatement to propose that access to courts is the
sword that protects all other rights. Access cases involve allega-

tions that the prisoner is blocked from communicating with the courts. If communication is blocked, then recognized rights are worthless because there is no way to protect them when they are denied. If courts don't hear the cases, no one can protect the inmate against illegal deprivations. Even during the so-called "hands-off" era, the Supreme Court made it clear that state officials could not interfere with access to courts.

In *Ex parte Hull* (1941), a Michigan prison regulation required inmates to submit all legal documents (briefs, petitions, motions, habeas corpus proceedings, and appeals) to the institutional welfare official and the legal adviser for the Parole Board. Only if these officials believed that the legal documents were valid and properly written would they be forwarded to the court. The Supreme Court found this regulation invalid.

In *Johnson v. Avery* (1969), the Supreme Court held that a state could not punish a jailhouse lawyer for helping inmates with their cases if the state provided no alternative means for inmates to receive legal assistance. Early cases merely removed barriers to court access, such as regulations that stopped a petitioner's claims from going forward. Once these barriers were removed, later challenges took up issues of real as opposed to "apparent" access. For instance, illiterate and unschooled inmates must have help if they are to have "real" access to the courts. In *Wolff v. McDonnell* (1974), the Court held that protection of writ writers extended to those helping with Section 1983 claims, not just those who helped with habeas corpus petitions.

The Court has been extremely protective of the right of inmates to communicate and air their grievances and constitutional claims. Access cases might cover other real access issues, such as providing to indigents free of charge things like transcripts, postage, photocopying, and expanded visitation rights with attorneys or attorney representatives to assist in case preparation. "Legal mail" is correspondence addressed to a court, attorney, or legislator. It is distinguished from regular mail and has been awarded special protections. For instance, outgoing legal mail can be sealed (most mail is open for spot checks for escape plans or smuggling) and incoming legal mail cannot be read by prison officials. However, the Supreme Court also ruled in *Wolff v. McDonnell* (1974) that a Nebraska prison rule that permitted corrections officials to open and inspect legal mail in the presence of prisoners was constitutional. The prison officers could not read the mail, but they could check it for contraband in the prisoner's presence.

Several cases have dealt with the right of prisoners to have special rights of visitation with attorneys. In *Procunier v. Martinez* (1974), the Supreme Court held that prisoners were entitled to visits from paralegals or law students who were working on their cases. Officials can observe a legal visit, but they cannot breach the attorney-client privilege by listening.

After *Johnson v. Avery*, states that had no provisions for assisting inmates in their legal claims were required to institute changes. The most common method of meeting the Court's demand for real access was the creation of law libraries and some version of inmate or officer clerks to help inmates research legal questions. *Bounds v. Smith* (1977) was a holding that has been widely held as a "win" for prisoners, but in reality the beginning of the deference period can be heard in the Court's holding. The Court reaffirmed its earlier holdings in *Younger v. Gilmore* and *Johnson v. Avery* that inmates were entitled to meaningful access even though that access could be accomplished in a number of different ways (mentioning paralegals, paraprofessionals and law students, volunteer attorneys, or full-time staff attorneys). However, they rejected the prisoners' challenge that having to travel to a law library at another prison was unduly burdensome. They evidently were not concerned that in order to access a library, the prisoner might have to be transferred for a temporary period, thereby having to give up his cell, his place on any waiting list for programs, or his place in a coveted program.

There have been limits placed on the right of the individual to access the court. In *Murray v. Giarratano* (1989), the Supreme Court majority held that indigent death row inmates did not have a right to counsel in collateral appeals of their sentence (collateral appeals are those that come after the first, direct appeal process). This followed *Pennsylvania v. Finley* (1987), an earlier case that denied such a right to inmates seeking collateral appeals of sentences other than the death penalty.

Some believe that prisoners' rights to law libraries or other programs of assistance in filing legal claims have been more or less eviscerated by *Lewis v. Casey* (1996). In this case, the Supreme Court held that a prisoner must demonstrate that alleged shortcomings of the prison's library (or other type of legal assistance program) caused actual injury and hindered the prisoner's efforts to build a case in order to win. According to the Court's ruling, if the prisoner cannot show actual injury, then evidently the program, however superficial or inadequate, will be deemed sufficient.

Disciplinary Proceedings

As stated before, the Supreme Court has identified several sources for the existence of individual rights. Rights may come from the Constitution (or state constitution), by statute or agency procedural rules, or a right may be "inherent," meaning that the right exists whether or not it has been stated in a man-made document. This third source is controversial, as we shall see.

If there is a protected liberty interest at stake, then due process is determined by the seriousness of the threatened deprivation, with more serious deprivations deserving more elaborate due process protections. Only if there has been a fair trial and sentencing can the state (or federal government) send a person to prison. But once in prison, the individual is still protected; not by the Sixth Amendment, which is no longer applicable because of the criminal conviction, but rather by the Fourteenth Amendment.

In *Wolff v. McDonnell* (1974), an "adjustment committee" in a Nebraska prison found an inmate guilty of a prison infraction and took away good time. The inmate argued he should have had the same due process safeguards given to parolees facing revocation. These rights include advance notice, an impartial hearing body, the conditional right to present witnesses and evidence, the conditional right to confront and cross-examine, the right to a statement of fact-finding, the right to appeal, and a conditional right to counsel.

The Supreme Court majority found that prisoners did have a protected liberty interest, at least in good time, and held that some procedural protections must be in place before taking good time away. The Court held that the loss of good time was a protected liberty interest because of the statutory language creating it. That is, although there was no "right" to good time inherent in the Due Process Clause, such a right could be state-created. No inmate has a right to good time, and several states have now eliminated good time entirely with no constitutional violation. However, according to the *Wolff* analysis, once a state creates good time and statutory language promises it and specifies when it might be taken away, then a protected liberty interest has been established. The Court held at a minimum that the procedural protections necessary included a disciplinary proceeding by an impartial body, 24 hours advance written notice of the claimed violation, a written statement from the fact finders as to the evidence relied upon and the reasons for the disciplinary action, and an opportunity for the inmate to call witnesses and to present documentary evidence (provided this is not hazardous to institutional safety or correctional goals). The Court held that the prison setting may restrict the right to call witnesses and cross-examine, and so these rights would be conditional. Prisoners were not awarded the right to counsel except those who were illiterate or otherwise unable to defend their claims themselves (*Wolff v. McDonnell* 1974, 566).

The Court also extended due process protections to solitary confinement. Evidently, the Court grouped the two together because both affected the length and nature of confinement. Solitary confinement was described as a "major change" and the Court also discussed the possibility that a sanction of punitive segregation could later ruin the prisoner's chance for an early parole.

It should be noted that although *Wolff v. McDonnell* has been widely hailed as an important "win" for prisoners, in reality, the prisoners lost in the case. Nebraska was already providing many of the due process protections in the above list, as were many progressive states during that time period. The inmate was given notice (although it was oral); there was an adjustment committee hearing and a written record. The case was groundbreaking because of the number of states that had purely arbitrary and discretionary discipline procedures. For these states, the minimal protections awarded in *Wolff* were a dramatic change from prior practices.

After *Wolff*, states were required to hold some form of disciplinary hearings. Most adopted the two-tier procedure suggested in *Wolff* whereby minor infractions that might be punished by less severe sanctions were separated from major infractions with potential loss of good time and/or segregation. Only the latter charges were processed through the disciplinary hearing procedures. Disciplinary hearings are often conducted by "adjustment committees," with both classification and treatment represented. Some states employ outside hearing officers.

One should also note that most inmates describe such proceedings as little more than kangaroo courts, where their guilt is decided ahead of time. With rare opportunity to present witnesses or evidence or have outside counsel, and with the hearing officer usually a superior of the officer who filed the original "ticket," there is often the merest patina of due process in such proceedings. "Counsel substitutes" are often either correctional officers or other inmates; their ability to provide an aggressive defense is questionable. Further, according to *Superintendent v. Hill* (1985), the level of proof necessary to determine guilt in a prison disciplinary case is merely "some evidence."

Later cases have further eroded the reach of the *Wolff* decision. Prisons ordinarily have two types of segregation. In addition to punitive segregation (or solitary confinement), there is also administrative segregation. It operates in much the same way as punitive segregation but is reserved for those awaiting transfer, newly transferred prisoners, those seeking protective custody, and others for a variety of reasons. It is virtually indistinguishable from punitive segregation. Prisoners are locked in their cells for 23 hours a day, they have no access to programs or yard recreation, they have isolated visitation schedules, and they cannot visit the law library, although they can request that law books be brought to them in their cells.

In *Hewitt v. Helms* (1983), an inmate who was sent to administrative segregation challenged the transfer, arguing that he deserved the same due process protections as those awarded in *Wolff v. McDonnell.* Aaron Helms was removed from the general population in connection with a riot that occurred at the State Correctional Institution at Huntingdon, Pennsylvania. He was accused of assaulting prison officers and of conspiracy to disrupt the institution. After a number of hearings, officials charged him with assault and ordered him to disciplinary segregation for six months. Helms sued, claiming that his confinement in administrative segregation prior to his sentencing violated his due process rights. In this prison, administrative segregation was used for those inmates who posed a threat to security, when disciplinary charges were pending, or when an inmate required protective custody.

The Supreme Court, in a holding written by Justice Rehnquist, illustrated the shift to a deference approach in their identification of the source of rights and their decision as to what process was due. They did find that prisoners in this state had a protected liberty interest in the transfer to administrative segregation, but only because it was created by state statute and prison regulations. According to the Court, when states explicitly mandate administrative segregation for certain violations, some due process is required. Note the importance of this shift in rights. The Court did not say that the move from general population freedoms to extremely restricted living conditions, by itself, was a grievous loss; only that the state may create a right to due process by statute or procedural rules.

Justice Rehnquist held that a "liberty interest arises when the action taken by the prison is not 'within the terms of confinement ordinarily contemplated by a prison sentence'" (*Hewitt v. Helms* 1983, 869). However, according to Justice Rehnquist, the transfer of an inmate to "more restrictive quarters for non-punitive reasons was well within the terms of confinement ordinarily contemplated by a prison sentence" (*Hewitt v. Helms* 1983, 468). Thus, the majority opinion in this case concluded that the inmate possessed due process protections when being transferred to administrative segregation only when it was created by statutory language. In this case, the prison regulations required only an informal, nonadversary review of information with the inmate's statement of events. This review was to be done within a "reasonable time" after confinement to administrative segregation. The Court agreed that these minimal due process protections were sufficient to protect the liberty interest created; therefore, the state won.

In *Sandin v. Conner* (1995), the Supreme Court overruled its *Hewitt* decision and completed its evisceration of the *Wolff v. McDonnell* holding, at least as it regarded transfer to segregation. Demont Conner, a Hawaiian prisoner, complained that prior to his disciplinary hearing he wasn't given a summary of facts relevant to the charge, he was not permitted to question the guard who charged him with the offense, he was not allowed to call witnesses at the hearing, and prison officials "doctored his testimony" and used it against him. According to Hawaii's regulations, an adjustment committee could only find guilt when the inmate admitted the violation or upon "substantial evidence."

The Court of Appeals applied the *Hewitt v. Helms* "source of rights" rationale and concluded that Hawaii's regulations created a liberty interest in remaining free from disciplinary segregation and these same regulations mandated the specific due process elements that must be met before transfer to punitive segregation could occur. The Court of Appeals held that the adjustment committee did not have "substantial evidence" of guilt, and therefore the sanction of punitive segregation violated Conner's due process rights. Connor won, but the state appealed the decision to the Supreme Court.

The Supreme Court overturned the Court of Appeals ruling. Justice Rehnquist wrote the opinion for the 5 to 4 decision, and in this opinion he rejected the statutory source of right and instructed lower courts to look only at the nature of the deprivation. The Court argued that the practice of searching for statutory rights "encouraged prisoners to comb regulations in search of mandatory language on which to base entitlements to various state-conferred privileges," created disincentives for states to codify prison management procedures, and involved the courts in day-to-day management of prisons and did not allow "appropriate deference and flexibility to state officials trying to manage a volatile environment" (*Sandin v. Conner* 1995, 2299).

The majority were no doubt responding to the explosion in prisoners' rights litigation and perhaps also to the public's increasing impatience with "frivolous" due process complaints. Certainly, after the *Hewitt* decision, a rash of cases emerged in which prisoners sought to find liberty interests in mandatory language of prison rules and regulations. Another issue that evidently was on the justices' minds was that the states that had attempted to provide guidance and develop some restrictions on unrestrained discretion of prison officers found themselves in litigation more often than those states that did not provide extensive guidance through policies and procedures. The Court noted that this was an unfortunate side effect of the state-created right analysis and discouraged greater codification of procedures.

Thus, according to the *Sandin* majority, the source of the liberty interest, if there is one, should be found in the nature of the deprivation. Now, only when the deprivation constitutes an "atypical, significant deprivation" and is not "within the range of confinement to be normally expected" does a liberty interest exist and due process is required.

In *Hewitt v. Helms*, the Court, in dictum, opined that the nature of the deprivation (in that case administrative segregation) wasn't atypical or outside the scope or range of the original sentence because it was similar to disciplinary segregation. Now, in *Sandin*, the Court utilized that argument to dismiss the deprivations of disciplinary segregation as well, arguing that it is similar to administrative segregation and thus not atypical. The Court also noted that the general inmate population often spent many hours in their cells because of lockdowns in the prison; thus, the longer period of time in disciplinary segregation wasn't relatively more burdensome.

Although the Court argued that it was merely reverting back to the analysis first proposed in *Wolff*, in truth this decision overturns *Wolff* as well because in that earlier case the majority did believe that being locked in one's cell for 23 hours a day and having no opportunity to take part in any programs or education was "atypical" and implicated a significant liberty interest. Evidently, the only liberty interest left to inmates that deserves due process protection is any deprivation that fundamentally alters the length of the original prison sentence (such as taking away one's good time).

The four justices who dissented in *Sandin* strenuously objected to the majority's definition of what would constitute a liberty interest. Justice Ginsburg, joined by Justice Stevens, also disagreed with the notion of looking for liberty interests in mandatory language. She argued that this would create the strange situation where "fundamental rights" were different from state to state, a situation that ran counter to the concepts and tradition of due process protections. However, they felt that disciplinary segregation was substantially different from administrative segregation and deserved due process protection. While both types of segregation restricted liberty, only punitive segregation might substantially affect the length of sentence by affecting the parole board's decision.

Thus, prisoners who face administrative segregation or punitive segregation today arguably have no rights of due process protections. States could evidently abandon the disciplinary proceedings that were instituted after *Wolff* for every sanction except, perhaps, the loss of good time with no argument from the Court.

Other Deprivations

The above discussion concerned transfers to administrative or punitive segregation. Other cases have dealt with other types of transfers. In *Meachum v. Fano* (1976), the Court held that inmates had no due process rights when being transferred to a prison where conditions were harsher. This case has had far-reaching effects, even beyond correctional law, because of its "source of rights" analysis. In this case, officials removed Arthur Fano and five other prisoners from Norfolk to Walpole prison in Massachusetts. Living conditions were substantially less favorable in Walpole because it is a maximum-security prison. Fano and others were suspected of setting nine serious fires. The prison classification board held individual classification hearings, and inmates were represented by counsel. Each prisoner was allowed to present evidence but was not given transcripts or summaries of the testimony. Fano alleged violation of due process.

In a surprising retreat from the due process line of cases decided up to that point, all of which had accorded the liberty interest definition and due process protections to discipline and transfer decisions (such as parole and probation revocation), the Court held that there was no liberty interest at stake. According to Justice White, there was no right to be in any particular prison; therefore, transfers deserved no due process.

The case became important because of Justice White's discussion regarding the source of rights. In *Meachum*, the Court identified that liberty interests either came from the Constitution or through some statute or state regulation and had no existence apart from these sources. However, Justice Stevens and other dissenters argued passionately that rights were not merely man-made. In their discussion, utilizing natural law concepts, such sources were not the sole harbinger of rights; rather, they were only man-made notations of rights that existed independent of judicial or statutory recognition of them. Each individual is endowed with certain "inalienable" rights by virtue of being.

Laws and statutes merely recognize such rights. Justice Stevens, in his dissent, joined by Justices Brennan and Marshall, argued that even inmates retained fundamental liberty interests or, at minimum, the right to be treated with dignity—which the Constitution may never ignore.

> If a man were a creature of the State, the analysis [regarding source of rights] would be correct. But neither the Bill of Rights nor the laws of sovereign States create the liberty which the Due Process Clause protects. The relevant constitutional provisions are limitations on the power of the sovereign to infringe on the liberty of the citizen. . . . I had thought it self-evident that all men were endowed by their Creator with liberty as one of the cardinal unalienable rights. It is that basic freedom which the Due Process Clause protects, rather than the particular rights or privileges conferred by specific laws or regulations . . . the inmate retains an unalienable interest in liberty—at the very minimum the right to be treated with dignity—which the Constitution may never ignore. (Justice Stevens in *Meachum v. Fano* 1976, 233)

The *Meachum* analysis that prisoners had no rights regarding transfer was applied to a challenge of a state prisoner being transferred to a federal prison in *Howe v. Smith* (1981) and to a state prisoner being transferred to another state prison in *Olim v. Wakinekona* (1983). Evidently, prisoners have no due process protections, even when such transfers involve being transferred to worse living conditions or cause great hardship to the prisoner and/or his or her family.

The dissent in *Wakinekona* was troubled by the Court's cavalier dismissal of such a transfer as not "atypical" or "within the normal limits or range of custody." Although logically it makes sense to conclude that a prisoner must expect to be imprisoned in any prison in his or her state, why would there or should there be an expectation that the transfer may be to any state in the union? Incarceration in a state far away from one's home creates a number of hardships. Visitation is impossible or nearly so for families, ongoing legal proceedings are hampered (for instance, family court proceedings concerning custody or deprivation of parental rights), there may be fewer program offerings, and classification committee hearings that allocate good time and custody level changes are made more difficult. Justice Marshall was deeply troubled by the decision and dissented: "[W]hether it is called banishment, exile, deportation, relegation or transportation, compelling a person 'to quit a city, place, or country, for a specified period of time, or for life,' has long been considered a unique and severe deprivation" (*Olim v. Wakinekona* 1983, 252).

The only transfer case that has turned out differently involved a transfer to a mental hospital. As of this point, it is still good law. In *Vitek v. Jones* (1980), the Court ruled that involuntary transfer from a prison to a mental hospital setting did involve a liberty interest and necessitated a due process hearing. This was because a mental hospital was qualitatively different from a prison, residents had greater limitations on their freedom, there is stigma attached to a stay in a mental hospital (evidently worse than or at least different from that attached to a prison sentence), and there was a mandatory behavior modification program in operation. These elements created a "major change in the conditions of confinement" amounting to a "grievous loss."

The Supreme Court held that before an inmate can be transferred to a mental hospital, the same due process protections as required before civilians can be committed must be in place. This meant that inmates deserved all of the *Wolff* protections plus cross-examination. Specifically, they deserve written notice, a hearing, disclosure of evidence relied upon, an opportunity to be heard in person and present documentary evidence, an opportunity to present testimony and to confront and cross-examine witnesses (except upon a finding, not arbitrarily made, of good cause for not permitting such presentation, confrontation, or cross-examination), an independent decision maker, a written statement by a fact-finder as to evidence relied upon and reasons for transferring the inmate, legal counsel (furnished by state if indigent), and effective and timely notice of all foregoing rights.

Other Due Process Issues

The Due Process Clause is implicated whenever there is a liberty interest threatened. Up to this point, the discussion has involved disciplinary or transfer cases in which prison officials seek to deprive the inmate of good time or transfer him or her to segregation, administrative segregation, or another prison (either in the same state or a different state). There are other official decisions that may implicate a liberty interest; however, the Court's decisions in these cases have clearly shown that it will take extreme circumstances before a liberty interest is recognized.

The only other case besides *Vitek v. Jones* in which the Supreme Court did find a liberty interest sufficient to require due process protection was in *Washington v. Harper* (1990). In this case, the Court decided that inmates had an inherent right to be free from involuntary administration of psychotropic drugs. However, the process due was extremely minimal, merely a finding from officials that the inmate was a danger to self or others.

Not surprisingly, an argument that inmates deserve due process before being deprived of property is met with little sympathy from the Supreme Court. In *Parratt v. Taylor* (1981), an inmate filed a Section 1983 claim, arguing that he lost a $23.50 hobby kit due to the negligence of officers. The Court held that negligence would never be sufficient to uphold a constitutional violation and that state actors must intentionally violate an individual's constitutional rights before a Section 1983 claim could be made. But then, in *Hudson v. Palmer* (1984), the Court further held that even if officers intentionally deprive an inmate of property, as long as there are some mechanisms for filing grievances, or if state tort claim actions exist, then these are sufficient to meet the due process protection requirements for property deprivation.

The Prisoner Litigation Reform Act

In 1996, Congress passed the Prison Litigation Reform Act (PLRA). This act has been responsible, no doubt, for a dramatic reduction in the number of prisoners' rights suits filed in the federal courts.

This sedulously crafted piece of legal language is so vicious, detailed, and sweeping that is has baffled journalists and academics into near-total silence. (Parenti 1999, 177)

One of the elements of the PLRA is that an inmate must exhaust all administrative remedies before filing a Section 1983 suit (a civil suit alleging that an agent of the state has violated one's constitutional rights). Further, the inmate must show physical injury—emotional or mental suffering is no longer sufficient to justify a claim. A $120 court filing fee was instituted, even for poor inmates, unless they show absolutely no income for a six-month period prior to filing. Another element of the act is that attorneys no longer are paid by the defendant state if they win. Their earnings must be taken out of the award to the plaintiff inmate. Such awards may not be very large, since often the victories are injunctive rather than financial. Finally, the act permanently bars an inmate from ever filing any other suit if he has had three suits declared frivolous or malicious. While this may seem fair, it should be understood that inmates may have legitimate cases thrown out as frivolous because they did not understand how to write the writ or present their evidence. In essence, this inmate is without recourse to the courts regardless of what happens to him.

The ire of the writers of the PLRA was also directed to activist judges who sought to reform the prison system. Elements of the act prohibit judges from imposing indefinite consent decrees (the vehicle by which many state prisons were brought into compliance with humane standards) and limit a special master's (court monitor's) pay to $40 an hour (even if these masters are lawyers, whose pay is usually many times that amount). Obviously, this has meant that few highly skilled individuals are remaining in special master positions.

The Supreme Court has upheld the PLRA and, according to many, the rights of prisoners must be defended in state courts, using state constitutions, because the federal courts have been effectively silenced (Roots 2002; Harding 1998).

Conclusion

This chapter includes a review of "access" cases, those cases that have created the right of inmates to have their grievances heard by the court. We have seen that the early sensitivity to the importance of access has dissipated. In a number of decisions, the court has closed doors to prisoner writ writers and made their entry more difficult. The final and most troubling blow was the *Lewis v. Casey* decision, which held that only if the inmate could show specific injury or harm, could the actions of prison officials in hampering his access to the court be considered a constitutional violation. If there are situations that block or impair access to the court (such as inadequate law libraries or legal assistance), then it is hard to see how the prisoner is going to be able to get his grievance to court in the first place, much less be able to show specific harm.

In disciplinary and transfer proceedings, the Supreme Court has overturned prior decisions that recognized liberty interests could be created by statutory language. The Court has returned to the "grievous loss" analysis, as first presented in *Wolff*: however, today the Court majority seems to believe that almost any deprivation endured by prisoners should be considered "typical" and characteristic of imprisonment. Being pulled from the general population and spending 23 hours in a cell—removed from programs, educational opportunities, and certain visitation opportunities—is considered "typical," as is being sent thousands of miles away from one's family and legal counselors in the ever-increasing interstate transfers. These transfers may be to a facility designed to be used as a jail rather than a prison, and outside recreation, programs, and cell design may be inappropriate or inadequate for longer periods of confinement.

James Jacobs (1980), a legal analyst and early observer of prisoners' rights, postulated a number of hypotheses regarding the impact of prisoners' rights on the legal landscape. They were:

1. The prisoners' rights movement contributed to the bureaucratization of the prison.
2. The prisoners' rights movement has produced a new generation of administrators.
3. The prisoners' rights movement expanded the procedural protections available to prisoners.
4. The prisoners' rights movement has heightened public awareness of prison conditions.
5. The prisoners' rights movement has politicized prisoners and heightened their expectations.
6. The prisoners' rights movement has demoralized prison staff.
7. The prisoners' rights movement has made it more difficult to maintain control over prisoners.

8. The prisoners' rights movement has contributed to a professional movement within corrections to establish national standards.

One could also add the following:
9. The prisoners' rights movement and subsequent court decisions helped to increase correctional budgets.
10. The prisoners' rights movement is over.

Today, in the Supreme Court's current "due deference" approach, prison administrators have been given broad latitude to run their prisons in the way they see fit. Although prisoners still possess certain fundamental rights (of minimal medical care, sanitation, and safety), there are few other recognized rights. Inmates may be transferred at will, sometimes across the country or to a private prison with no notice or reason. They may correspond or visit with their family, marry, practice their religion, and write or speak freely only when it has been approved by prison officials. Some states have taken their cue from recent Supreme Court decisions and completely barred any media interviews with inmates; others have shut down or said they will no longer update law libraries (Parenti 1999, 181). Those who continue to argue that prisoners have too many rights are simply out of touch with current case law.

Study Questions

1. Describe the hands-off era and the activist era of the Supreme Court and federal courts regarding prisoners' rights litigation.
2. Describe the source(s) of prisoners' rights.
3. What prisoners' rights might be recognized as coming from the First Amendment?
4. What prisoners' rights might be recognized as coming from the Eighth Amendment?
5. What prisoners' rights might be recognized as coming from the Fourteenth Amendment?

Chapter 8

Prisons for Women

We controlled every moment of the lives of the women we guarded. We told them when and where they could go, when they could eat, shower, sleep, when and with whom they could talk. We strip-searched them after an afternoon visit with their children. We made them work to acquire skills, but told them they were capable only of sewing, mopping floors, or preparing food. We confiscated their personal belongings. We read their mail. . . . We were the ones who took away their dignity. . . . [W]e were disempowering them and setting them up for failure once back on the street. (a prison guard, reported in Faith 1993, 162)

Only about 7 percent of the prisoner population in this country are women (Harrison and Karberg 2003). Up until recently, women constituted an even smaller percentage. This means that women's institutions have always been considered the stepchild of the corrections system. A typical statement of correctional managers is that there are prisons and then there are *women's prisons*. Historically, women's prisons had different staffing patterns and even a different mission from that of men's. About the mid-1980s, roughly corresponding with the spike in prison populations, there was a trend in correctional management to "straighten up" the management of women's prisons. This meant that women's prisons were to be brought into line with men's prisons. In some ways this has been a benefit, but in other ways the changes have hurt the prisons' ability to meet the needs of women.

Increasing Numbers

Table 8.1 shows the precipitous increase in the number of women sent to prison. The rate of growth has been nothing short of phenomenal. The impact on American families is unknown. The number of women incarcerated in state prisons actually decreased by almost 1,000 from 2000 to 2001, although the number of women sentenced to federal prisons went up by about 500 for a net decline to 93,031 (Greene and Schiraldi 2002, 12; Harrison and Beck 2002, 5). However, the number of women increased again in 2002 to 96,099 (an increase of 1.9 percent) (Harrison and Karberg 2003, 5).

Table 8.1 Number of Women Incarcerated

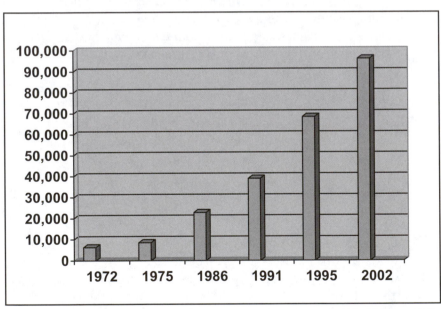

Adapted from T. Snell, *Women in Jail: 1989*. B.J.S. Special Report (Washington, D.C.: U.S. Department of Justice, 1994); P. Harrison and A. Beck, B.J.S.: *Prisoners in 2001* (Washington, D.C.: U.S. Department of Justice, 2002); P. Harrison and J. Karberg, *B.J.S. Bulletin: Prison and Jail Inmates at Midyear 2002* (Washington, D.C.: Department of Justice, 2003), 3.

Although the total number of women incarcerated is dwarfed by the number of men in prison, the *percentage increase* of women sentenced to prison over the last two decades has been higher than the rate for men. Since 1990, the average annual growth rate has been 5.7 percent for men and 7.5 percent for women. Put another way, the number of men in prison has increased by 80 percent, whereas the number of women in prison has increased by 114 percent (Harrison and Beck 2002, 5). The national prison incarceration rate for women is 60 per 100,000, but the rate for men is 902 per 100,000, so there is still a huge difference in the numbers and likelihood of imprisonment for women and men (Harrison and Karberg 2003, 5). Belknap (2003) presents evidence that the rate of increase for minority women has been even higher than that experienced by white women. For instance, whereas the rate of incarceration in prisons and jails for white women was 67 per 100,000 in 2001, the rate for African-American women was 380 and the rate for Hispanic women was 119. Of course, even black women's rate comes nowhere near the rate of men: white (705), Hispanic (1,668), and African-American (4,848) (Beck, Karberg, and Harrison 2002, 12).

In 2001, Texas held the largest number of female prisoners (12,369), followed by the federal system (10,973) and California (9,921). Florida (4,245) has recently surpassed New York (3,273) as the state with the fourth largest female prisoner population (Harrison and Beck 2002, 6). The states with the highest incarceration rates for women were Oklahoma (130), Mississippi (113), Louisiana (99), and Texas (96). The lowest incarceration rates for women were in Maine (8), Rhode Island (10), and Massachusetts (13) (Harrison and Beck 2002, 6–7). This pattern of increase is present in jail and community corrections populations as well. Today, women constitute a little under 20 percent of the probation population, about 11 percent of the parole population, and 11 percent of jail inmates (Beck 1998).

Are we sentencing more women to prison because they are committing more crime? Yes and no. As one can see in Table 8.2, while women's contribution to violent crime has not risen substantially, except for assault categories, they have increased their participation in property crimes (Pollock 1999, 2002; Belknap 2000). The increase seems to be due to the same pressures that have been driving the tremendous growth in the population of male prisoners, along with special factors that affect women. Determinate sentencing and sentencing guidelines take away judicial discretion to some extent, and if judges had been more likely to sentence women leniently in the past, they are no longer able to do so. Further, they

Table 8.2 Percentage of Arrests of Women by Crime

Crime	Percent of All Arrests		
Total	1988*	2000	2001
Violent crime (index)		17.4	17.3
Property crime (index)		29.9	30.4
Crime index total		26.4	26.7
Murder	12.5	10.6	12.5
Forcible rape	1.2	1.1	1.2
Robbery	8.1	10.1	10.1
Aggravated assault	13.3	20.1	20.1
Burglary	7.9	13.3	13.6
Larceny-theft	31.1	35.9	36.5
Motor vehicle theft	9.7	15.8	16.4
Arson	13.7	15.1	15.9
Other assaults	15.1	23.0	23.4
Forgery and counterfeiting	34.4	39	40.2
Fraud	43.5	44.9	45.4
Embezzlement	38.1	50	49.6
Receiving stolen property	11.6	17.4	17.9
Vandalism		15.5	16.2
Weapons violations		8.1	8.2
Prostitution/commercialized vice	64.8	37.9	66.6
Sex offenses (other than prostitution and rape)		7.4	8.0
Drug abuse violations		17.6	17.8
Gambling		11	9.5
Offenses against family and children	17.4	22.4	23.1
DUI		16.4	16.6
Liquor law violations		23	23.6
Drunkenness		13.1	13.7
Disorderly conduct		22.8	23.9
Vagrancy		20.9	19.1

(*Note: 1988 figures are only selected crime categories.)

Source: Uniform Crime Reports, "Arrests by Sex" (Washington, D.C.: Department of Justice, 2001, 2000, 1988).

may choose not to do so today in an effort to "equalize" sentencing between men and women, even if they have discretion. For whatever reason, the prison population explosion has reverberated in women's prisons as well, and the effect has been a mini-building boom, with states adding to their capacity either by constructing new buildings or adding on to existing facilities. When a state exceeds its own capacity for housing female offenders, women (like men) are transferred far away to other state systems. This has extremely troubling consequences for women because they are already struggling to maintain their role as mothers.

History of Women's Prisons

Originally women were housed with men, and terrible conditions and sexual exploitation prevailed. Even after they were segregated, they usually had no exercise or opportunity to get fresh air. Part of the reason for their ill-treatment was the fact that there were so few of them. Only women who committed crimes that shocked or enraged the public or those women who were chronic offenders were placed in confinement. Prisons were reserved for those females who were considered to be evil and irredeemable. Courts managed to find other solutions for most women who committed crimes.

In the 1800s, the number of female prisoners increased and some prison administrators began hiring female wardens to run the women's wing or section. There was also a growing perception that women were not evil, but misguided, and could benefit from the influence of proper "ladies" who could teach them how to be good housewives and mothers. This involved teaching them to read, cook, clean, and sew. Even music and art were added to the curriculum of some prisons.

In 1873, the first completely separate prison for women was built in Indiana. Several states followed in short order. Most women's prisons built in the late 1800s and early 1900s utilized a reformatory model (Freedman 1986; Rafter 1990). These institutions housed young women who were thought to be amenable to treatment. Many were not what we would consider even criminal today. Because of extremely flexible and broad sentencing authority, the "criminals" might have been young girls whose parents thought they were promiscuous, women who lived in "sin," or wives who ran away from their husbands (Rafter 1990). Even those states that opened separate reformatories usually kept open the wing or building at the prison for men for chronic or older female offenders. Minority offenders were also usually sent to custodial institutions (Rafter 1990).

In the South, incarceration followed a different path. Because the South followed an agricultural model, most prisoners were either leased to landowners or performed agricultural labor for the state. The few women who were incarcerated in these southern prison farms, usually minority women, worked in small garden plots for the prison staff's use or did domestic labor in the warden's and other members' homes (Rafter 1990).

It wasn't until the mid- to late 1970s, however, that all states had separate institutions for women. Even as late as the 1950s, many states had only a wing or a building on the grounds of a prison for men. Some states transferred the handful of female prisoners they felt needed secure facilities to neighboring states. Rafter (1990) reported that between 1930 and 1950, only three or four women's prisons were built in each decade; however, in the 1980s, 34 prisons were built for women.

Prisons for women have always been different from prisons for men. Until recently, female wardens had restricted career paths; their experience running a facility for women seldom helped them move up the administrative ladder in a system dominated by men's institutions. Also, wardens of prisons for women have had to fight for resources. Because women's institutions have never posed the threat of riots or major disturbances, their needs have been relegated to the end of the list.

Programming in women's institutions has continued to be a product of the beliefs regarding women's place in society. For most of this century, whereas some type of basic educational programming in prison was common, other opportunities were extremely limited. College classes or educational release programs were much less common in women's prisons than in men's. Classes in typing, food service, and hairdressing was about the extent of vocational programs typically offered. It was only in the 1980s and 1990s that prisons began to provide programs that had some chance of helping women achieve economic success. Nontraditional programs, found in a few women's prisons, have included auto repair, heavy machinery operation, and commercial cleaning.

Computer training has also been a highly attractive program offering in those prison systems that offer it.

Today, women's prisons have gained greater attention, partly because there are many more incarcerated women and state systems can no longer ignore the female prisoner population. There has also been litigation in several states that has forced them to equalize programming and improve medical care. For instance, *Glover v. Johnson* (1979) dealt with a challenge to the dearth of programming for women in the Michigan prison system.

Finally, state correctional officials tend to feel that women's prisons have not been managed well, and tighter security is needed for them to become more like men's prisons. This trend, no doubt, is at least partly due to the cross-sex supervision that now permeates most state systems. Men who have been trained and have worked in men's institutions and then transfer to women's prisons want the prison to run the way they are used to. Sometimes this is extremely frustrating to correctional managers in women's prisons, who must deal with real differences between the populations. Women's institutions are no longer stepchildren but now "problem children" that need to be "fixed."

Try explaining to a table full of men why female prisoners use three times as much toilet paper as the same size of prison housing men! It's obvious but I still need to justify it. (a female warden, private conversation 1993)

Who Are the Women in Prison?

Women in prison share some characteristics with men in prison, but there are also differences. Women are less likely to be in prison for violent crime: They continue to commit a consistently small percentage (less than 20 percent) of violent crime. While certainly there are women serving time in prison for violent crimes, including gang violence, few studies conclude that women as a whole are becoming increasingly violent. The problem of the "new violent female criminal" seems to be a recurring myth in criminal justice and popular literature and one that may well have contributed to harsher prison sentences imposed on female offenders. If one looks at arrest rates, conviction rates, or other objective evidence of violent crime, there is great consistency over time in women's homicide and robbery crime rates (Pollock 1999; Chesney-Lind 1997; Belknap 2000).

There has been a small increase in women's arrest rates for assault. In 1965, women accounted for 13.5 percent of all arrests for aggravated assault; in 1995, 17.7 percent; and in 2001, women accounted for 20.1 percent of all arrests for aggravated assaults (Uniform Crime Reports 1965, 1995, 2001). What this increase means, however, is unclear. One possible explanation is that mandatory arrest policies for domestic violence have led to police officers arresting both parties, creating this increase in reported crime.

There is no doubt that women's contribution to various property crimes is increasing, although the rapid rate of increase that appeared in the 1990s has slowed. As one can see in Table 8.2, women accounted for about 36 percent of all arrests for larceny-theft and 45 percent of all arrests for fraud in 2001 (Uniform Crime Report 2001).

Explanations for such an increase in crime can be categorized into the general explanations of "opportunity theory" or "economic necessity." Opportunity theories speculate that women are involved in the workplace and in public life more than in the past, so they are utilizing that opportunity for illegitimate as well as legitimate activities. Economic necessity theories speculate that because of no-fault divorce, abysmal child support enforcement, and reduced national and state public assistance, women and their children form the largest poverty class and some of these women commit property crimes to survive (See Pollock 1999, 2002; Belknap 2000).

Several authors have argued that the increase of women offenders in prisons and correctional populations is largely due to the increased number of women arrested for drug crimes. Bloom and her colleagues report that the percentage of women admitted to prison for drugs in California increased from 14.2 percent of total admissions in 1982 to 42.2 percent of total admissions in 1992 (Bloom and Steinhart 1993). About one in 10 women were in prison for drug crimes in 1979, but in 1991, that figure had risen to one in three (Deschenes and Anglin 1992). More current figures indicate that about 34 percent of women in prison are serving time for a drug offense (Greene and Schiraldi 2002, 12).

The women inside these walls are very real, human, mainly conservative, and often depressingly dependent. Their problems are not bizarre or complicated. In the main, over eighty percent are addicted to drugs and/or alcohol. . . . An equally high percentage are victims of incest, rape, and/or battering. The likelihood of these traumas contributing in part to addiction is very high. (a Canadian female inmate, Mayhew 2002, 156)

Drug use forecasting figures indicate that female arrestees are more likely than male arrestees to have drugs in their system and self-report more drug use. Needs assessment studies of prisoners also indicate that women self-report more drug use. However, it does not seem to be true that women are playing increasingly more powerful roles in drug distribution systems. Evidence indicates that women continue to have fairly minor participation in drug dealing, acting as "mules" or low-level dealers (Wellisch, Prendergast, and Wellisch 1994). It is reported that drug use by women seems to be associated with prostitution, small-scale drug sales, and larceny/theft crimes (Webb, Katz, and Klosky 1995).

The increasing numbers of women in prison and other correctional populations is most probably due to a combination of increased participation in criminal activities and changing patterns of sentencing. Determinate sentencing systems, drug laws, and a more punitive sentencing culture, as well as increased arrests especially in property crime areas, all account for the increased numbers of women in corrections.

Background Characteristics

Women in prison have usually encountered hardships and abuse as children, have been exposed to drugs and alcohol very early, and have engaged in self-destructive behavior and relationships. They tend to be young, single, economically disadvantaged, and disproportionately minority. They are likely to be mothers. Women are sentenced to prison most often for drug offenses and/or property crimes, usually larceny. They are also slightly older than male prisoners, and do not have as extensive criminal histories as do men in prison. They are also less likely to have been employed before incarceration. They are more likely to have come from dysfunctional families (with histories of sexual and physical abuse) and report more drug use (whereas men report more alcohol use). They are also more likely to have been custodial parents of children before incarceration and more likely to plan on being primary providers for their children upon release (Pollock 2002).

I started using marijuana at age of eight, with my sisters and my cousin. I started drinking about that time too. Then I started cocaine binges. I started running away when I was eleven. It seems like I have always been in trouble. (a female offender quoted in Owen 1998, 46)

Needs assessment surveys of female prisoners have been conducted in California, Oklahoma, and Texas (Owen and Bloom 1994; Fletcher, Shaver, and Moon 1993; Pollock 1998a). Findings from these state studies were consistent with a national study of female prisoners (Snell 1994). What these studies show is that because of their criminal history, most women in prison present little risk to the public. Because of their family and drug backgrounds, they may need more intensive programming. Also, because of their status as primary caregivers, they desperately need tools to help them in that role, including the ability to earn a living and the skills to be better parents to their children.

Women in prison today are more likely to have criminal histories than in the past, but they are still less likely to recidivate than men (Pollock 2002). Almost all women in prison are classified as low risk. Even so, because there are usually fewer women's prisons, all women tend to be held at medium/maximum custody levels.

One of the most consistent findings of women in prison is that they are more likely than men in prison to have experienced both childhood and adult abuse—both physical and sexual. In most surveys, one-third to one-half of the women surveyed have experienced sexual or physical abuse as children and even more as adults. Women who have been involved in the sex industry were more likely to have experienced abuse, as have women with a history of drugs (Pollock 2002). The Bureau of Justice Statistics reported that 41 percent of female probationers, 48 percent of female jail inmates, and 57 percent of female prisoners reported either sexual or physical abuse (Greenfield and Snell 1999, 8; also see Harlow 1999).

Most studies report very consistent findings. In one study, half of the women interviewed for the study had experienced some form of sexual abuse in childhood or adolescence. Thirty-eight percent had been a victim of a violent assault, one-third had been a victim of a violent sexual assault, and 28 percent had been shot at or knifed (Browne, Miller, and Maguin 1999). These experiences are obviously traumatic and influence the women's life in a variety of ways.

When I was eight or nine, my mother's boyfriend molested me. I was afraid to say anything. He did it again and I told my mother; they got in a fight and she killed him with a knife. When she went away to prison, nobody talked to me. They acted like it was my fault. It was my fault, I should have stayed silent. I started to drink when I was eleven. A boy raped me on the roof when we were drinking. I was too afraid to tell anyone, even when I became pregnant. Everyone was shocked when I gave birth at thirteen years old. (a female prisoner, quoted in Bedell 1997, 28)

While there seems to be a correlation between childhood abuse and violent crime with men, the same pattern does not hold for female offenders (Widom 1989, 1996). Women evidently are much more likely to react to childhood abuse with self-destructive behavior (drugs, alcohol, suicide, mutilation) and depression. Prior abuse seems to be related to female prisoners' bad choices regarding drugs, alcohol, and relationships. The correlation between victimization and female criminality cannot be ignored. Some women's prisons today run survivor groups to help women discuss and understand the effects of childhood incest and molestation, as well as battering.

Living in Prison

> What bothers me most back here is these stinking ass women. . . . (an inmate, quoted in Owen 1998, 116)

Women's prisons have a different atmosphere than prisons for men. There is less of the incipient threat of violence. There is more laughter. But there are also more tears. Officers say that women are more emotional than men (Pollock 1986). That may be true; at least women seem to feel free to express their emotions. Some women report that they feel that they have to put on a front, and some women are fearful, but overall there is less of the "jungle" atmosphere in women's prisons.

One of the interesting things discovered by talking to women is that many appreciate the programs offered. A common theme is "if it wasn't for prison, I'd be dead now." Prison offers a respite from the streets. Some women choose to re-create the street in prison by fighting, engaging in destructive relationships, and using drugs. Many female offenders, however, use the time in prison to reflect on their lives, take advantage of educational and therapeutic opportunities, and make plans to do better when they are released. Unfortunately, prisons do not have the resources to offer enough programs to all of the women who desire them. Vocational, educational, and therapeutic programs often have waiting lists. Many women are idle because the prison staff cannot create enough job slots for the burgeoning prison population. States are building more prisons for women and adding new beds to existing facilities. Unfortunately, at times, once a new prison is built, there is no money left to provide programs. One thing that we have learned from history is that once a prison is built, it almost never closes. The same is definitely not true of prison programs.

Women's social interactions and subcultural norms are somewhat different from male prisoner subcultures (Pollock 2002; Morash and Schram 2002; Sharp 2003). Men in prison are likely to form gang structures and have social/political organizations, but women tend to form small cliques and dyads (friendship pairs). If they do organize in larger groups, communication patterns tend to be less political and more familial.

Women also tend to form pseudo-families, or play families. These social structures involve several or many women who take on familial roles, such as mother, father, daughter, sister, and so on. The most common role is that of mother. However, roles can cross sexual identity lines. For instance, women will play male roles such as the authoritarian father or jealous husband. One can observe that these roles are played fairly stereotypically, but they seem to provide needed relationships for some women (Pollock 2002).

> I see it like maybe the reason they do that is 'cause they don't know who they [sic] father is, maybe they don't have any sisters or brothers, maybe their mother's passed away, maybe they don't have any kids and want kids, want a mother, want a father, want a brother, want a sister. I don't want none of it. It's not real, for one thing. (an inmate talking about make-believe families, quoted in Girshick 1999, 91)

Today, these roles seem to be changing somewhat. While Owen (1998) found that pseudo-families did exist, they were somewhat more diffuse than in past years. Fox (1990), Girshick (1999), and Greer (2000) argue that female prisoners do not bond in the way described in older research. Fox (1990), for instance, found that when he returned to the same women's prison about 10 years after his first visit, kinship systems were more fragmented. Greer (2000), utilizing a small sample, found that women reported less activity in kinship networks.

One of the most obvious differences between men's and women's relationship patterns is that homosexuality in women's prisons tends to be consensual while homosexuality in men's prisons is often coerced. For most women, prison homosexuality is a transitory adaptation to the deprivations of prison. Although the superficial indexes of a homosexual relationship are fairly apparent (hugging, hand holding, kissing), these relationships may or may not actually involve sexual contact. Many women admit that they engage in such activity just to have someone to "love them." Such relationships may cause trouble for the woman when she is released. It is not uncommon in prison visiting rooms to have fights erupt when a lover in prison observes her partner's visit with an outside loved one.

> The homosexuality that is done in the male facilities is usually masked, and there is a percentage of rapes, but I think a lot more of it is permissive, it is sold and so forth. In the female facilities it's not sold, it's not rape, it's just an agreement between two people that they're going to participate and there is a lot of participation. (a correctional officer, quoted in Pollock 1984, 86)

Women in a committed prison relationship will take great pains to hide their relationship from others and from staff. They often express great scorn for "jailhouse turnouts"; those who engage in a homosexual relationship only as a transitory adaptation to prison. In most prisons, women are punished for any sexual contact, and in some prisons, any form of physical contact, including hand-holding, is against the rules in an effort to control and suppress homosexuality. Of course, these absolute prohibitions against any physical affection are as unsuccessful as they are unnatural.

There is not as much violence in prisons for women, but there is always the threat of violence. Women have been known to rape (with an object) a prison "snitch," although the more common sanction is ostracism. There is fighting, usually caused by jealousy or hurt feelings. Since women do not have as organized a black market or as extensive a drug market as one finds in prisons for men, the fighting that ensues from business activities is relatively rare. Weapons are also not as prevalent in women's prisons (Pollock 2002). Some recent reports indicate that women's prisons may be becoming more violent than in past years (Girshick 1999; Greer 2000).

While men in prison form racial gangs and a good proportion of violence is directly or indirectly attributed to racial tension and hostility, women do not seem to be as racially divided. In fact, many sexual dyads and pseudo-family structures are interracial. While there is some voluntary racial segregation while eating and in recreational activities, extreme patterns of segregation and hostility due to racial tension do not seem to be present in prisons for women (Pollock 2002).

Barbara Owen (1998) offers the most complete recent ethnography of a women's prison. In her study, she finds that the earlier descriptions of prison life hold true today with a few changes. While pseudo-family structures are somewhat more diffuse, they still exist. "Homegirls" (those who come from the same neighborhood) provide a network of friends and supporters in prison. Fellow gang members also provide companionship and share resources. Drugs are more prevalent than in the past. In Owen's description of a very large California prison, "the mix" was the term used for the subcultural activity of those comfortable in prison. The "drug mix" involved those who sold, traded, and used drugs; the "homosexual mix" involved those who were involved in pseudo-families and homosexual dyads; and the "fighting mix" involved those who established themselves as fighters (Owen 1998).

Inmates who wanted to do their time quietly avoided the mix by avoiding the yard. "Programming" meant volunteering and participating in prison programs. Some women entered into programming enthusiastically, some did not. Old-timers or "convicts" avoided officers and avoided programming. As in the earlier studies, Owen found that the relationships between staff and inmates could be cordial, even helpful, if the staff members interacted with the women with fairness and kindness. Women who were ready to change entered into programs, sought out good jobs in prison, and avoided the mix (Owen 1998).

Prison Programs for Women

Although nontraditional programs (such as auto mechanics, heavy machinery operation, and carpentry) have been offered in some state systems, women's prisons still bear the legacy of sex stereotyping. Recent research efforts (Morash and Schram 2002; Sharp 2003) provide current information concerning what is happening in women's prisons as far as programming is concerned.

Gender-specific programming is a new buzzword in corrections. It means designing programming that takes into account the special needs of women. This approach recognizes the possibility that although women's programming should be equal to men's, it doesn't have to be the same as men's and, in fact, sameness may not meet the needs of female offenders. National studies indicate women's programming in prisons is improving but does not currently meet the many needs of female offenders (Morash and Bynum 1995; Pollock 2002; Owen and Bloom 1994, 1995). For instance, nontraditional programs have been offered, but, ironically, many women have the mistaken impression that these programs are merely borrowed from facilities for men and that the programs are offered because of a neglect or ignorance of the needs of women. Unfortunately, women who enter such programs sometimes do so unwillingly and report that they plan to ignore their training and get a job as a beautician or nurse's assistant upon release because they "like helping people" (Pollock 1998a). The lesson to be learned from this example is that programming must match women's interests and needs, or at least there must be an effort to educate participants as to the benefits of nontraditional vocational programming.

Needs assessment surveys have found that more than half of women in prison have grown up in a household without both parents and are more likely than male prisoners to have relatives incarcerated and/or have relatives with drug or alcohol problems. They also report abuse, as discussed above (Owen and Bloom 1994, 1995; Fletcher, Shaver, and Moon 1993; Snell 1994; Pollock 1998, 2002).

We know that women in prison are amenable to treatment. In needs assessments, women indicate that they appreciate all forms of programming and specifically ask for more programs that will help them overcome drug addiction, get a job upon release, and become better parents to their children (Pollock 1998). We also know, however, that many states do not even screen for such things as childhood abuse or battering. Further, many states do not know how the female offender has arranged for her children to be cared for during her imprisonment. Some states do not even collect information on whether or not incoming female inmates have children (Pollock 2000).

Drug treatment programs for women have often been copied from programs for men, yet some point out that women and men are different in their motivations for drug use and incentives for change. Women have been found to have higher scores on the Addiction Severity Index and also to be more likely to report serious psychiatric problems such as depression and anxiety (reported in Peters and Steinberg 2000). Even though more female offenders than male offenders report drug problems, only about 11 percent of them are in a prison program (Predergast, Wellisch, and Falkin 1995). Like men, women are likely to have co-occurring disorders, such as drug addiction and depression or drug addiction and personality disorder (Morash and Schram 2002).

Drug treatment programs designed for men do not necessarily work as well for women. For instance, while women tend to be more open and show less resistance to introspection, this advantage can be circumvented by forcing them into treatment groups with men. Also, women may not need the confrontational tactics common in some group therapy programs directed to male offenders and may respond less well to them (Pollock 1998a).

If it is true that female offenders are more likely than males to have dysfunctional family backgrounds, then it is important to create gender-specific programming that responds to this fact. Groups that deal with incest, sexual abuse, and the like are in demand when they are offered and often have waiting lists, despite the inmate subcultural prohibition against self-disclosure. However, these programs are not often evaluated.

Studies of correctional programs have typically either ignored programs for women or included them in general findings where they have been eclipsed by the much larger samples of programs for men. It may be that certain characteristics of female offenders make them especially amenable to particular programs and not so amenable to others. There has been virtually no research that uses gender as an independent variable when evaluating correctional programming. It is important to isolate and evaluate programs for women separately from larger evaluation efforts. Only then will we be able to test whether programs affect men and women differently.

The body of research that explores correctional programs for female offenders is extremely small. Meta-analyses of correctional programs have not studied programs for female offenders, and if such programs were included in the sample, the findings from such evaluations have not been presented in a gender-specific manner. Morash and Bynum's (1995) survey of correctional programming for women is perhaps the only study available that specifically evaluates women's programming. In their study, they found that their sample of programs most often offered drug treatment (54.9 percent), but the programs sampled also offered "life skills" (40.3 percent), parenting skills (40 percent), information on relationships (30.6 percent), and basic education (29 percent). This study concludes that there are very few innovative programs for women across the country and those that might be described as innovative are gender-specific and individualized.

Morash and Schram (2002) explain the need for programs that address co-occurring disorders, such as drug addiction and bipolar disorder or alcoholism and depression. Elements of good programs for female offenders should address a number of different but related issues. First, the program should address the woman's specific needs, including the cycles of poverty, violence, poor parenting, marital discord, parental psychopathology/mental illness/depression, lack of education, parenting issues, addictions, childhood incest or physical abuse, criminal behavior, and survival strategies (Bedell 1997; Pollock 1998a).

Vocational programs should offer opportunities to acquire skills with the potential to be used to earn a decent wage. If the programs are nontraditional, the staff may have to convince women that they are valuable. However, if women acquire nontraditional skills only to discover they cannot find work outside, then such programs are a waste of time and money. Brewster (2003) found, in an Oklahoma study, that educational programs for women resulting in a GED were successful in reducing recidivism but vocational-technical programs were not. What this means is unclear, but it could be that vo-tech programs may not lead to employment after release.

Prisoners as Mothers

Women in prison are very often mothers of small children (McGowan and Blumenthal 1978; Hungerford 1993; Pollock 1998a; Pollock 2002; Enos 2001). Estimates of the number of women prisoners who have children under 18 range from 60 percent to about 85 percent (McGowan and Blumenthal 1978; Bloom and Steinhart 1993; Pollock 1998a; Henriques 1996; Hungerford 1993; Pollock 2000). There seems to be consensus that about 70 percent of women in prison have at least one child under 18 and women have an average of two or three children (Pollock 1998a; Greenfield and Snell

1999). A large number of these women were the primary caregivers of their children before their imprisonment. A recent study reports that whereas 64 percent of female prisoners were living with their children before incarceration, only 44 percent of men had been (Mumola 2000).

What happens to these children when their mother is imprisoned? Surprisingly, only about 10 percent enter foster care (Immarigeon 1994; Pollock 1998a; Mumola 2000). Of those who retained custody during imprisonment, most placed their children with relatives, usually the maternal grandmother (Block and Potthast 1997; Pollock 2000). It is also true, however, that the children are moved around several times during the prison sentence. Placement and arrangements for guardianship of the children is often informal, ad hoc, and without resources. Women fear that state protection agencies will permanently take away their children, and so they don't involve the state. However, this means that there are no financial resources to help care for the children, necessitating already overburdened families with few resources to care for them. Most states do not keep records on children's placement in the community, so we have very little knowledge about what happens to these children.

Some women in prison never see their children (Courturier 1995; Bloom 1995). Bloom and Steinhart (1993) found that 54 percent of mothers in a national sample reported no visits. This compared with only 2 percent of those surveyed in a similar study in 1978 who reported no visit. Why there is such an increase in the number of women who never receive visits is attributed to a restriction of prison telephone privileges to collect calls only, the construction of new women's prisons in rural areas, and lack of financial support from social service agencies for travel (Bloom 1995). Bloom and Steinhart (1993) reported that visitation frequency was related to pre-prison factors. Whereas 46 percent of those who lived with children prior to imprisonment received no visits, 72 percent of those who did not live with children prior to prison or jail received no visits.

Visits are difficult because of the long distances between the prison and home and the expense of traveling. Also, there may be hesitancy on the part of caregivers to take the children to the prison and/or anger at the mother for her actions that led to the situation.

Many social workers may feel it is traumatic for children to see their mothers in prison and resist accommodating such visits. Finally, the mother herself may not want her children to see her in prison or to subject them to the search and admission procedures required for visitation. She may feel guilty and ashamed over her imprisonment and refuse to let her children see her in such a setting. Furthermore, visits necessarily include saying good-bye—an experience that is so painful to both mother and child that many women in prison prefer to avoid it.

I myself have a son who is 19 years old and he's sitting in a county jail . . . that's all he saw . . . motorcycles, drugs, guns, and his mom in and out of prison. His dad was never around. He left when he was a child. (a female inmate, reported in Pollock 1999, 108)

Some women may give birth during the time they are imprisoned. About 6 to 10 percent of women in prison on any given day are pregnant (Henriques 1996; Pollock 1998a, 2000). This percentage may mean a few women a year in those states with small prison populations, but it could mean close to 100 women in larger states. These pregnancies are often high risk, since women in prison may have been drug users, have avoided or neglected medical treatment, and/or have had difficult previous pregnancies.

One report, for instance, indicated that 77 percent of imprisoned women had exposed their fetuses to drugs (Johnston 1995b). Some research indicates a higher than average rate of miscarriage for women in prison. Part of the reason for this is attributed to the fact that women must be transported to outside hospitals for delivery and for medical emergencies.

Recently, Amnesty International (1999) published a critical report on the imprisonment of women in this country and one of the major criticisms was the way in which pregnant women were treated. Prison policies included lack of prenatal care even when there were medical problems with the pregnancy, being shackled to the hospital bed during labor, delays in transporting a woman in labor to an outside hospital, and immediate separation from the infant with no opportunity to bond.

Parenting programs should address the children's needs, including the provision of a safe, non-intimidating location to visit the mother in prison, and preferably offer a long uninterrupted time for such a visit to take place. Also, there should be support for children outside of prison, either counseling or support groups. In the few published studies that evaluated parenting programs in women's prisons, a reduction of recidivism is rarely stated as a goal or objective. However, there is some evidence to indicate that family ties, and frequent visitation, are correlated with a reduction in recidivism (Block and Potthast 1997). In a 1991 study of Camp Retreat in New Jersey, it was found that not one of the 70 women who participated thus far had returned to prison (Stumbo and Little 1991).

Martin (1997) examined mothers who were incarcerated in the Minnesota Correctional Facility at Shakopee in 1985 five years after their release. This study establishes the fact that frequent contact with children in a child-centered institution supports future reunification with children. Nearly two-thirds of the women studied who were imprisoned in Shakopee in 1985 emerged five years later as "primary, highly involved parents to at least one of their children." One-third of the women were no longer connected with their children; the difficulties were too great to overcome and too complex to allow them to care for children. There was no relationship between seriousness of crime and ongoing connection with children. Mothers who were "connected" with their children were three times more likely than nonconnected mothers to be drug-free and to have no history of chemical abuse. Connected mothers were more likely to be married. Whereas 80 percent of connected mothers committed no new crimes, only 57 percent of nonconnected mothers had not committed subsequent crimes. However, 28 percent of the mothers were still in prison (Martin 1997, 4–9).

The mothers described as unconnected did not parent well; they let children control interactions and had histories of drug use, erratic contact, and repeated criminal activity. Connected mothers had legal custody, emotional connection, and a mature grasp of their children's needs. Mothers in Shakopee saw their children twice a month. Nationally, only 10 percent of mothers saw children more than once a month, and only 12 percent were allowed overnight or weekend visits. The frequency of visitation was related to whether the mother was described as connected five years later (Martin 1997, 18).

Although it seems obvious that the children of incarcerated parents are at high risk for future incarceration themselves, there does not seem to be a national will to intervene. Programs for prison mothers are few and often paper-only programs that do not meet the needs of prisoner mothers (Pollock 2000; Sandiver and Kurth 2000). This is despite the fact that many female prisoners will leave prison to resume their caregiving duties. If prison does not provide them with any insight into what happened with their own lives, they will be unable to assist their children in avoiding the temptations they fell victim to.

Health Care

In *Todaro v. Ward* (1977), female prisoners in New York were successful in proving that the lack of appropriate medical care provided by the prison system was unconstitutional. The Court found that there were arbitrary procedures, failure to perform laboratory tests, long delays in diagnoses, a grossly inadequate record-keeping system, and inappropriate screening. The state of New York was forced to meet court-ordered standards for improvement. Unfortunately, the facts cited in this case over 25 years ago are still the subject of legal actions today, if not in New York, then certainly in other states.

Women in prison suffer from a multitude of health problems, some of them self-induced. Drug addiction, alcoholism, smoking, promiscuity, untreated sexual diseases, inherited and untreated hypertension, diabetes, asthma, AIDS, and many other medical problems characterize the female prisoner population. While advocates don't expect women in prison to receive better care than those outside, prisoners do have a right to expect minimal care. Some don't get that care and die for that reason.

One of the biggest concerns regarding female prisoners is their special needs for gynecological care and prenatal care. Some women have miscarried in prison, arguably because of improper or absent medical care. In the report by Amnesty International (1999), cases were presented in which women giving birth were shackled to the hospital bed. In many cases, women who give birth in prison must be transported to an outside hospital and so there is always the risk that the birth will occur in the prison or en route.

I was . . . put on eyeball status, stripped of belongings, clothing, placed in a room with nothing but a plastic mattress on the floor. Watched 24 hours a day by a man or woman. I was hemorrhaging but because of my status not allowed to have tampons or underwear. I was very humiliated, degraded. Being on eyeball status with male officers, my depression intensified. I didn't want to be violated any more than I already was, so I put the mattress up against the window. When I did that I was in violation because they couldn't see me. The door was forced open, I was physically restrained in four point restraints—arms, legs spreadeagled, tied to the floor, naked, helmet on head, men and women in the room. (a woman who was considered a suicide risk in a Massachusetts prison; reported in Amnesty International 1999, 78)

Management Issues

As discussed previously, there has been a trend to equalize prison institutions, which of course means that women's institutions were supposed to be brought into line with the men's. In some ways this is a good thing, but in other ways it is clear that women are not men, not even in prison, and differences must be addressed. These differences pose a host of management issues for correctional administrators.

One of the current issues in administering women's prisons is the prevalence of cross-sex supervision. This has led to male officers strip-searching and conducting intimate pat-downs of female offenders. When female inmates challenge such treatment utilizing right-to-privacy arguments, some courts have agreed that women and men are different and experience different realities. In this instance, the fact that so many women in prison have experienced sexual abuse by men arguably makes them different from male prisoners who do not share that history and, therefore, do not experience the same level of anxiety or violation as do women when undergoing a search conducted by a guard of the opposite sex (Pollock 2002).

> It seems like every time you use the toilet or begin to un-
> dress for bed, he's standing there in front of your cell
> gawking at you. Sometimes he rubs his crotch and makes
> some crude comment about wanting to do something to
> you or have you do something to him. It's so disgusting,
> and there's nothing you can do about it because he's to-
> tally in charge. (a female inmate, quoted in Kupers 1999,
> 128)

The negative reaction of some female prisoners to their male guards is unfortunately supported by recent findings that indicate that sexual abuse and exploitation of women in prison has occurred and continues to occur across the country. Women's prisons utilized very few male correctional officers until the Equal Employment Opportunity Commission and litigation opened the doors to cross-sex supervision. Now some state systems have a majority of male officers supervising women in women's prisons. Evidence of sexual exploitation and abuse has emerged in Hawaii, Texas, Michigan, New York, Georgia, and other states (Amnesty International 1999).

In Washington, D.C. jails, legal advocates began hearing cases of sexual abuse and exploitation that were too widespread and consistent to be ignored. Female inmates became pregnant in a system that did not allow conjugal visits and came forward with stories of male officers threatening women with violence or withdrawal of privileges if they didn't provide sex. Over a dozen women testified regarding their experiences with officers who raped or coerced sex from them. It wasn't just officers. Chaplains, administrators, deputy wardens, contractors, and food service workers were implicated (Parenti 1999, 190; also see Siegal 2002). Incidents included those where officers and inmates forced other female prisoners to strip and dance (*Daskalea v. District of Columbia* 2000; Parker 2002). In Georgia, a similar pattern emerged. Inmates working with legal advocates came forward with stories of sexual extortion, sexual harassment, and assault. In this case, 17 staff members were indicted, although only one was convicted (Siegal 2002).

One of the most shocking cases to date of prison rape occurred in Pleasanton, California, at FCI Dublin. This was a federal prison that inexplicably housed women prisoners in the segregation unit of the prison for men. In *Lucas v. White* (1998), the court found that three women were, in essence, sold to male prisoners by correctional officers who also opened the women's cells so the male prisoners could go in and rape them. Eight prison officials were forced to resign over the incident and the prisoners settled their civil lawsuit for $500,000 (Parenti 1999, 191; Siegal 2002). Observers note that the case has had an impact on policies and practices in federal institutions (Siegal 2002).

> Nearly every inmate we interviewed reported various sexually aggressive acts of guards. A number of women reported that officers routinely "corner" women in their cells or on their work details in the kitchen or laundry room and press their bodies against them, mocking sexual intercourse. Women described incidents where guards exposed their genitals while making sexually suggestive remarks. (Amnesty International 1999, 38)

All but about a dozen states now have legislation that criminalizes sexual abuse and/or any sexual contact with prisoners (Siegal 2002). But abuse still continues across the country in prisons and jails. More pervasive than sexual assault is a widespread sexual harassment or a "sexually charged" atmosphere that is created when men guard women. Observers and advocates relate instances where officers show off erections, make inappropriate sexual comments, needlessly touch and grope women, and remark on the appearance of female prisoners.

> If I need Tylenol, all I need to do is ask him for a pelvic and he will give me whatever I want. (an inmate describing sexually inappropriate behavior by a prison doctor, cited in Siegal 2002, 137)

Some state officials, faced with such scandals, have responded with proposed policies that would completely bar male officers from working with female inmates or bar them from searching female inmates. In some cases, courts have upheld states' regulations prohibiting supervision or searching by male officers. For instance, in *Jordan v. Gardner* 1993), the court held that because the women's prison population had a higher percentage of prior sexual victimization than did male prison populations, being searched, even patted down, by male officers might be "cruel and unusual punishment." This case has not been followed in other jurisdictions, however, and the law is not settled in this area.

Female inmates have never been as litigious as male prisoners (Pollock 2002). When suits have been filed, they have typically concerned equal protection challenges to the lack of programming or the lack of adequate medical services. In *Glover v. Johnson* (1979), the court held that the state must provide roughly equal program opportunities to men and women and that the small numbers of women are not reason enough to deny them opportunities. Of course, as some writers have noted, courts only mandate equal opportunities for men and women; the state can choose to increase program offerings for women or reduce program offerings for men to meet such a mandate (Chesney-Lind and Pollock 1994).

Release

Women released from prison face many challenges. The biggest challenge is attempting to reunite with their children. Some mothers have permanently lost their children to the state; some have to wrest them away from relatives. Some children don't want anything to do with their mothers. For those mothers who want to regain custody, it is a struggle to make enough money to support themselves and her children. Very few women return to homes with husbands and providers.

One of the added burdens placed upon them has been the federal law creating a lifetime ban on receiving federal aid from TANF (Temporary Assistance for Needy Families) if convicted of a drug offense. A state may opt out of this ban, but if it doesn't, women who would otherwise be eligible for financial assistance would be denied. Ironically, this law would bar assistance to a woman with a minor drug conviction, but an offender with a violent crime would be eligible. This law, combined with the federal law that prohibits those with felony drug convictions from living in public housing, makes it extremely difficult for any woman leaving prison with a drug conviction to make a new life for herself and her children. It is no wonder that so many retreat into the netherworld of drug abuse again.

Conclusion

It is clear that convictions for drug crimes account for many women's involvement in the criminal justice system. The criminalization of drug use has resulted in huge increases in the number of women we imprison and the number of children who are affected by their mothers' imprisonment. Although these women admit that drugs have been a negative influence in their lives, prison is usually not the best answer for them, their families, or society in general. Women may benefit from treatment programs in prison, but in general prison is a negative world, and women benefit very little from putting their lives on hold. Further, their children suffer and the dislocation in some children's lives is severe. Because of the nonviolent nature of many women in prison, it would pose very little risk to the public to explore community alternatives to incarceration. Wherever they serve their sentence, they typically need assistance in learning how to take care of themselves and their children.

Study Questions

1. What differences can be noted between prisons for men and for women historically and today?
2. Describe the demographic profile of the female prisoners.
3. What special management problems are there in prisons for women?
4. What do we know about the children of incarcerated women?
5. What are the differences in violence and homosexuality between prisons for men and women?

Chapter 9

'Doing Time Eight to Five'

Out in the free world, people have only two notions of how prisons are run. Some believe prisons are staffed by sadistic guards, and others believe social-worker types are in control. Both kinds can be found working in prisons, but neither has any say at all about how a prison is operated. Bureaucrats run prisons. Sadists and social workers come and go but the paper-shuffling bureaucrats endure forever. (an ex-prisoner, Martin and Sussman 1993, 101)

Up until this point, the discussion has focused on prisoners. However, three distinct groups exist in prison—the inmates, the correctional officers, and the administration. There is conflict between the "keepers" and the "kept." There is also conflict between correctional officers and the administration. In fact, as will be discussed, correctional officers report feeling more stress stemming from administration policies than they do from inmate behavior. Officers are both workers and supervisors. They are the lowest level of line staff, taking orders from everyone above them, but they are also supervisors of all inmates. How they treat inmates may have a great deal to do with how they are treated by management.

Correctional Officers

There is an inherent conflict between inmates and officers. At times, the power and authority all officers possess by virtue of their uniform is abused. Other officers, however, go out of their way to instill a bit of humanity in the prison world of violence and depersonalization. Stereotypes of correctional officers as sadistic brutes are present in books and movies and are reinforced by some works written by inmates. But the reality is, of course, much more complex.

The Changing Role of the Guard

Crouch (1995, 184), in a discussion of the changes throughout the 1970s and 1980s that affected the guard force, noted that three factors combined to change the prison world for inmates and officers alike. First there was a new emphasis on rehabilitation that led to a loosening of the tight controls that characterized prisons in early years, as well as an expectation that officers would do more than just "lock and unlock" doors. The second factor was a change in the size and composition of the inmate population. There were more inmates entering the system and more of them had serious drug problems. Finally, judicial intervention eventually affected every policy and procedure, leading to a belief that "the courts ruled the prison."

It [legal reform] has resulted in the absolute abdication of control by the people of Texas, handing what was once their prison system to the federal courts. The civilian Board of Criminal Justice has been reduced to a political correctness monitor for a legislature that runs for cover every time a federal judge even hints that some convict may not be receiving his court-mandated gym class. (a retired and disgruntled Texas warden, Glenn 2001)

Crouch (1995) examined how these three events created role conflict and ambiguity, danger, loss of control, stress, racial and sexual integration, and deviant behavior among officers. Other factors that have changed the role of the guard include unionization, professionalism, and bureaucratization (Crouch 1995; Silberman 1995; Johnson 1997; Irwin 1980; Crouch and Marquart 1989).

It wasn't until the 1960s that the role of correctional officer (CO) expanded to include the idea that the CO might have some influence on the prisoner. In fact, prisoners, when polled, more often cite officers than treatment staff as influential. This is not surprising, considering that inmates spend much more time with custodial staff than treatment staff. With an expanded role came a different title—correctional officer. Some old-timers refused the offer, preferring to continue calling themselves guards. Even today, one hears correctional officers use the term guard as often as correctional officer. There is a definite split between the custody-oriented officer and the "professional" officer who welcomes a more diverse agenda and role (Freeman 1997a).

In the 1960s and 1970s, treatment supplanted custody as the theme in many prisons and older methods of control were challenged and abandoned. Court holdings requiring due process protections for prisoners eliminated the unquestioned authority of correctional officers. Other prisoners' rights, such as to send and receive legal mail, to practice their religion, and to receive medical care, were recognized. Prison administrators rescinded strict rules of inmate movement and there were more privileges and freedoms granted, either as a result of court cases or in anticipation of a legal challenge. Ironically, curtailing "official oppression" opened the door to gangs and inmate cliques who filled the power vacuum and used violence to get what they wanted. Inmates in the 1980s had less to fear from guards but more to fear from each other as racial gangs and other powerful cliques or individuals solidified their control over prison black markets. As discussed in an earlier chapter, there was a time in the late 1970s and 1980s when officers described some prisons as "out of control." There were prisons where guards were afraid to walk into living units, and inmates literally controlled some parts of the prison.

In Texas, and a few other southern states, the prison system used inmates to control other inmates, usually through coercive force and fear. This allowed the state to operate with many fewer staff than those states that did not employ inmates in this manner. The Texas prison system, for instance, was run with an iron hand that was "brutal" or "just," depending on one's perception. Glenn (2001), a retired prison warden, described the Texas prison system in the early 1960s as fair and just, arguing that the allegations of abuse by guards and building tenders was slander (2001, 24).

He then describes the forms of punishment used. The "rail" was a two-by-four turned on its side. An inmate found guilty of a minor offense was required to stand on the rail for a period of four hours; if he fell off, the time would start again. If an inmate didn't pick enough cotton, he would be made to stand on a barrel for four or five hours. Up to four inmates might be placed on a single barrel, and if one fell off, the time would start again for them all. Other inmates would have their hands raised above their head and handcuffed to the bars in the inmate mess hall; their feet would be handcuffed too (2001, 25–26). He also described a situation where an inmate tried to escape, was shot, and then was hung on the front gate, bleeding, for the field hoe squads to see as they came back in from the fields. This was described as an "effective . . . object lesson" (2001, 44). Glenn also described a prison captain who played a "game" with inmates who he believed weren't working hard enough on the hoe squad. He would have them tied and stripped, and then he would lower his pants and threaten to sodomize them (2001, 69).

These, then, were the "golden years" of the Texas prison system that have been described by some as fair, just, and the best-run prison system in the country. In the mid-1970s, an inmate and legal aid attorney brought a case that eventually changed the Texas system completely. In *Ruiz v. Estelle* (1982), Judge Justice ruled on crowding, programs, sanitation, and a host of other subjects, but the biggest focus of the lawsuit was on brutality, especially by the building tenders, who were said to terrorize other inmates to maintain order. Judge Justice eliminated the building tender system in a sweeping court order that barred the state from using inmates to guard or in any way provide custodial supervision or discipline over other prisoners.

The vacuum of power was filled by inmate cliques and individual officers who felt compelled to enforce their own individual authority through violence at times. Inmates vied for power in a free-for-all where inmate-to-inmate violence increased at an incredible rate, as did reports of officer brutality. In 1983, there were three gang-related killings, but between 1984 and 1985, there were 52 inmate-on-inmate homicides (Glenn 2001, 125). But officer-on-inmate violence escalated as well. In 1984, for instance, 200 disciplinary actions were taken against officers who had used excessive force (Martin and Eckland-Olson 1987, 38).

In Rhode Island, a very similar transformation took place when officers, who felt betrayed by the courts and management, in effect gave up guarding. Carroll tracked the changes that occurred during the 1970s in Rhode Island and described how the events there were quite similar to those of Texas in the 1980s and other states when court decisions upset the balance of power (Carroll 1998).

> Assaults and stabbings became almost everyday events. On just one weekend near the end of May 1973 two officers were assaulted with a pipe, and another suffered a fractured foot when he was pushed down a flight of stairs; two inmates were likewise assaulted with pipes, and two others were stabbed, all requiring hospitalization. And on Saturday afternoon of the following weekend, an inmate was stabbed over 100 times, his body stuffed in a trash can and set on fire. (Carroll 1998, 82)

Mississippi, notorious for its brutality, slowly and reluctantly accommodated court orders to integrate, got rid of the trustee system, and improved physical conditions. Mississippi officers, feeling powerless and vulnerable, expressed their alienation.

> Nobody knows what to do. They [middle managers] tell you one thing one day, something else the next, and all the while you know they'll cut your balls off and save their own asses if someone in Jackson gets embarrassed or pissed off by something you do or don't do. (young Mississippi correctional officer quoted by Taylor 1993, 217)

Silberman (1995) argued that much of the violence escalation in the late 1970s, 1980s, and early 1990s has been eliminated or reduced. He compared prisons with grievance procedures and those without, and found that drops in group violence occurred in those jurisdictions that improved their response to civil rights complaints.

There is an interesting perspective difference one discovers when reading inmate authors and comparing them to penologists like Silberman (1995). As mentioned previously, many prisons went through periods of excessive violence either in the late 1970s or 1980s. By the end of the 1990s, most observers noted a dramatic lessening of violence (similar to the rise and fall of criminal violence on the outside). Analysts propose that the prisons were brought under control by able administrators and good management skills (Wright 1994; Lin 2000). According to inmate authors, however, the violence was partially caused by officers and administrators who pitted races against each other and managed the prison poorly: that is, by overutilizing informants or allowing incompetent and brutal guards to operate. They argue that the prisoners themselves "sorted it out" when they got tired of the violence. As in primitive societies, prisoners learned they had to control each other in order for all to live more comfortably. In this view, regardless of what administrators do, inmates still run the prison (Hassine 1999; Rolland 1997). Of course, the truth, as always, is probably a complicated shade of gray.

Correctional Officers Today

There were approximately 457,000 correctional officers working in state, federal, and county facilities in 2000. About six out of 10 worked in state prisons, 15,000 worked in federal prisons, and 19,000 worked in private correctional facilities (Occupational Outlook Handbook 2003). Growing percentages are minority or female. In 1988, 14 percent of the guard force were women, but this percentage increased to almost 21 percent by 1997. Minority representation did not grow as fast; it went from 30.4 percent to 32.2 percent in the same years (Carlson 1999a, 186). The need for correctional officers is expected to rise 50 percent between 1995 and 2005 (Bales 1997, 5).

The salary of correctional officers varies quite a bit from state to state. In the late 1990s, for instance, new officers in California earned about $55,000, but the average salary for new officers in New Jersey was only $30,000 (Bales 1997, 5). Carlson (1999a, 183) reports that starting pay has greatly improved over the last decade and now ranges from $14,000 to a high of $32,000. Other sources report that the median salary in 2000 was $31,170. In the federal system, the starting salary was about $27,600 in 2001 (Occupational Outlook Handbook 2003). Average salaries have ranged from a low of $17,300 in South Carolina to a high of $41,700 in Rhode Island (Occupational Outlook Handbook 1999).

Officers usually also have the opportunity to make substantial overtime, sometimes up to double their salary. For instance, in the California prison system, a few officers make a great deal of money: a lieutenant made $140,000 in 1999, which was double his stated salary (Gladstone and Arax 2000). In 2002, 10 officers made over $100,000 because of overtime (Morain 2002b). Contracts negotiated with the correctional officers' union require that a watch commander must offer the overtime opportunity to the most senior officers first, which means that the cost of the overtime will be much more expensive than if less senior officers filled the slots (because overtime is paid as time and one-half or double one's salary). In 2001 negotiations with the union, the state relinquished its discipline policy, resulting in a surge of sick leave and a concomitant increase in overtime paid (over $200 million in 2001) (Morain 2002b).

Texas officers, on the other hand, are woefully underpaid. There were about 28,000 guards for about 150,000 inmates in 2000. The staffing levels were 1,700 officers short of what had been approved by the legislature. A correctional officer's killing in December 1999 was attributed to staffing shortages (there had been no officers killed in Texas prisons for over 17 years). Texas ranks 46th in pay for prison guards. The first-year salary for officers is about $21,744, compared with the national average of $22,300. After two and one-half years, an officer's salary tops out at $26,724, compared with a national average of $34,404 (Associated Press 2000a, B3; Hendricks 2000; Fikae 2000).

Qualifications for correctional officers are usually merely good health and a high-school diploma or a GED. About 24 percent of states use psychological testing to screen out inappropriate job candidates (Josi and Sechrest 1998, 24). About 80 percent of states use a written civil service exam to hire correctional officers. Training of new officers ranges from a low of 17 days to a high of 16 weeks (Michigan), but the average number of training hours for new hires is about 221 hours. About 75 percent of the states also require about 40 hours of in-service training for all officers (Josi and Sechrest 1998, 28).

Freeman reports there is about 20 percent turnover every year (Freeman 1999, 59). The reasons include low pay, the nature of the job, long hours, stress, and a poor fit between person and job.

States and local entities are finding it harder and harder to fill academy classes with qualified entrants, although the recent recession may make it easier as qualified applicants find it harder to locate other jobs. Studies indicate that over two-thirds of correctional officers wished they were in a different job and their satisfaction level was lower than that of most other occupations measured (cited in Johnson 2002, 207).

> Forces seemed to conspire against the better impulses of the employees. Their pay was low, with a scale that began around $15,000 a year, and awarded captains, who'd put in years of service, about $30,000. At night they were locked alone inside dorms with sixty-four convicts. The guards were unarmed and, in most cases, didn't even have a walkie-talkie, just a signal box that would bring help guaranteed to arrive within three minutes. As a means of containing disturbances, the doors were bolted from the outside. The "key guards" were instructed not to free a colleague until backup was present. (Bergner, describing Angola, 1998, 83)

In the last 30 years, the trend has been to increase hiring qualifications, standards, and training of correctional officers. Although the overcrowding problem of the 1980s limited and slowed the trend toward professionalism, most states now have quite extensive training academies. In these academies, officers experience training somewhat similar to law enforcement, a combination of practical how-to courses and a sampling of sociological and psychological offerings such as communication, cultural sensitivity, criminology, and legal rights of prisoners. One list of subjects in a training curriculum included relevant legal knowledge, rules of the institution, administrative policies and procedures, elementary personality development, methods of counseling, self-defense tactics and use of firearms, report writing, inmate rules and regulations, inmates' rights and responsibilities, race relations, basic first aid and CPR techniques, radio communication, substance abuse awareness, and how to deal with special inmate populations like the mentally ill (Josi and Sechrest 1998, 37).

Officers often say they are "doing time" in eight- or ten-hour installments. There is some truth to the idea that officers are the "other inmates." They spend a great deal of time inside the prison walls and must adapt to the prison world just as surely as do the inmates who live there (Lombardo 1989). What makes the analogy even more salient is the prevalence of overtime, sometimes forced or coerced; officers may spend up to 18 hours in the prison without going home. Some prisons even have (or have had) officers' quarters that don't look all that much different from prisoners' living quarters, where officers live part-time or full-time if the prison is far away from their home.

'Structured Conflict'

The relationship between officers and inmates is one of structured conflict (Jacobs and Kraft 1978). This term refers to the inherent tension between the two groups arising from the role conflict of the keepers and the kept. This "structured conflict" permeates the prison and the relationship between officers and inmates. It is present in even the most cordial of relationships and influences every interaction between the two groups. It is why officers say "you can be friendly with an inmate, but you can't trust them," and why inmates, despite their surface friendliness, could never look upon an officer as a friend.

Of course, this situation varies tremendously from institution to institution, especially between institutions of different custody levels. Whereas minimum-security work camps are fairly calm, with generally cordial relationships between officers and inmates, maximum-security institutions often seethe with a high level of tension and frequent altercations between inmates and staff. Lin (2000) describes several institutions, and the general atmosphere, inmate-officer relationships, and central values of the institutions were quite strikingly different. A so-called treatment institution had an atmosphere in which both inmates and officers felt more relaxed and trusting of each other. Of course, part of the dynamics might have been the custody level of the inmates, but part of the difference was no doubt the leadership and general culture, which did not discourage interaction. One thing is clear: Prisons, even at the same custody level, can be very different institutions because of the "social climate" that is created and nurtured by a clear vision, strong leadership, and competent management.

> [At other prisons] you always had to have a mask on—you show no emotions, you be a hard convict. Antelope Valley [pseudonym] . . . it's the first place I've laughed or smiled since I've been in. . . . (an inmate describing the atmosphere of a treatment-oriented prison, quoted in Lin 2000, 100)

Only a small fraction of inmates are so hostile and antagonistic to guards that they erupt in frequent outbursts and/or assaults. Likewise, only a small percentage of officers are actively abusive—either physically or psychologically—to inmates. The majority of both guards and inmates prefer to live in peace and understand that they need to treat each other with some modicum of respect to get along. Unfortunately, both feel they must take sides when conflict occurs. Inmates must support their fellow inmates and guards must support their fellow guards, regardless of how little support the individual deserves. Thus, a brutal guard may be protected by his fellows and a racist guard will not be informally or formally sanctioned. Likewise, an assaultive inmate will not be kept in check by his peer group unless his actions are perceived to hurt their interests.

> Seventy to seventy-five percent there's no problems with. Tell them to do things and they do it. They look at the CO as doing a job. But fifteen to thirty percent you have problems with regardless. They hate the world and the CO's because they deal with the CO's most frequently and the CO's represent the state. Those guys give you lots of problems with drugs, extortion and verbal abuse. They're constantly into something. (an officer quoted by Lombardo 1989, 115)

Many guards believe that other guards think all inmates are dishonest, lazy, and manipulative. This constructed reality that all inmates are scum is part of the guard subculture. Riley (2000) discusses how officers construct a reality of who they think prisoners are. This "sense-making" links belief with action and attaches meaning to ambiguous situations. Officers very quickly develop a working understanding of inmates as "untrustworthy, manipulative, and dangerous" (Riley 2000, 363). Further characteristics include immature, unpredictable, weak, perverse, and trouble for staff (Riley 2000, 371). If newcomers or others challenge this stereotype, then certain activities will be engaged in to enlighten the naïve. "Reading the record" is where the officer will provide the criminal offense sheet to prove what a "bad character" the inmate is. Yet despite this tendency to place all inmates into a category of inmate rather than treat him or her as an individual, many officers will point to one inmate and say "he's different" or "he may be like that, but he's alright because . . . ," and the "because" may be because he's a vet, or he comes from the same city, or he's worked with him for years.

The most productive relationships between COs and inmates are when each treats the other as an individual and they understand each other, or try to. The most unproductive, but all too common, relationship is when all officers see inmates as a group—where individual differences are not recognized. Officers are outnumbered and unarmed, and live with the constant knowledge that they may be assaulted, taken hostage, and/or killed. Because of this, inmates are perceived with suspicion, distrust, cynicism, and bitterness, especially by those officers who have been tricked and/or threatened.

As early as the 1950s, Sykes discusses the concept of reciprocity, which he used to describe the reliance officers have on inmates to help them do their job (Sykes 1956). The experts in prison operations are sometimes the inmates themselves. New officers learning their jobs find themselves slowly and insidiously dependent on inmates to help them learn the tasks and get things done. Before long, the inmates have become indispensable and the officers may find themselves allowing special favors and rewards to the inmates who help them (Lombardo 1989; Crouch 1995). They, in effect, give up a certain amount of their power to the inmates.

Reciprocity also occurs when officers accept goods and gifts from inmates. The gift-giving may be innocuous at first. For instance, an officer on a duty station may accept a cold soda on a hot day from an inmate. However, such small gifts may result in the officer doing favors for the inmate. Relationships also develop when officers come to rely on inmates to control or "keep the lid on." These relationships eventually become corrupting when inmates expect the officer to overlook their own transgressions in return for controlling others (Stojkovic 1990). Over time, the power balance shifts between officer and inmate because the officer knows the inmate could report him for numerous rule violations. Although officers are trained to avoid this type of manipulation in the training academy, the process is so slow and insidious that many officers still get trapped by the process.

Despite the inherent "structured conflict" between inmates and officers, and despite the presence of some officers who abuse their power, there is a good deal of positive interaction that occurs between officers and inmates. Because officers spend the most time with inmates, some inmates report that it is an officer who has helped them by acting as a role model or informally talking about life's problems. Johnson (1981) described the type of officer who performed an expanded role and discussed his or her role in rehabilitation. Silberman (1995) reported in his study that inmate respondents described surprisingly positive interactions with correctional officers. Good officers are obviously invaluable in running a safe and secure facility. Their careful observations of inmates can avert riots, suicides, and assaults.

> We can't solve much, but we can communicate with the inmates. I get along with them pretty well. . . . I can get the job done. . . . When you start out, they'll test you. I let them think they're fooling me; then I turn the tables on them to let them see where the line is. It's entertainment to them, and that's how I look at it too. . . . (an officer, quoted from Lin 2000, 50)

The officer's interactions with inmates will depend on what type of job assignment he or she has. Some assignments have direct, all-day contact with inmates. Some have almost none at all (such as the tower officer). Job assignments may include block officer, work detail officer, transportation officer, industrial shop and school officer, yard officer, administration building officer, hospital/infirmary officer, wall post officer, and relief officer (Freeman 1997a).

Hepburn's (1985) typology of power is useful for understanding the interactions between inmates and officers. In this typology, there are several kinds of power an officer might employ to perform the functions of the role. Legal authority is what comes with the uniform. In other words, every officer, just by wearing his uniform, has this type of authority. Coercive power is the implicit power behind the uniform. If an inmate does not follow orders, coercive power is always the next potential alternative. It includes taking away privileges and segregation or loss of good time, as well as the power to use brute force to move the inmate or compel him to comply. Reward power is the ability of officers to provide inmates with things in order to gain compliance. Expert power is the officer's ability to depend on some special skill, ability, or expertise. For instance, an officer supervising a work detail might possess this power because of his superior knowledge of carpentry or some other skill. Finally, referent power is personal authority that comes from the officer's individual personality, especially his ability to deal with inmates fairly and with respect. An officer with referent power will be able to elicit inmate compliance because of respect the inmates have for him, not necessarily the uniform.

... guards ... slowly but surely become cogs in the machinery of "The System." Like policemen or firemen, they enlist to obtain steady pay with accompanying benefits; they don a uniform and patch badge; they acquire power and assume the role of public servants, but at a personal cost. While participating, tacitly or actively, in the daily dehumanization of others, they themselves betray and barter their human instincts away. ... (a prisoner with a fairly negative view of officers, Hairgrove 2000, 148)

One of the most well-known psychological experiments, and one which directly led to protections for human subjects, illustrates that, for some, the power attendant with the officer role corrupts. In this experiment, conducted at Stanford University, young male college students were randomly assigned the role of guards or inmates. The experiment was abandoned after only six days because of the transformation of the students into brutal, sadistic "guards" who took pleasure in cruelty. About one-third of the guards became "tyrannical in their arbitrary use of power" (Zimbardo 1982, 196). The experiment illustrates the potential of the "power corrupts" truism. Although many argue that the experiment was very different from real prison in that prisons today are governed by a panoply of laws, regulations, policies, and procedures, the specter of students turning into the worst stereotypes of brutal guards is a cautionary lesson in the danger of power and how easy it is for some people to abuse that power when they receive messages from the institutional culture that it is acceptable.

The Officer Subculture

Just as one can observe a prisoner subculture consisting of values that are sometimes antithetical to dominant society, there is also an observable correctional officer subculture. As with the prisoner subculture, the officer subculture is formed by the needs and realities of the officers. The norms or values of the officer culture include the following:

- Always go to the aid of an officer in distress.
- Never make a fellow officer look bad in front of inmates.
- Always support an officer in a dispute with an inmate.
- Always support another officer's sanctions against an inmate.
- Show concern for fellow officers.
- Don't lug drugs.
- Don't be a "white hat" (sympathetic to inmates). (Kauffman 1988)

These norms promote safety and a unified front, but they also encourage a curtain of secrecy for those officers who exceed their authority.

Farkas (1997) found officers adhered to these important principles:

- Always go to the aid of an officer in real or perceived physical danger.
- Do not get too friendly with inmates.

- Do not abuse your authority with inmates.
- Keep your cool.
- Back your fellow officers in decisions and actions.
- Do not stab a coworker in the back.
- Do not admit to mistakes.
- Carry your own weight.
- Defer to the experience and wisdom of veteran officers.
- Mind your own business.

According to Farkas, the code engenders solidarity among officers, provides meanings for their actions, and supports the officer through relationships and shared values.

Some argue that the officer culture is not monolithic. Klofas and Toch (1982; also see Toch 1981) propose that only some officers uphold those values of the officer subculture that are representative of pure custody and anti-inmate. In their view, officers are divided into the "subculture custodians," who are anti-treatment and place high value on security and control; the "supported majority," who are pro-treatment and professional; and the "lonely braves," who are pro-treatment but feel custodians overwhelm institutions and have trouble expressing support for pro-treatment initiatives.

Freeman (1997a) also discusses role types of officers. He notes the differences between "custody-oriented" officers and "professional officers" in their use of control (custody officers use more formal means), affective ties, informal relationships, social distance (social distance is greater between inmates and custody officers), and use of discretion. Both types are present in prisons today.

Gilbert (1997) parallels correctional officers and police officers, using Muir's (1977) typology of "professional," "enforcer," "reciprocator," and "avoider." These types are described on the basis of their use of discretion, coercion, and human relations. The professional is reasonable, innovative, and able to make exceptions when called for. The enforcer is aggressive, allows no exceptions to rules, and is cynical. The reciprocator has a counseling orientation, has difficulty using coercion even when it is called for, and is easily frustrated. The avoider uses means to avoid confrontations or even interaction with clients. While acknowledging that some adaptations are necessary to apply these police types to correctional officers, Gilbert goes on to note that they help in understanding the role of correctional officers and the part discretion plays in their interactions with inmates.

Additional evidence indicates that Klofas and Toch may be right. In a study of pre-service officers, it was found that officers today hold less positive views toward treatment than officers did in the 1970s, but even so there is still a good deal of support expressed by officers for treatment efforts. Variables that affected attitudes toward treatment in a positive direction included age, the size of town an officer came from, and race. Younger officers, officers from larger cities, and African-American and Hispanic officers were more positively oriented toward treatment. Gender, interestingly, was not found to be significant in views toward treatment (Paboojian and Teske 1997).

Other studies find that correctional administrators express a fairly high degree of support for treatment as well and perhaps higher than officers (Cullen et al. 1993). In a national study of prison wardens, it was found that they obviously considered security the first priority of prison management, but treatment was viewed as an important secondary goal. They also favored the expansion of treatment programs. Although some individual and institutional variables had moderate effects on support for treatment, none were strong. That is, it didn't matter much what the race was of the warden, how old he or she was, or what type of prison he or she managed (Cullen et al. 1993).

Farkas (1999), in a study of 125 county correctional officers, found that many officers expressed support for rehabilitation. For instance, over 70 percent disagreed with the statement "Rehabilitative programs are a waste of time and money." These officers also overwhelmingly agreed that you couldn't trust an inmate (84 percent) and that a personal relationship with an inmate invites corruption (95 percent). Further, she found that older officers expressed greater support for a counseling orientation. This finding is inconsistent with the findings of Paboojian and Teske (1997) but consistent with those of Toch and Klofas (1982).

In Farkas' (1999) study, female officers were more likely to express both high agreement with counseling principles and a punitive approach. However, work variables (i.e., shift, contact hours, job satisfaction, role conflict) were more influential on officer orientation than individual characteristics, although some of the relationships are a bit puzzling. For instance, high job satisfaction correlated with less support for a counseling role and less agreement with harsher conditions. High job satisfaction correlated with a desire for greater social distance from inmates. Whether these findings can be applied to a prison guard sample is debatable, but it does seem clear that there are differences between officers and these differences aren't always simply limited to age, race, and sex.

Britton (1997) reviewed a number of studies of correctional officers, including their adherence to the correctional officer subculture and their views toward rehabilitation and inmates. She found that most studies reported there were differences in how minority and female officers responded, although female officers were not substantively more likely to express support for rehabilitation or have higher positive regard for inmates. In Britton's own study, she found that women reported higher levels of job satisfaction than white men, and African-American men reported feeling greater efficacy in handling inmates. Further, she found that officers with more experience reported more satisfaction but also higher stress and less efficacy in working with inmates.

The role of discretion is particularly troublesome for officers who feel "damned if they do and damned if they don't." The myriad of rules present in the prison makes it virtually impossible to enforce all of them. The officers must learn which rules are sacrosanct, which are overlooked, and which are overlooked only in some situations or by some inmates. If they make a mistake in either direction, they are vilified—by the inmates if they enforce too stringently rules that are usually ignored and by the administration if they do not enforce a rule that is viewed as more important. Sometimes, they receive informal training by officers, more often by inmates, but they also learn by trial and error. The result, of course, is a pervasive defensiveness that officers live with and learn to deal with (Conover 2000).

There's a constant changing of orders brought on by directives from the central office. It creates a state of confusion on the blocks. Among the inmates it's dangerous, among the officers it's chaos. The constant state of turmoil drives everyone crazy. (an officer, quoted in Lombardo 1989, 52)

Violence

Prison is a world where violence and the threat of violence are more the norm than the aberration and officers are affected by the reality of this world just as surely as inmates. Thus, we need to revisit two forms of violence—that of inmates assaulting officers and the reverse situation, where officers assault inmates.

I gave up trying to figure out if the inmates arrived on the row behaving like animals or if the unit made them that way. Just working in the place was degrading. The environment was charged with anger and open hatred between convicts and guards. Inmates routinely threw feces and urine at us, flooded their cells, and stopped up toilets. Officers and trusty workers—patience depleted and nerves frayed—responded with brute force. (a former officer, Cabana 1996, 81)

Silberman (1995) reports that the rate of inmate-on-officer assaults is decreasing from a high in the 1980s. He reports situations wherein some guards have been killed or severely beaten during hostage-taking incidents or individual attacks, as well as rapes of both male and female guards by inmates. Ross (1996) reports that there were 6,850 assaults on officers in 1994 and that figure is lower than the reported 9,269 reported assaults in 1988. Other sources indicate much higher numbers—14,165 inmate assaults on staff in 1995, with the highest rate occurring in maximum-security institutions (Stephan 1997).

Other sources indicate that assaults on guards nationwide have more than doubled in the past five years. Texas, for instance, had 6,001 attacks on guards between 1995 and 1999 (Associated Press 2000a, B3). Of course, if the number of inmates doubled during that period, one would expect the number of assaults to also have doubled; but this would not mean there was an increase in the tendency of inmates to assault. To determine whether officers are more or less likely to be assaulted, one must compute rates—that is, divide the number of assaults into the number of inmates.

Light (1999, 211–212) conducted an analysis of 694 incidents of assaults on guards in New York State. Findings indicated that much of the violence directed at officers was unplanned and unpredictable. Fully 25 percent of the incidents fell into the category of "unexplained." The next most frequent category was violent retaliation in response to an officer's command (13 percent). In an earlier project, Light (1991) pointed out that the deprivations of imprisonment compel inmates to resist attempts to deprive them of perceived "rights."

In one study of inmate attacks, it was found that there was an association between inmate alienation and expressions of hostility toward the staff. Those who expressed hostility toward the staff (and engaged in actual incidents of assault against officers) were also more likely to assault other inmates (Silberman 1995, 85). Another study found a correlation between a number of variables and the frequency of assaults on the staff. Prisons that reported higher numbers of staff assaults were more likely to be those with open designs, those that had a high percentage of black prisoners and young, inexperienced staff, and those with a high percentage of sex offenders. Although this was a study of the British prison system, there is no reason to believe that the findings are not applicable to American prisons (Ditchfield and Harries 1996).

An American study collected information on 604 assault incidents in 21 state and federal prisons. After analyzing the incidents, the authors concluded that the typical assaulter was 26 years old and was 10 years younger than the victimized officer. The prisoner was almost as likely to be African-American as white and was likely to have had prior incarcerations, to be incarcerated for a violent crime, and to be serving a long sentence. The assault took place during the course of basic job tasks, such as enforcing institutional rules, giving orders, conducting searches, and supervising. Officers were likely to be assaulted with hands (i.e., punch, slap, kick), and the most common injury was a back injury or a fracture. The most frequent victims of inmate assaults are officers with five to eight years of experience who are between the ages of 30 and 45 (Ross 1996).

Officers also assault inmates. Obviously all officers may at times have to use force to subdue a violent inmate, separate two fighting inmates, or move a recalcitrant prisoner by legitimate force. It becomes assault and unlawful when the officer uses violence beyond what is necessary to accomplish the legitimate goal.

In the prison world, officers have historically used physical coercion against those inmates who disrespected or assaulted officers. Crouch and Marquart (1989) described Texas "tune-ups"— abuse administered to those inmates who did not show proper respect. These incidents involved profanity, shoving, kicks, and slaps. Inmates who attacked officers were severely beaten. There is evidence to indicate that these "lessons" continue to occur in today's prisons, albeit less frequently.

In a 1994 study, 424 use-of-force reports were examined from 27 Florida prisons. The authors of this study found that most use-of-force incidents were in response to inmate fights (36 percent) or inmate disobedience (35 percent). Inmates physically resisted the guards in 42 percent of the cases. The authors then undertook a national survey and found that 60 percent of use-of-force incidents were in response to inmates fighting or disobeying orders. Note that these use-of-force incidents were almost always determined to be legitimate use of force (Henry, Senese, and Ingley 1994). Information on those incidents where guards' use of force was illegitimate and illegal is harder to come by.

Silberman (1995) reported that officers respect those who could dish it out to inmates and were not afraid to use violence. The use of violence has been seen as a rite of passage for officers (Marquart and Crouch 1985). "War stories" indoctrinate new officers and include stories of officers who were murdered by inmates, as well as incidents of officers beating inmates (Silberman 1995). State-sanctioned violence violates the Eighth Amendment protection against cruel and unusual punishment. There is no question that officer-on-inmate violence, undertaken to teach a lesson to a disrespectful inmate, is not only unethical but also illegal.

Silberman (1995, 222) surveyed 96 inmates and none reported being abused by officers, although they did report threats and believed that such beatings occurred in segregation. These results led Silberman to conclude that officer-to-inmate violence occurs much less often today than in years past.

However, Hamm and his colleagues (1994) have evidence that times have not changed all that much. They first describe the history of violence against prisoners, including beatings, whippings, use of "the hole" or "doghouse," and the Tucker telephone (an electrical device attached to earlobes, genitals, and other sensitive parts of the body to administer shocks). The authors report on a study they did on officer abuse that utilized a survey questionnaire. First, they noted severe problems with distribution, partly because of active resistance and repression on the part of some state prison staff. The survey was printed in prison newspapers, but many states confiscated all copies of the newspaper and punished inmates for having copies of the questionnaire. Also, guards read the surveys before they were mailed, thus reducing the likelihood of inmates accurately reporting the incidence of officer assaults. Despite these problems, the authors received 605 surveys from 41 different states (for a return rate of 10 percent) (1994, 181).

According to inmate respondents, abuse seemed uniform across the country. About 62 percent of the sample had observed physical beatings (almost 50 percent said they occurred routinely). Inmates reported that the two most frequently mentioned reasons for the abuse were being verbally abusive to guards and not following orders. The survey respondents also indicated that "jailhouse lawyers" were beaten (Hamm et al. 1994). Although some may argue that inmates may not be the most accurate and unbiased source for such information, the trends and patterns that seemed to exist, as well as the reinforcing information from other sources (such as officers), lends credibility to the proposition that officer-on-inmate violence is neither rare nor unsupported by the officer subculture.

Special response teams or disturbance teams are the prison world's version of law enforcement SWAT teams. The stated advantage of such teams is that they result in reduced injury to officers. The action is videotaped for the protection of both inmates and officers, and highly trained officers are less likely to hurt inmates. However, others allege that abuses continue to occur.

The training, uniforms, and practices of the team create a mystique among officers and inmates. In some prisons, inmates have such antipathy for team members that their identities are kept secret. This safeguard may be necessary, since it has been noted that in some hostage-taking situations, officers on such squads are often on "hit lists" of inmates. In actuality, when professionally run, this approach probably reduces injury for both inmate and officer. However, as stated before, we have very little information on incidents of abuse—either from a special response team or an individual officer.

Stress

Prison officers have high levels of medical and social problems related to stress (Cheek and Miller 1983; Williamson 1990; Kauffman 1988). Heart disease, smoking, alcoholism, and divorce are high among officer groups. One of the major reasons for disability leave is stress-related alcoholism, cardiac problems, and emotional disorders (Gross et al. 1994). Kamerman (1995) notes that correctional officer suicides may be at least as great a problem as law enforcement officer suicides.

Freeman (1999) reviewed the literature on correctional officer stress. He found that some reports showed higher than normal levels of stress, while others indicated that stress may be related to the period of time on the job. What possibly occurs is that some individuals are not suited for a corrections job and leave, since older officers report lower levels of stress. However, other reports indicate divorce, hypertension, and alcoholism are all elevated in correctional officer populations.

Stress is caused by the pervasive sense of potential danger in the prison, the lack of predictability, feeling trapped in the job, low salaries, inadequate training, an absence of standardized policies, procedures, and rules, lack of communication with management, and little participation in decision making. What is clear from the above list is that management can alleviate or exacerbate a good many of these elements.

Stohr et al. (1994, 489), in a survey analysis of management approach and social climate in jails, inadvertently found that jail officers reported higher levels of stress-related symptomatology than did the psychiatric patient group the instrument was designed for. Although there are differences in the working conditions and management of jails versus prisons, these results should be viewed as important and possibly reflective of prisons as well.

Jail officers had higher than average scores on obsessive-compulsive, anxiety, hostility, phobic anxiety, and psychosis scales. The authors concluded that those jails that employed personnel investment strategies (training, benefits, and so forth) also had higher job satisfaction, and officers reported fewer psychosomatic stress symptoms. There was also more organizational identification and a reduction in turnover (Stohr et al. 1994, 495).

Another study conducted in the federal prison system studied the effects of job autonomy and participation on job satisfaction, commitment, stress, and efficacy in working with inmates (Wright et al. 1997). These authors found that, contrary to Diulio's (1987) argument that the best management approach for a prison was a bureaucracy with little input from staff, indexes of job satisfaction and commitment were positively correlated with a feeling of autonomy and participation in management decisions. Thus, in many surveys, it is found that officers identify stress as arising not from inmates but from management. The lack of control over rules and procedures, shift work, and a feeling of lack of support create the negative feelings officers have for prison management (Freeman 1997b).

Management in prisons follows very traditional bureaucratic patterns. Discipline follows the progression of verbal instruction, verbal warning, written memo of instruction, letter of reprimand, disciplinary reduction in pay, disciplinary suspension without pay, demotion, and discharge (Wright 1999). As in many organizations, officers often feel unfairly treated and observe that certain officers get away with more than others.

The Human Service Officer

Johnson (2002) has long been an advocate of an expanded role for the correctional officer. He urges recognition of the fact that some officers do and many other officers should be encouraged to play a very positive role in the lives of inmates. The "human service" officer may be at his or her most effective simply by being honest, straightforward, and caring. Many inmates, at least in private, admit that an officer has helped them by listening, giving advice, or helping them get a phone call or a doctor's appointment.

> Here was a guy . . . who saw gallery work as an art, something you could perform creatively. Interpersonal skills were a big part of it . . . [he] melded toughness with an attitude of respect for the inmates. In turn, he was respected back. (Conover 2000, 91)

Research shows that those guards who take on a more enriched role have greater job satisfaction (Hepburn and Knepper 1993). Further, human service orientations may come with seniority; older officers expressed more positive views toward an enriched role and more positive attitudes toward inmates in some studies (Toch and Grant 1982; Jurik 1985).

One of the changes in prison that has perhaps changed the role of the guard is that increased liberties for inmates made the guards' role less salient. While guards used to be able to help an inmate get a phone call and, thus, obtain at least some level of gratitude on the part of the inmate, today in some prisons, pay phones are in dayrooms for all to use. Grievance counselors, ombudsmen, and other job titles usurp informal roles held by guards. This point should not be overstated, however, since there are many ways in which the officer can help inmates.

> They get bad news letters, they stay in and brood about it. I call the service unit and get a "it's none of your business." We took care of all these things before the service unit was set up. (an officer, quoted in Lombardo 1989, 68)

The job of the correctional officer is not an easy one. Supervising inmates, who are held in captivity against their will, requires a good deal of human relations skills. If one also aspires to help in the process of reformation, or even make the experience less debilitating, it is an even harder task. In the past several decades, officers have seen their role responsibilities change and change again. Their world was virtually turned upside down by court orders, inmate population changes, and the pressures of overcrowding. They continue to struggle to control an increasingly frustrated inmate population with inadequate programming and little innovation, and do so in some states with abysmal salaries or expectations for advancement.

Yet despite these handicaps, some officers do make a difference and the prison becomes, for some at least, a place to effect change.

Managing the Prison

Wardens used to rule their prisons out of the sight of public scrutiny. They were promoted from the guard ranks and, typically, the toughest guards became tough wardens. Today, prisons are just as likely to be administered by professionally trained managers as those who have been promoted from the ranks of officers. Administrators must now respond to a multitude of legal, political, social, and economic pressures (Freeman 1997b; Carroll 1998). Correctional administrators face a variety of pressures from the courts, officers' unions, the media, ex-prisoner and family groups, and legislators. Centralization is the trend, and the needs or unique characteristics of each prison are becoming less important in a policy of homogenization.

A well-run prison is one where inmates and officers are safe. There are productive activities for inmates, with a balance of self-improvement programs and work. There is little or no corruption on the part of officers or inmates. How close prisons come to these ideals depends, to a great extent, on the expertise and skill of the managers and the managers' ability to hire and retain good people. Carlson (1999b, 43) identifies some elements necessary to reach these goals: well-articulated policies, adequate training, compliance audits, "benchmarking" (comparing the institution to others), accreditation, identification of corruption, and strategic planning.

Wright (1994) describes how leadership can dramatically affect the management of a prison. Effective leaders are those who demonstrate their commitment, provide training and education, create a climate of change, trust staff to take responsibility, listen, share management tasks, and institutionalize feedback (Wright 1994, 9). Further, he argues that an important aspect of management and leadership is integrity. If leaders do not provide a moral example, then they will not be effective in other areas either. Good leaders in corrections provide an institutional culture for staff through their actions and words that convey important values and missions. Staff who don't have a clear sense of where they are going and what they are doing have low morale. Wright (1994) promotes the four "c's" of management—candor, caring, commitment, and confidence.

The challenges for correctional administrators have been described as including the impact of the rehabilitative model, increasing accountability, civil service system, unions, judicial intervention, legislative action and prison overcrowding, workforce diversity, the media, special needs inmates, and improving the quality of staff (Freeman 1997b, 285–294). However, the biggest challenge facing prison management over the last 25 years has been finding beds for the massive influx of prisoners.

Unionization

Where they exist, correctional officers' unions have developed into powerful political bodies that can affect policy as management struggles to accommodate union demands for pay, benefits, and the bidding system. Correctional officers' unions tend to act as a resistant force to treatment initiatives. For instance, unions fight vigorously to defend the "bidding" system whereby senior officers get first choice over assignments. Because many, if not most, officers prefer posts away from inmates, what occurs is that officers with the least experience are left in the undesirable posts with the most inmate-officer interaction. Thus, those with the least experience are given the most difficult positions.

In the 1980s, unions became increasingly powerful in the Northeast and California. Carroll (1998, 269) notes their power in Rhode Island. In California, the correctional officers' union has become so powerful that it has become a real political force in gubernatorial races and other political contests. In the 1994 political race, the union contributed more than any other donor to Governor Wilson's campaign. One source reported that only the California Medical Association spent more on the gubernatorial race than the correctional officers' union (Josi and Sechrest 1998, 160). The California Correctional Peace Officers Association (CCPOA) represents over 29,000 officers and has a budget of $17 million. It employs 22 in-house lawyers and distributed over $1 million in political contributions in the first half of 1998 (Parenti 1999, 226).

Don Novey has stepped down, but until recently he had been the head of the California union since 1980. During the more than 20 years he held the position, he greatly expanded the pay and benefits of officers, secured money for a training academy, built a large headquarters for the union in Sacramento, and became a political powerhouse. California legislators who disagreed with him often found to their detriment that the union could indeed change elections (Warren 2000). The union not only supports legislators it likes, it also torpedoes bills it doesn't, such as the proposal to allow the attorney general to prosecute all claims of abusive guards, rather than the local district attorney (which is a political seat heavily dependent on union support in the county in which the prison is located) (Warren 2000).

More recently, the California Correctional Peace Officers Association endorsed the 2002 re-election bid of Governor Davis to the tune of over $1 million. They spent about $2 million to get him elected in 1998 and were rewarded with a pay raise, signed into legislation in January of 2002, of as much as 37 percent, paid out over five years (Morain 2002a). In California's current budget crunch, corrections was one of the few governmental agencies that was not cut.

In other states, correctional officers often belong to the American Federation of State, County, and Municipal Employees (AFSCME). The political power of guards' unions is important because, unlike unions in the private sector, the power of guards' unions to call for a strike is limited by legislative or executive action that makes strikes by public employees illegal. The unions that can dispense large monetary contributions to members of the legislature do not need the power of the strike to affect raises and other benefits, since a legislative vote is what determines these benefits for its members.

Unions have so far been seen by researchers as a force resistant to rehabilitation and concerned only with individual benefits for members rather than the mission or goal of corrections. Unions provide legal assistance to officers in personnel and legal attacks and often support officers who, many would argue, have no business working in corrections. In California, for instance, unions have provided legal assistance to officers who have been accused of assaulting inmates, having sex with inmates, giving drugs to inmates, and setting up gladiator fights between inmates (Josi and Sechrest 1998). Governor Davis attempted to direct $4 million to the correctional officers' union for its defense fund. In effect, the public would have ended up paying for both the prosecution and the defense of errant officers, as well as their salary. Criticism was so strong that the administration canceled the funding, although the officers still received the money to be used for other things, and they obtained the pay raise and other concessions demanded in contract negotiations (Salladay 1999).

Civil Service and Workforce Diversity

In the past, wardens and superintendents had absolute authority over who they would hire and who the would fire. Not any longer. Civil service eliminates political patronage and protects individual workers against arbitrary and biased hiring, promotion, and firing decisions. It also makes it more difficult to fire employees and tends to make it difficult to promote promising staff quickly. Although it does tend to be a barrier to quickly firing errant officers, civil service has done a great deal to protect workers from arbitrary decision making. Two groups that have benefited include minorities and women. Since the 1960s, ethnic minorities and women have entered corrections in increasing numbers. Whereas women have always worked in facilities for juveniles and women, they began to work in prisons for men starting in the 1980s.

Female officers. Women enter corrections largely for the same reasons that men do—security and pay. Women report that they "drifted" into corrections after exploring other jobs. Female officers are in virtually all maximum-security institutions for men and in every part of those prisons. Because they are still fewer in number than male guards, women still experience some features of tokenism. Criticism of female officers in prisons for men has centered on the fact that they tend to be weaker and less able to protect themselves, that they may be subject to intimidation or seduction from inmates, and that they create sexual tension in the prison.

Evaluations of female officers in prisons for men have found that they perform the job duties as well as men. Management and male officers feared that women would not be able to handle aggressive inmates, would be subject to harassment and assault, and would be co-opted by inmates (Freeman 1999). Evaluations indicated, however, that women officers did their jobs adequately. By most measuring sticks, there were few differences between male and female officers.

Freeman (1997) indicates that female COs respond as aggressively as male COs in similar situations. There is no statistical evidence to indicate they are more subject to assault. They write approximately the same number of misconduct reports. Some studies report that women experience more stress (Zupan 1992). Other researchers report that female officers do not experience more stress than male officers. They do, however, exhibit significantly less intense feelings of cynical attitudes that depersonalize inmates (Gross et al. 1994).

Some authors report that women may perform their job functions in a manner different from their male colleagues. For instance, one hypothesis is that women employ a more nurturing, "listening" style of supervision, while male staff members are more likely to employ an authoritarian, formal mode of interaction (Pollock 1995). Evidence to support such an assertion tends to be anecdotal and phenomenological, since paper-and-pencil tests of attitudes toward inmates fail to uncover any differences between male and female correctional staff. Jenne and Kersting (1996), for instance, used hypothetical situations and asked male and female officers to respond. They discovered few differences between the sexes in the use of aggression in resolving hypothetical situations. When differences were observed, they were in the opposite direction from that predicted; that is, it was female officers who were more likely to use aggressive responses.

Zimmer (1986) observed three role types emerge among female officers. The institutional role (rule-oriented, professional stance), the modified role (feared inmates, avoided contact, relied heavily on male workers for backup), and the inventive role (looked to inmates for support, expressed little fear, preferred work that involved direct inmate contact). Later observations indicated that these adaptations were not necessarily unique to women. Male officers also have a variety of adaptations to the role and some avoided inmates, while others sought them out and participated fully in the more complex nature of the treatment role offered (Johnson 1981).

Attitudinal surveys among male co-workers and inmates show that male co-workers exhibit more resistance to female officers than do male inmates. Also, male inmates rate female officers more highly on "listening" capability but feel that female officers are less able to protect them against physical threats (Pollock 1995).

Inmates indicated a generally positive regard for the entry of women as officers, not necessarily for reasons that were desired. Evidently female officers were perceived as "sexual objects" and made life more interesting. Male inmates express mixed views regarding female officers. Understandably, they object to having women watch them take showers or go to the bathroom. Some also complain that women engender desire and fantasies. However, male inmates also report appreciating the presence of women, who seem to care more than male officers and are able to treat them with respect.

> Personally, I came to regret the existence of female guards. Being a prisoner in a world devoid of sex I would rather not even see them, because it was frustrating to be around women who were off-limits and untouchable.. .. For the most part, they were a reminder of what was missing, and in that regard, their mere presence was painful. (Terry in Richards, Terry, and Murphy 2002, 212)

Thinly veiled sexism still exists in some prisons. Ironically, by some accounts, women were more resented than African-American officers. Speculation as to why male officers were so hostile to women entering their workforce included the idea that it destroyed the macho character of the job (Freeman 1997b). One recent study conducted in a midwestern prison discovered that there is still a degree of male resistance to the presence of women officers. In a sample of men and women, male officers were less likely than their female counterparts to agree with a statement that "male staff accepted women as corrections officers" (47 percent to 67 percent) and also less likely to agree with the statement "most inmates accept women as corrections officers" (44 percent to 74 percent). Interestingly, however, 80 percent agreed that women "should be hired as corrections officers." Male officers were more likely than female officers to believe that female officers were in more danger than male officers (61 percent to 32 percent) and that male officers' safety is endangered when working with a female officer (37 percent to 16 percent). Only 44 percent of the male officers believed that women could control a fight between inmates (compared with 96 percent of the responding female officers), and only 52 percent of the male officers agreed that the presence of women officers improved the prison environment (compared with 89 percent of the women) (Lawrence and Mahan 1998). These results indicate that there is still a good deal of hostility and cynicism regarding the presence of female officers in prisons for men.

Objections to women officers in prisons for men also included the fact that inmates would lose a certain amount of privacy by having opposite-sex guards watching them shower and perform other private bodily functions. In most court cases, there was little sympathy for this challenge, at least when presented by male inmates arguing against the entry of female officers. As was discussed in a previous chapter, courts have been more sympathetic to female prisoners who argued against the entry of male corrections officers. Most states, however, interpreted equal opportunity to mean that if they could not bar women from entering institutions for men, they also could not bar men from working in institutions for women. The consequence has been a complete reversal of the trend of same-sex guards in women's institutions. This issue will be discussed in a later section.

African-American officers. The entry of African-American and other minority officers into the ranks of corrections officers in large rural prisons occurred in the 1970s, when prison administrators actively sought to dispel the image that prisons were places with mostly African-American inmates being guarded by mostly white guards. The first minority officers were subjected to racial slurs from their white colleagues and other forms of discrimination. Initially, white officers mistrusted minority officers, believing them to be sympathetic to inmates and therefore not to be trusted. African-American officers felt completely unprotected by white colleagues and depended on inmates to keep them safe (Owen 1985).

Some research indicates that neither race nor ethnicity is related to job satisfaction, although minority officers report more feelings of effectiveness in working with inmates (Wright and Saylor 1992). In another study of 2,979 correctional officers, using the Prison Social Climate Survey, it was found that race and sex did influence the officers' perception of their work environment

(Britton 1997). In an interesting study on officers' perceptions of job opportunities, it was discovered there was a wide gap between African-American and white officers in their perceptions of the available opportunities for advancement for minority officers. The white officers perceived greater advancement opportunities for minority officers than did minority officers themselves (Camp et al. 1997).

It is probably true that the blatant racism that correctional officers experienced in the 1960s and 1970s has been eliminated; however, more subtle evidence of discrimination may still be present in corrections. There is no indication that minority officers perform their jobs differently from white officers, but it would be helpful to have more information on how they perceive their jobs, their advancement, and their interactions with inmates.

Cross-Sex Supervision

Cross-sex supervision is emerging as a volatile issue in the management of prisons. In the seventeenth and eighteenth centuries female prisoners were housed together with men in jails, with predictable results. Women were raped and sexually exploited, and sold themselves for food and other goods. With the development of the Walnut Street Jail and penitentiaries, women were separated from male inmates but still guarded by men, and sexual exploitation continued. Various scandals and exposés of prostitution rings led to women's reform groups pressuring legislatures to build completely separate institutions for women in the late 1800s and early 1900s. Finally, women were guarded by women, although men often held the highest administrative positions in these institutions.

This pattern continued until the mid-1970s, when female officers challenged state prison systems hiring patterns that barred them from working in institutions for men. Female officers had a very constricted career path in corrections when they were only allowed in institutions for women—few could get promoted, and they often had to move great distances to the only facility in the state for women even if one for men was located in their hometown. States resisted assigning women to prisons for men because of a fear that they would be victimized, that they would have less control over the inmates, and that they would "sexually excite" the inmates, leading to disruption in the institution. In *Dothard v.*

Rawlinson (1977), the Supreme Court agreed with these fears, but only because the Alabama prison where Diane Rawlinson wanted to work had such high levels of violence that it was already under a federal monitor. The dictum of this case convinced many state systems that, despite the holding that Rawlinson could be prohibited from the Alabama prison, in most situations women would have to be allowed in. And so they were, and early evaluations showed that they did their jobs about as well as male officers (Zimmer 1986; Zupan 1992; Pollock 1995). Inmates tended to appreciate the presence of women, although evaluations indicated inmates had concerns over privacy and the ability of female officers to protect them. Male officers were much more antagonistic toward their presence.

By the mid-1980s, female correctional officers could be found in most prisons for men. Today, about 20 percent of the state correctional officer force and 30 percent of the federal correctional officer force are women. Women work in prisons for men in 46 states (Reichel 1997, 379). There is great variability, however, in how many women work in prisons for men. In some states, only about 1 percent of the force in prisons for men are women, while in others the percentage is closer to 10 percent (Reichel 1997, 379).

The ironic effect of these court cases and the entry of women into prisons for men was that male officers were no longer barred from working in prisons for women. In the early 1980s, fairly small percentages of male officers could be found in prisons for women and they were restricted to public places. Now, male officers are assigned to all posts inside prisons for women, including sleeping and shower areas. Thus, male officers again are in positions of power over women; and again, abuses are occurring. An increasing number of incidents in which male officers have coerced female prisoners to have sex or, in some cases, sexually assaulted them have been substantiated. Amnesty International (1999) condemned the practice of allowing male officers to guard female inmates and cited many court cases across the nation that resulted in officers being fired or indicted and convicted of sexual assault or misfeasance.

Of course, not all instances of sexual contact between a guard and an inmate involve a male guard and a female inmate. There are homosexual contacts, as well as female officers and male inmates.

Some estimate that as much as 19 to 45 percent of all sexual interactions in the prison involve officers (Struckman-Johnson et al. 1996). The majority of incidents, however, do involve male guards and female inmates. Sex between an officer and an inmate is always coercive because of the vast power differential between the two parties.

It is clear that the reality of cross-sex supervision has created a major problem for administrators. Management's task is to eliminate or minimize the incidents of officers sexually abusing or exploiting inmates. Selection, training, and supervision are the key elements in protecting inmates. Some states are considering reducing and restricting job assignments of male officers in women's institutions. Officers' unions have been resistant to this solution, and the dispute will inevitably end up being resolved in a courtroom. It is likely, however, that courts will decide that there is a rational state interest in protecting female inmates from sexual exploitation, especially given their histories of sexual and physical abuse. Further, it could be argued that given the differences between male and female officers in the way they interact with female inmates, female and male officers are not "similarly situated" and so do not need to be treated equally.

Corruption and Unethical Practices

Pollock (2003) and others (McCarthy 1991; Souryal 1999) describe some ethical issues of correctional officers relating to their use of discretion and authority. Unfortunately, one does not need to look very hard to find examples of unethical and illegal behavior on the part of correctional workers.

Trafficking in contraband, theft, warehouse sabotage, sexual relations with inmates, bartering with inmates, assisting in escape, theft of weapons, and brutality are a partial list of the types of unethical behaviors that occur (McCarthy 1991). Souryal (1999), in another typology, describes the types of corruption as falling into the following categories: arbitrary use of power (treating workers or inmates preferentially or in a biased fashion), oppression, failure to demonstrate compassion/caring, and abusing authority for personal gain (extortion, smuggling, theft).

Periodically, news stories will describe officers who committed illegal and/or unethical acts. For instance, four state prison guards faced felony bribery charges after they agreed to "launder" money for inmates. One received $60,000 with the understanding that he would get $10,000 for his services (Associated Press 2000b, B3). In 1990, wide-scale corruption involving smuggling drugs into Florida's Martin Correctional Institution resulted in 15 arrests of corrections officers (Houston 1999, 360).

As mentioned in an earlier chapter, Corcoran guards in California were accused of setting up "gladiator"-type fights between inmates and encouraging or allowing prisoner rapes. One former guard testified that a "loudmouth" prisoner was placed with a prison rapist known as the "Booty Bandit" (Arax 1999a). Other guards were accused of an unlawful use of force by shooting an inmate during one of the "gladiator fights." Eventually, several guards received federal indictments and were tried for the killing, as well as the other acts of oppression. They were acquitted even though former guards and other experts supported the inmate's allegations ("Guards Acquitted" 2000). Some argue that the officers' union "tainted" the jury pool by running television ads before the jury selection that showed officers as tough, brave, and underappreciated. The television ads, with the tagline of "Corcoran officers: they walk the toughest beat in the state," aired only in the Fresno area, where the trial was held (Lewis 1999).

Nine Florida guards were indicted in 1999 for the murder of an inmate. The inmate died from injuries, including broken ribs, swollen testicles, and innumerable cuts and bruises. He was on death row for killing a prison guard in a botched escape attempt in 1983. Prosecutors alleged he was killed because he was planning to go to the media with allegations of widespread abuse in the prison. Accused guards insisted he killed himself by flinging himself against the concrete wall of his cell or, alternatively, that he was killed by other guards (Cox 2000). The first three officers who were tried were acquitted in February 2002 ("Three Guards Acquitted" 2002).

Pollock (2003) and Carroll (1998) present other examples where investigations uncovered abuses, including sexual abuse of inmates, brutality, and bribery at the highest levels of corrections departments. Officers have extreme difficulty when they testify against each other or in any way break the code of silence. This is very similar to the police subculture.

If an incident went down, there was no one to cover my back. That's a very important lesson to learn. You need your back covered and my back wasn't covered there at all. And at one point I was in fear of being set up by guards. I was put in dangerous situations purposely. That really happened to me. (an officer, Houston 1999, 365)

Thus in corrections, as in law enforcement, even if only a small number of officers are engaged in illegal or unethical practices, they are protected by the large silent majority, who are afraid to come forward because of the powerful subcultural prohibitions against exposing fellow officers.

A Florida news article reported that prison guards were more than twice as likely as police officers to violate state standards of conduct. An analysis of the state records for disciplinary actions showed that from January 1998 to June 1999, 769 corrections officers (29.6 per 1,000) were brought up on disciplinary charges, including sexual assault, shoplifting, and excessive force. During the same period, 559 law enforcement officers from city, county, and state police forces were sanctioned (14.0 per 1,000) (Kleindienst 1999). What can be made of this statistic? Perhaps nothing, but if it is true that correctional officers have a higher pattern of misconduct, then it would be important to identify the cause and remedy the situation. It may be that there is less of a culture of professionalism, it may be the hiring incentives and standards, or it may be that training is lacking the component of ethics. One would expect that state corrections departments would want to know and understand the reasons why officers misbehave.

To reduce corruption in corrections, there must be a concerted effort to improve hiring practices (background checks and psychological testing), institute training, and employ supervisory devices to reduce temptation and punish wrongdoers. By most accounts, law enforcement seems to be ahead of corrections in ethics training for its officers. The trickle-down theory of ethical management predicts that officers will treat inmates the way they perceive they are being treated. If they feel they are being treated with fairness, compassion, and respect, they will treat inmates in a like manner. If they feel they are being exploited, treated unfairly and with disrespect, they will treat inmates that way. It becomes easier to justify unethical actions if one feels victimized (Houston 1999; Souryal 1999; Pollock 2003). Furthermore, staff who are coerced into unethical or illegal actions by management are more likely to behave in unethical and illegal ways by their own initiative.

Conclusion

In this chapter we have shifted the focus from the inmates to those who guard them. It also bears repeating that most officers are professional, effective, even compassionate in their treatment of inmates. The problem may be that the subculture requires a closing of the ranks to protect those officers who behave corruptly and/or with brutality. Officers who come forward to testify against the officers who abuse their position are treated as traitors. Just as in the "blue curtain of secrecy" of law enforcement, the "silent majority" allow transgressors to sully the names of all and even help them do it by remaining silent.

Part of the reason this may be so is that officers often feel just as distrustful of the administration as they do of inmates. Similar to law enforcement, correctional management is a hierarchical model that is somewhat militaristic and bureaucratic; but there are also remnants of the old individual "charismatic" style of management. In this amalgam of management styles, there does seem to be the tendency to perceive that discipline and promotion decisions are unfair and that certain cliques of officers receive preferential treatment. This lowers morale and results in officers "taking care of themselves" rather than upholding the mission of the organization.

The biggest challenge of correctional management is to create a social climate within an institution where officers feel valued and trusted. Once that is achieved, then the trickle-down effect will be that officers will treat inmates with respect. Only in this atmosphere can anything positive come out of the prison experience. It should be noted that prisons are different. In some institutions, enthusiastic staff members are given the support necessary to create an environment where change can occur. Unfortunately, all too many institutions are simply warehouses, where disgruntled staff and bitter inmates consider it a good day when there are no serious assaults on either side.

Study Questions

1. Describe the concept of "structured conflict."
2. Describe the officer subculture.
3. What do we know about officer-on-inmate and inmate-on-officer violence?
4. Describe the major challenges to correctional management.
5. What types of unethical behavior do some officers engage in?

Chapter 10

'We Shall Be Released'

. . . the fight to keep my freedom had only begun. There were many reasons, but the main one was the uncertainty I had about being able to stay out of trouble and away from all those old friends and places that got me in trouble in the first place. Most of the public doesn't understand that after five and a half years in prison, those old friends and old places are the only things we remember; therefore, they are likely to call us back to them. (an inmate being released; Padron in Johnson and Toch 2000, 199)

One of the most obvious facts about incarceration is that almost everyone serving a prison sentence will be released—eventually. Except for the few who will die in prison, these individuals will be released to live among us. Even those who do not favor rehabilitation should pause and reflect on the reality of this fact. An individual will exit prison either better able to face the rigors and temptations of life or less able to because of the suspended animation of a prison sentence.

Prison does change a person. Of that there is no doubt. Whether it is positive or negative change depends on the individual's willingness and readiness to take advantage of vocational training, education, drug treatment programs, and other opportunities in prison; but partly it depends on whether or not those opportunities exist and what ravages prison has taken on the individual's personality, self-esteem, and capacity to live with "straights."

Getting out is a weird and alien experience. . . . Prison has a way of eating at your self-esteem. Upon release into the "normal" world, you find yourself feeling less and less normal every day. (an ex-prisoner, Martin and Sussman 1993, 301)

Parole

There are about 5 million people on probation or parole in this country (Mauer and Chesney-Lind 2002), so it may be surprising to find that the use of parole has declined over the last 25 years. Fifteen states have abolished parole and five additional states have eliminated parole for some categories of offenders (Greene and Schiraldi 2002, 19). Other states have informally cut their use of parole drastically through parole release decisions. In Texas, for instance, about 80 percent of prisoners eligible for parole received it in 1991, but by 1999, only about 20 percent of eligible prisoners received parole. Political pressure finally shifted the strict policies of parole in the early 2000s so that the decision rate has begun to creep upward again. In a recent report, it was noted that parole approval rates had risen from about 20 percent in 1999 to close to 30 percent in 2000 (Fabelo 2001, 3).

Reduced use of parole means that prison populations back up and become bloated by the closing of the "back door." It also means that those who are released are more likely to be "maxed out," having served their full sentence. Once released, they are under no supervision or oversight at all. In fact, they may be maxed out from the super-max prisons where they have not had much of any human interaction for years, or from solitary confinement for being unable to live within the general population of the prison. They may be released from prison while under the effects of Thorazine or other antipsychotic drugs with the admonition to seek medical assistance from a community mental health center to receive their "meds," but with no supervision to see that they do. These individuals have paid their debt to society, but are they ready to survive back in society with no assistance and no supervision?

One important, but overlooked, contribution to the rise of this nation's prison population has been increased parole violations and returns to prison. From 1990 to 1998, new commitments rose by 7.5 percent, but parole violation returns rose 54 percent (Butterfield 2000). California has eliminated early release through parole, but every prisoner is supervised for a mandatory term after release. Fully 65 percent of prison admissions in California are for violations of this mandatory supervision. It should be noted that a large number of these cases may be for criminal charges, but often the charges are minor and would not have, by themselves, warranted a prison sentence (Petersilia 1999).

A study of Nevada prisoners reported that about one-sixth of all prison admissions were parole or probation violators. The violations included such things as failing to report, failing to pay supervision fees, failed drug tests, failing to maintain employment, and so on (cited in Austin and Irwin 2001, 146). In Texas 36 percent of its prison admissions in 1998 were parole violators and another 40 percent were probation violators (cited in Austin and Irwin 2001, 144). However, in more recent years, along with higher parole approval rates, have been lower revocation rates in Texas. There were over 2,000 fewer revocations in 2001 than there were in 2000, a trend that will probably continue as parole-hearing board officials are given the green light to make graduated sanctions for violators available (Fabelo 2001, 5).

Graduated sanctions, rather than a return to prison, make sense despite being politically unpopular. It is possible to respond to parole violators with a sanction short of a return to prison. For instance, failed drug tests could result in a mandated residential drug program; absconding could result in some type of curfew or expanded monitoring; and technical violations could require stricter monitoring. It is possible to reduce the number sent back to prison, but only if there are alternatives available for parole supervisors.

Re-entry and Recidivism

It is estimated that roughly 600,000 prisoners are re-entering our communities each year from prisons and jails (King and Mauer 2002b, 3). In fact, the number of releasees has increased in recent years. The number of individuals released in 2000 represented an 8.4 percent increase over the number released in 1998 (Harrison and Beck 2002, 7).

Most of those released have the same low levels of education and vocational skills that they had going into prison. Many of them return to prison. In fact, according to a recent Justice Department study, 67 percent of released inmates were charged with at least one serious crime within three years. The study tracked 272,111 released inmates in 15 states. Other study findings indicated that the recidivism rate of offenders is worse than 20 years ago, not better, despite longer sentences imposed. Men were more likely to recidivate than women (68 percent compared with 57 percent), African-Americans were more likely to recidivate than whites (73 percent compared with 63 percent), and young people under 18 were more likely to recidivate than older offenders 45 and over (80 percent compared with 45 percent). Offenders with the highest recidivism rates included car thieves, those convicted of receipt of stolen property, burglars, and those convicted of robbery (Murphy 2002a). The Bureau of Justice Statistics reports that in 2000, there were 350,431 prison admittees for new court convictions and 203,569 returned for probation or parole violations. Almost a third of the total number entering prison each year are parole violators (Harrison and Beck 2002, 7).

Civil Liberties

One should remember that for offenders, their punishment often does not end when they leave prison. Many states suspend civil rights, such as voting—either permanently, during the course of their sentence and parole supervision, for some legislated period of time after correctional supervision has ceased, or to be granted only after the individual petitions for reinstatement. Estimates indicate about four million ex-offenders are permanently barred from voting because of their state's laws. Thirteen states currently permanently bar ex-felons from voting (Richey 2002). Twenty-seven states bar anyone in prison or on probation or parole from voting (P. Ward 2002). Only two states (Maine and Vermont) allow prisoners to vote.

In Georgia, one out of every 15 adults is barred from voting, at least until the expiration of their supervision by the state. No state has a bigger percentage of its adult population under some form of correctional supervision. Observers argued that a state like Florida, which has a very high population of African-Americans, can actually have elections determined by removing a large percentage of the minority population from voter eligibility. In fact, roughly a quarter of the state's African-American men are not allowed to vote. Consider, for example, that in the Bush-Gore election, Florida's popular vote was determined by less than 600 votes and there were 400,000 Floridians unable to vote because of their criminal history (Cernetig 2002, A9; Richey 2002; P. Ward 2002).

In recent years, states have been changing their laws that bar ex-felons the vote. According to a recent Harris Poll, 80 percent of Americans feel ex-felons that have served their time should be allowed to vote (Richey 2002). Delaware, for instance, recently changed their lifetime ban to only a five-year restriction. Maryland also changed their lifetime ban to a three year restriction and New Mexico completely eliminated their ban (P. Ward 2002).

Barriers to Re-entry

Why do ex-inmates recidivate? Some prisoners leave with the idea that they will just commit smarter crimes. They often end up not smarter but just older prisoners. Others have the best of intentions. Yet despite declarations that they will never come back, that they are going to stop using drugs and get a job and stay out of trouble, they end up coming back to prison. Some of these individuals end up violating their parole for technical reasons, disobeying rules that are not new crimes. Others, however, do commit new crimes and/or go back to using drugs. The main barriers for them in their journey out of prison are employment, housing, family adjustments, and the lure of old friends combined with the difficulties and loneliness of the outside. It has been said that the three basic needs of ex-prisoners are a place to stay, employment, and someone to believe in them (which also gives them something to lose) (Ross and Richards 2003, 3).

Obtaining gainful, interesting employment is difficult for most of us. Having the millstone of being an ex-offender is a weight that is almost insurmountable. It should be noted that many offenders have had gainful employment before prison. Having the ex-felon status, however, makes a return to their old employment sometimes impossible or finding new employment difficult as well, even if they are willing to settle for less. Many ex-offenders who have no help on the outside are released with from $20 to $200 from the state to help them get started. With that money, they are supposed to buy clothes, get a place to live, and eat while they look for work. It is no wonder that some use the money to get drunk or buy drugs. The anxiety of release is sometimes overwhelming to an individual who has, for perhaps years, been awakened, told where and when to work, and been fed and clothed by the state. Prison is a terrible, dangerous place to be, but prisoners never wonder whether or not they will eat. Once released, hunger is a very real possibility.

Inmates often have no families to return to. They may find that missions or halfway houses are the only homes they can arrange on the outside. Sometimes release plans, including housing promised by relatives, is just a sham for the paroling authorities and there is no such arrangement offered, or if it is, the ex-inmate feels compelled to leave quickly so as not to be a burden to a parent, sibling or other relative. Recently, the crackdown on drugs has made it even more difficult for ex-offenders. Federal laws have mandated that public-housing management exclude those with felony convictions or drug convictions from living in low-income housing. What this means is that if a man is released from prison and his wife and children are living in a low-income housing project, he cannot live with them. If he does, they will all be evicted. A released woman, attempting to regain custody of her children from foster care, may have a job but still need public housing in order to make ends meet. Because she is barred from low-income housing eligibility due to a drug conviction, she may not ever get her children back.

Besides employment and housing, there are very real adjustment problems facing releasees. Stresses that do not exist in prison suddenly confront them. Women can't get their children back but feel they cannot live without them. Men either can't return to their families because their wives have divorced them, or they return and find that they are unneeded and unnecessary and wives and children are resentful and angry at them for being away. Parents and relatives, at first jubilant and grateful for the releasee's return, quickly move on and may vent years of stored-up frustration and disappointment. The releasee's first thoughts may be to relax and "party" a little—alcohol, sex, and fun are natural and predictable as the releasee's agenda. Parole officers obviously have a different viewpoint. Single parolees are often told to have no relationships for a year, or to inform their parole officer when they begin "seeing" someone.

If the preceding are barriers to success, what elements seem to be correlated with a crime-free lifestyle for ex-offenders? One of the strongest correlates is just getting older. Offenders past the age of 35 are much less likely to re-offend. Other correlates include marriage with children, job stability, and being drug free (Maruna 2001).

Murphy (2002a) reports that 49 states will share $100 million in federal aid for programs that will give ex-cons education, job, and life skills training and substance abuse treatment. It is a part of the Justice Department's Serious and Violent Offender Reentry Initiative. Programs will coordinate the efforts of prosecutors, prison staff, parole officers, workforce investment boards, and other community-based service providers. This type of program is a hopeful alternative to more prisons.

Cutting Back on Prison

One of the most effective solutions to the problems of re-entry is not to imprison in the first place. If an offender is punished in the community, there is no re-entry issue. If prison sentences are shortened, at least the adjustment problems are minimized. There are growing numbers who advocate either abolition or a drastic curtailment of the use of prison. West and Morris (2000), for instance, present the argument for penal abolition: religious and spiritual support for forgiveness eclipses such support for vengeance; research indicates prisons have failed to deter or rehabilitate; and the practice of incarceration dehumanizes all who are engaged in it and leads to inhumanity.

There are good examples across the country of states that are reducing their prison populations through an array of options, including drug courts, sentencing guidelines, repealing mandatory sentencing laws, reducing security classifications, increasing the use of parole and early release options, restitution programs, and compassionate release programs for elderly prisoners (Greene and Schiraldi 2002). In recent years, some states have relaxed mandatory minimums (Connecticut, Louisiana, Mississippi, and North Dakota); others have utilized drug treatment instead of prison as a sentencing option (Arkansas, California, Idaho, Oregon, and Texas); and still other states have passed legislation to ease overcrowded prisons (Arkansas, Iowa, Mississippi, Montana, North Carolina, Texas, and Virginia) (King and Mauer 2002b, 3).

There are indications across the country that citizens can make an impact if they choose to make their voices heard regarding the ever-expanding prison boom. Alameda County in California was set to begin construction on what would have been one of the biggest juvenile detention centers in the country, with close to 500 beds. In a pro forma public meeting before the board of corrections was expected to rubber-stamp the $2.3 million construction request from county officials, a youth movement, "Books Not Bars," energetically argued against the need for such a facility, given declining youth crime and stretched state revenues for education and other youth services. Surprisingly, this grassroots organization was successful in blocking construction of the prison, as the county commissioners voted against it.

Chanting, waving placards and raising 70 clenched fists in the air a colorful throng of youth and their allies marched into the "belly of the beast" today—flooding and overflowing the stuffy confines of a California Board of Corrections (BOC) meeting . . . at the eleventh hour and against all odds—the young crusaders accomplished the impossible. (press release, Ella Baker Center, "Books Not Bars" Campaign 2001, as cited in Schiraldi and Jones 2001)

There is increasing evidence that our practice of incarceration is devastating communities. Whole neighborhoods are affected when a large percentage of their population is sent away for years at a time. Wacquant (2001) discusses the situation wherein children raised in public-housing communities with razor wire and armed guards view prison as an almost inevitable part of their future. Generational effects are obvious; we know that children of inmates are six times as likely to be delinquent. More subtle effects exist as well. The economy and social fabric of a community are also affected when large numbers of young people are removed (Mauer, Chesney-Lind, and Clear 2002).

Like an overused antibiotic, it [the use of prison] has left the prisoner untreated and unchastened, the community unprotected and the whole society demonstrably worse off. (columnist William Raspberry 2002, A13)

One good reason for looking for alternatives is that prisons are "breaking the bank" of state budgets. The growing behemoths have eclipsed spending for education and other areas of public services. With the economy in a downward decline, state budget-makers will have to find politically feasible ways of turning off the spigot of ever-increasing prison budgets. It will not be easy.

The Prison Industrial Complex

The "prison industrial complex" refers to the massive buildup of prisons in this country and the incestuous relationship between politicians who approve the budget and those who reap the profits, similar to the military industrial complex in the Vietnam and post–Vietnam War years (Dyer 2000). The fact of the matter is that crime does pay, although not necessarily for criminals, but it has been profitable for those who build and maintain prison facilities. When stock profits surge, someone is getting rich. The economic rewards of prison building act as a barrier to deinstitutionalization. Small towns will not give up their prison "factories" without a fight. Private prison profiteers, who have been contributing huge amounts of money to politicians, do not want to see crime rate decreases translate into declining incarceration rates— why would they?

Dyer (2000) details the rise of the prison-industrial complex and details its benefits for the different groups that participate in it. Politicians benefit because they are able to convince the public that they are doing something about crime. The media contributes by creating the climate of fear. The emphasis on violent crime misleads the public as to the true risk of crime in society and promotes the idea that prison is the best solution to the problem. The vast array of prison profiteers, either those in the private prison industry or the vendors who contract with prisons, certainly have everything to gain by seeing prison rates rise.

The economics of private prisons is that desperately poor towns look at the promise of a private prison as an economic boon.

They are promised jobs and contracts for everything from food to mattresses. In return, the towns and counties vying for these institutions are willing to offer free land, tax rebates, and other incentives so that they are chosen over other contenders for the right to have the prison. Many of these areas surround military bases that were closed in the federal downsizing of the 1980s and 1990s. Florence, Colorado, offered 600 acres to the federal government and no less than four detention facilities were promptly built. Some towns cut out the middleman and build their own institutions. Observers note that the small rural communities that experienced an economic boost with the arrival of state or private prisons are not going to give up their "factories" without a fight, even if there are fewer inmates to be housed (Rohde 2001).

A huge network of profitable enterprises has sprung up because of the "corrections industry." At the American Correctional Association, twice a year delegates are enticed to a huge ballroom or conference hall filled from front to back with vendors selling their wares. Participants pick up "freebies" of pens, water bottles, candy, and other items while they stroll the aisles and look at prison wares—everything from riot batons to stainless steel stools are displayed. High tech is represented, too. Corrections is big business and it supports a huge number of ancillary businesses. "Prisoner brokers" are the middlemen between states or private agencies who are seeking to fill beds and states with more prisoners than beds. Evidently the profits involved in making the deals are quite substantial (Dyer 2000).

Profits seem to be even more important than security in some situations. Fifty years ago, or even 20, prisoners could not use the telephone except as a very limited privilege (i.e., once a month) or because of an emergency and with a counselor's approval. Today, some prisons allow virtually unlimited calling and phones are placed in dayrooms or in the yard. Officers grumble about this and mutter darkly about courts giving inmates more rights than guards, but it isn't the courts that spur the widespread availability of telephones—it is telephone companies offering high incentives to states to allow them to provide the service, at an exorbitant cost. Prisoners must call collect and families end up paying several times more for the call than free-world collect calls would be. In effect, telephone companies are gouging prisoners' families and acquiring huge profits, which they then split with the states and counties (in jails). WorldCom is one company that was fined $522,458 for overcharging in California, but the practice is widespread ("WorldCom Must" . . . 2001).

So there is profit in prison, but at what cost to the rest of us? It is not an understatement to say that whole segments of society are embittered and disenfranchised because of our zeal to incarcerate. No one can ignore the fact that young black men are disproportionately imprisoned, and no one can deny the fact that the injustices that occur in prison are equal to or worse than the crimes that some prisoners have committed on the outside. Further, the costs involved in supporting such a massive industry are literally forcing choices between funding education and prison. There is no doubt that states have seen the corrections piece of the budget grow exponentially and absorb resources that would have gone to other governmental programs.

> We are only now beginning to glimpse the social and financial costs of this institution in terms of: reduced state budgets for other spending; the alienation of whole sectors of the population; the normalization of the prison experience and the transfer of prison culture into the community; the criminogenic consequences of custody for inmates and their families and their children; and the disenfranchisement of whole sectors of the community. (Garland 2001, 2)

Conclusion

We are at a crossroads. We can continue down the path we have been taking for the last 20 years and incarcerate more and more people. This policy will continue to alienate and disenfranchise large segments of our population and condemn millions more to fractured lives and multigenerations in this nation's prisons and jails. The alternative is that we can stop and re-evaluate the imprisonment response. We can start with drug offenders. Even changing our punitive policies regarding simple possession would drastically reduce the numbers of people in prison. If we substituted treatment instead of prison, and invested resources to find better treatment options, that would do even more by reducing the number of people who relapse. Next, we could look at some innovative ways to substitute other forms of punishment for property offenders. Electronic monitoring, house arrest, restitution, and community justice centers all have their place if they are used as diversions rather than widening the net of offenders who are dealt with by our justice system. The result of these two campaigns would be a dramatic reduction in the population in prisons, which would, in turn, free up money for other social programs. Drug treatment and early childhood intervention programs are much more cost-effective than bars and guards. Prisons could then be utilized, as they were used in the earlier part of this century, for those who truly pose a danger to society.

The resistance to such a change in policy is very strong. It comes from guards who don't want to see their jobs disappear, private prison companies that don't want to see their profits decline, the thousands of companies that build facilities, and/or provide goods and services to the prison industry, the public who have been indoctrinated to the belief that prison will reduce crime, and politicians who don't want to seem soft on crime. "Follow the money" is an old piece of advice how to solve a crime. It works here, too, on the mystery of why this country seems so intent on spending more and more money incarcerating nondangerous people, sacrificing education, health, and other governmental services in the process.

Prison is banishment. Prison is a place where few come out better people than when they went in. It should be used sparingly, with gravity, and with full knowledge that we are altering that person's life in fundamental ways. Prison should be reserved for those few who are truly frightening. It should not be an industry because people should be more important than profits.

Study Questions

1. What is the prison-industrial complex?
2. What other rights do prisoners lose upon a felony sentence?
3. What alternatives to prison exist?
4. What are the greatest challenges facing those who are released from prison?

Table of Cases

Sources

Abbott, J. 1981. *In the Belly of the Beast*. New York: Vintage Books.

Abramsky, S. 2002. *Hard Time Blues: How Politics Built a Prison Nation*. New York: St. Martin's.

Akers, R., N. Hayner, and W. Grunninger. 1977. "Prisonization in Five Countries." *Criminology* 14: 527–554.

Altman, L. 1999. "Much More AIDS in Prisons Than in General Population." *New York Times*. url: *nytimes.com/library/national/science/aids/090199hth-aids-prison.html*.

Amnesty International. 1999. *"Not Part of My Sentence": Violations of the Human Rights of Women in Custody*. London, England: Amnesty International.

Andrews, D., I. Zinger, R. Hoge, J. Bonta, P. Gendreau, and F. Cullen. 1990. "Does Correctional Treatment Work? A Clinically Relevant and Psychologically Informal Meta-analysis." *Criminology* 28, 3: 369–404.

Annin, P. 1998. "Inside the New Alcatraz." *Newsweek*, July 13, 1998, 13–15.

Arax, M. 1999a. "Ex-Guard Says 4 Men Set Up Rape of Inmate." *Los Angeles Times*, October 14, 1999, A6.

——. 1999b. "Ex-Guard Tells of Brutality, Code of Silence at Corcoran." *Los Angeles Times*, July 6, 1999, B4.

Archambeault, W. 2003. "Soar Like an Eagle, Dive Like a Loon." In J. Ross and S. Richards, *Convict Criminology*, pp. 287–308. Belmont, CA: Wadsworth, ITP.

Arriens, J. 1991. *Welcome to Hell*. Boston: Northeastern University Press.

Associated Press. 2000a. "Prison Guards Send Plea to Bush." *Austin American Statesman*, January 11, 2000, B3.

——. 2000b. "Prison Guards Suspected of Money Laundering." *Austin American Statesman*, January 27, 2000, B3.

——. 2001a. "New Jersey Prison Population Declined 5.4% in 2000." *New Jersey News*, August 14, 2001, A12.

——. 2001b. "Record Number Held in Prison. State Rise Slows." *New York Times*. Retrieved March 26, 2001, from *www.nytimes.com/2001/03/26/national/26PRIS.html*.

——. 2002. "Study: Measure Effect Inconclusive." *Statesman Journal.com.* Retrieved August 7, 2002, from *http://www.news.statesmanjournal.com/article.cfm?i=46305.*

Austin, J. 1999. "Rehabilitation: Reality or Myth." In P. Carlson and J. Garrett (eds.), *Prison and Jail Administration,* pp. 287–294. Gaithersburg, MD: Aspen.

Austin, J., B. Bloom, and T. Donahue. 1992. *Female Offenders in the Community. An Analysis of Innovative Strategies and Programs.* Report prepared by the National Council on Crime and Delinquency. Washington, DC: National Institute of Corrections.

Austin, J., and J. Irwin. 2001. *It's About Time: America's Imprisonment Binge.* Belmont, CA: Wadsworth.

Austin American Statesman. 2002. "Protect Prison Reforms Along With Inmates." *Austin American Statesman,* June 19, 2002, A12.

Bales, D. 1997. *Correctional Officer Resource Guide.* Lanham, MD: American Correctional Association.

Barnes, H., and N. Teeters. 1952. *New Horizons in Criminology.* New York: Prentice-Hall.

Baunach, P. 1984. *Mothers in Prison.* New Brunswick, NJ: Rutgers/Transaction Press.

Beaumont, G., and A. de Tocqueville. 1833/1964. *On the Penitentiary System in the United States and Its Application to France.* Carbondale, IL: Southern Illinois University.

Beck, A. 1995. *Bureau of Justice Statistics Bulletin: Profile of Jail Inmates, 1989.* Washington, DC: U.S. Department of Justice.

——. 1998. *Bureau of Justice Statistics Bulletin: Profile of Jail Inmates, 1996.* Washington, DC: U.S. Department of Justice.

Beck, A., and J. Karberg. 2001. *Bureau of Justice Statistics Bulletin: Prison and Jail Inmates at Midyear 2000.* Washington, DC: U.S. Department of Justice.

Beck, A., J. Karberg, and P. Harrison. 2002. *Bureau of Justice Statistics Bulletin: Prison and Jail Inmates at Midyear 2001.* Washington, DC: U.S. Department of Justice.

Beck, A., and C. Mumola. 1999. *Bureau of Justice Statistics Bulletin: Prisoners in 1998.* Washington, DC: U.S. Department of Justice.

Becker, R. 1997. "The Privatization of Prisons." In J. Pollock (ed.), *Prisons: Today and Tomorrow,* pp. 382–413. Gaithersburg, MD: Aspen.

Beckerman, A. 1994. "Mothers in Prison: Meeting the Prerequisite Conditions for Permanency Planning." *Social Work* 39, 1: 9–14.

Beckett, K., and B. Western. 2001. "Governing Social Marginality." In D. Garland (ed.), *Mass Imprisonment: Social Causes and Consequences,* pp. 35–48. Thousand Oaks, CA: Sage.

Bedell, P. 1997. "Resilient Women." Unpublished master's thesis, Vermont College of Norwich University.

Belknap, J. 2000. *The Invisible Woman.* Albany, NY: SUNY Press.

——. 2003. "Responding to the Needs of Women Prisoners." In S. Sharp, *The Incarcerated Woman,* pp. 93–106. Upper Saddle River, NJ: Prentice-Hall.

Bergner, D. 1998. *God of the Rodeo: The Quest for Redemption in Louisiana's Angola Prison.* New York: Ballantine.

Bernstein, N. 2001. "Out of the Big House." *Salon Magazine.* Retrieved August 30, 2001, from *salon.com/mwt/feature/2001/08/30/clemency_women/index.html.*

Bianculli, L. 1997. "The War on Drugs: Fact, Fiction and Controversy." *Seton Hall Legislative Journal* 21: 169–200.

Blakely, S. 1995. "California Program to Focus on New Mothers." *Corrections Today* (December): 128–130.

Block, K., and M. Potthast. 1997. "Living Apart and Getting Together: Inmate Mothers and Enhanced Visitation Through Girl Scouts." Paper presented at Academy of Criminal Justice Sciences, March 1997.

Bloom, B. 1995. "Imprisoned Mothers." In K. Gabel and D. Johnston (eds.), *Children of Incarcerated Parents,* pp. 21–30. New York: Lexington Books.

Bloom, B., and D. Steinhart. 1993. *Why Punish the Children? A Reappraisal of the Children of Incarcerated Mothers in America.* San Francisco: National Council on Crime and Delinquency.

Blumstein, A., and J. Wallman. 2000. *The Crime Drop in America.* New York City: University Press.

Bonner, R., and A. Rich. 1990. "Psychosocial Vulnerability, Life Stress, and Suicide Ideation in a Jail Population." *Suicide and Life-Threatening Behavior* 20, 3: 213–224.

Boudouris, J. 1996/1998. *Prisons and Kids.* College Park, MD: American Correctional Association.

Bourge, C. 2002. "Sparks Fly Over Private v. Public Prisons." UPI. Retrieved February 21, 2002, from *www.upi./com/view.cfm?storyID= 20022002-064851-41221.*

Braswell, M., R. Montgomery, and L. Lombardo. 1994. *Prison Violence in America.* Cincinnati, OH: Anderson.

Brennan, P. 1999. "Male and Female Prison Populations: Differential Effects of Technical Violations of Probation and Parole." Paper presented at the American Society of Criminology meeting, Toronto, Ontario, November 1999.

Brewster, D. 2003. "Does Rehabilitative Justice Decrease Recidivism for Women Prisoners in Oklahoma?" In S. Sharp, *The Incarcerated Woman,* pp. 29–45. Upper Saddle River, NJ: Prentice-Hall.

Britton, D. 1997. "Perceptions of the Work Environment Among Correctional Officers: Do Race and Sex Matter?" *Criminology* 35, 1: 85–105.

Brown, J. 2002. "Aging Prison Populations Drive Up State Costs." *Stateline.org.* Retrieved June 21, 2002, from *http://www1.stateline.org/story.dojjsessionid=518djegth1?storyID=243927.*

Browne, A. 1987. *When Battered Women Kill.* New York: Free Press.

Browne, A., B. Miller, and E. Maguin. 1999. "Prevalence and Severity of Lifetime Physical and Sexual Victimization Among Incarcerated Women." *International Journal of Law and Psychiatry* 22, 3–4: 301–322.

Browne, D. 1989. "Incarcerated Mothers and Parenting." *Journal of Family Violence* 4, 2: 211–221.

Bryce, R. 1999. "Louder Than Words." *Salon Magazine.* Retrieved August 24, 1999, from *salonmagazine.com/newsfeature/1999/08/24/texas/html.*

Bureau of Justice Statistics. 2000. *Correctional Populations in the U.S., 1997.* Washington, DC: U.S. Department of Justice.

Butterfield, F. 1996. "Tough Law on Sentences Is Criminal." *New York Times,* March 8, 1996, A14.

——. 1999. "Report Shows Jump in Number of Inmates." *San Antonio Express,* A2.

——. 2000. "Getting Out: A Special Report." *New York Times,* November 29, 2000.

——. 2001. "U.S. State Prison Population Declining in Last Half of 2000." *New York Times,* August 13, 2001, A7.

——. 2002a. "States Ease Sentencing Laws as Prison Numbers Rise." *Austin American Statesman,* September 2, 2001, A15.

——. 2002b. "Father Steals Best: Crime in an American Family." *New York Times.* Retrieved August 15, 2002 from *www.nytimes.com/2002/08/21/national/21FAMI.html.*

Cabana, D. 1996. *Death at Midnight.* Boston: Northeastern Press.

Camp, G., and G. Camp. 1997. *The Corrections Yearbook, 1997.* South Salem, NY: Criminal Justice Institute.

Camp, S., T. Steiger, K. Wright, W. Saylor, and E. Gilman. 1997. "Affirmative Action and the 'Level Playing Field': Comparing Perceptions of Own and Minority Job Advancement Opportunities." *Prison Journal* 77, 3: 313–334.

Carlson, P. 1999a. "Correctional Officers Today: The Changing Face of the Workforce." In P. Carlson and J. Garrett (eds.), *Prison and Jail Administration: Practice and Theory,* pp. 183–188. Gaithersburg, MD: Aspen.

——. 1999b. "Management and Accountability." In P. Carlson and J. Garrett (eds.), *Prison and Jail Administration: Practice and Theory,* pp. 41–46. Gaithersburg, MD: Aspen.

Carroll, L. 1974. *Hacks, Blacks, and Cons.* Lexington, KY: Lexington Books.

C.A.S.A. National Center on Addiction and Substance Abuse. 2001. "Shoveling Up: The Impact of Substance Abuse on State Budgets." Retrieved August 14, 2002, from *casacolumbia.org/publications1456/pubications_show.htm?doc_id=47299.*

——. 1998. *Lawful Order: A Case Study of Correctional Crisis and Reform.* New York: Garland Press.

Cernetig, M. 2002. "U.S. Solidifies Its Rankings as the World's Biggest Jailer." *Globe and Mail,* Retrieved from *http://www.theglobeandmail.com/servlet/ArticleNews/PEstory/TGAM/20020827/UPRISN/International/international/international_temp/2/2/20/.*

Cheek, F., and M. Miller. 1983. "The Experience of Stress for Correction Officers: A Double-Bind Theory of Correctional Stress." *Journal of Criminal Justice* 11: 105–120.

Chen, D. 2000. "Ex-Attica Inmates Recount Shattered Lives and Dreams." *New York Times on the Web.* Retrieved February 15, 2000, from *www.nytimes.com/yr/mo/day/news/national/regional/ny-attica-case.html.*

Chesney-Lind, M. 1997. *The Female Offender: Girls, Women and Crime.* Thousand Oaks, CA: Sage.

Chesney-Lind, M., and J. Pollock. 1994. "Women's Prisons: Equality With a Vengeance." In A. Merlo and J. Pollock (eds.), *Women, Law and Social Control,* pp. 155–177. Boston: Allyn and Bacon.

Clark, J., J. Austin, and D. Henry. 1997. "Three Strikes and You're Out: A Review of State Legislation." *National Institute of Justice Research in Brief.* Washington, DC: U.S. Department of Justice.

Clement, M. 1993. "Parenting in Prisons: A National Survey of Programs for Incarcerated Women." *Journal of Offender Rehabilitation* 19, 1: 89–100.

Clemmer, D. 1940. *The Prison Community.* Boston: Christopher Publishing.

Cole, D. 1999. *No Equal Justice: Race and Class in the American Criminal Justice System.* New York: New Press.

Collins, M. 2002. "Prison Spending Outpaces Higher Education." *Cincinnati Post Online.* Retrieved August 29, 2002, from *http://www.cincypost.com/2002/aug/28/spend082802.html.*

Colvin, M. 1992. *The Penitentiary in Crisis: From Accommodation to Riot in New Mexico.* Albany, NY: SUNY Press.

Common Sense for Drug Policy. 2003. "CSDP Research Report: Revising the Federal Drug Control Budget Report: Changing the Methodology to Hide the Cost of the Drug War." Retrieved on May 30, 2003, from *www.csdp.org.*

Conley, J. 1992. "The Historical Relationship Among Punishment, Incarceration and Corrections." In S. Stojkovic and R. Lovell (eds.), *Corrections: An Introduction,* pp. 33–65. Cincinnati, OH: Anderson.

Conover, T. 2000. *Guarding Sing Sing.* New York: Random House.

Conrad, J. 1981. "Where There's Hope, There's Life." In D. Fogel and J. Hudson (eds.), *Justice as Fairness: Perspectives on the Justice Model,* pp. 17–23. Cincinnati, OH: Anderson.

Corrections Alert. 1997. *Corrections Alert* 4, 25: 8.

Corrections Digest. 2002. "Prisons Operate Above Capacity Despite Slowest Growth in 28 Years." *Corrections Digest* 33, 15: 1–3.

Couturier, L. 1995. "Inmates Benefit From Family Services Program." *Corrections Today* (December): 100–107.

Cox, D. 2000. "Grand Jury Inquiry Into Death of Inmate Extended." *Sun-Sentinel,* January 5, 2000.

Cox, V., P. Paulus, and G. McCain. 1984. "Prison Crowding Research." *American Psychologist* 39, 10: 1148–1160.

Crouch, B. 1995. "Guard Work in Transition." In K. Haas and G. Alpert (eds.), *The Dilemmas of Corrections,* 3rd ed., pp. 183–203. Prospect Heights, IL: Waveland Press.

Crouch, B., and J. Marquart. 1989. *An Appeal to Justice: Litigated Reform of Texas Prisons.* Austin: University of Texas Press.

———. 1990. "Resolving the Paradox of Reform: Litigation, Prisoners Violence and Perceptions of Risk." *Justice Quarterly* 7: 103–122.

Crow, I. 2001. *The Treatment and Rehabilitation of Offenders.* Thousand Oaks, CA: Sage.

Cullen, F. 1982. *Reaffirming Rehabilitation.* Cincinnati, OH: Anderson.

Cullen, F., E. Latessa, V. Burton, and L. Lombardo. 1993. "The Correctional Orientation of Prison Wardens: Is the Rehabilitative Ideal Supported?" *Criminology* 31, 1: 69–92.

Datesman, S., and G. Cales. 1983. "I'm Still the Same Mommy: Maintaining the Mother/Child Relationship in Prison." *Prison Journal* 63, 2: 142–154.

Davidson, R. 1974. *Chicano Prisoners: The Key to San Quentin.* Thousand Oaks, CA: Sage.

Deschenes, E., and D. Anglin. 1992. "Effects of Legal Supervision on Narcotic Addict Behavior: Ethnic and Gender Influences." In T. Mieczkowski (ed.), *Drugs, Crime and Social Policy*, pp. 167–196. Needham, MA: Allyn and Bacon.

Ditchfield, J., and R. Harries. 1996. "Assaults on Staff in Male Local Prisons and Remand Centres." *Home Office Research and Statistics Directorate Research Bulletin Issue* 38: 15–20.

Ditton, P. 1999. *Mental Health and Treatment of Inmates and Probationers.* Washington, DC: Bureau of Justice Statistics, Department of Justice.

Diulio, J., Jr. 1987. *Governing Prisons: A Comparative Study of Correctional Management.* New York: Free Press.

Donaldson, S. 2001. "A Million Jockers, Punks, and Queens." In D. Sabo, T. Kupers, and W. London, *Prison Masculinities*, pp. 118–126. Philadelphia: Temple University Press.

Dorsey, T., M. Zawitz, and P. Middleton. 2002. *Bureau of Justice Statistics Bulletin: Drug and Crime Facts.* Washington, DC: U.S. Department of Justice.

Dressel, P., and S. Barnhill. 1994. "Reframing Gerontological Thought and Practice: The Case of Grandmothers With Daughters in Prison." *The Gerontologist* 34, 5: 685–691.

Driscoll, D. 1985. "Mother's Day Once a Month." *Corrections Today* (August): 18–24.

Dumond, A. 2000. "Inmate Sexual Assault." *Prison Journal* 80, 4: 407–414.

Durham, A. 1994. *Crisis and Reform: Current Issues in American Punishment.* Boston: Little, Brown.

Dyer, J. 2000. *The Perpetual Prison Machine.* Boulder, CO: Westview.

Early, D. 1992. *The Hot House: Life Inside Leavenworth.* New York: Bantam.

Eisenberg, M. 2001. Evaluation of the Performance of the Texas Department of Criminal Justice Rehabilitation Tier Programs. Austin, TX: Criminal Justice Policy Council. Available through website.

Ekland-Olson, S. 1986. "Crowding, Social Control and Prison Violence: Evidence From the Post-Ruiz Years in Texas." *Law and Society Review* 20, 3: 389–421.

Enos, S. 2001. *Mothering From the Inside.* Albany, NY: SUNY Press.

Ewing., C. 1987. *Battered Women Who Kill.* Lexington, MA: Lexington Books.

Fabelo, T. 2001. *Texas Correctional Population Changes in Historical Perspective.* Austin, TX: Criminal Justice Policy Council.

Faith, K. 1993. *Unruly Women: The Politics of Confinement and Resistance.* Vancouver, British Columbia: Press Gang Publishing.

Farkas, M. 1997. "Normative Code Among Correctional Officers: An Exploration of Components and Functions." *Journal of Crime and Justice* 20, 1: 23–36.

——. 1999. "Correctional Officer Attitudes Toward Inmates and Working With Inmates in a 'Get Tough' Era." *Journal of Criminal Justice* 27, 6: 495–506.

Fecteau, L. 1999. "Private Prisons Warned." *Albuquerque Journal.* Retrieved August 30, 1999, from *wysiwyg://1http://www/abqjournal.com/news/2news08-27-99.htm.*

Feucht, T., and A. Keyser. 1999. "Reducing Drug Use in Prisons: Pennsylvania's Approach." *National Institute of Justice Journal* (October): 11–15.

Fields, G. 2001. "Mandatory Prison Time Is Being Rethought." *Wall Street Journal,* August 9, 2001.

Fikae, P. 2000. "Guards Petition for Pay Increase." *San Antonio Express News,* Tuesday, January 4, 2000, B1.

Flanagan, T. 1995. *Long Term Imprisonment: Policy, Science, and Correctional Practice.* Thousand Oaks, CA: Sage.

Fleisher, M. 1989. *Warehousing Violence.* Beverly Hills, CA: Sage.

Fleisher, M., and R. Rison. 1999. "Gang Management in Corrections." In P. Carlson and J. Garrett (eds.), *Prison and Jail Administration,* pp. 232–238. Gaithersburg, MD: Aspen.

Fletcher, B., L. Shaver, and D. Moon. 1993. *Women Prisoners: A Forgotten Population.* Westport, CT: Praeger.

Foucault, M. 1977. *Discipline and Punish: The Birth of the Prison.* New York: Pantheon.

Fox, J. 1982. *Organizational and Racial Conflict in Maximum Security Prisons.* Lexington, MA: Lexington Books.

——. 1990. "Women in Prison: A Case Study in the Social Reality of Stress." In R. Johnson and H. Toch, *The Pains of Imprisonment,* pp. 205–220. Newbury Park, CA: Sage.

Freedman, E. 1981/1986. *Their Sisters' Keepers: Women's Prison Reform in America, 1830–1930.* Ann Arbor: University of Michigan Press.

Freeman, R. 1997a. "Correctional Officers: Understudied and Misunderstood." In J. Pollock (ed.), *Prisons: Today and Tomorrow,* pp. 306–337. Gaithersburg, MD: Aspen.

——. 1997b. "Management and Administrative Issues." In J. Pollock (ed.), *Prisons: Today and Tomorrow,* pp. 270–299. Gaithersburg, MD: Aspen.

——. 1999. *Correctional Organization and Management: Public Policy Challenges, Behavior, and Structure.* Boston: Butterworth/Heinemann.

Gabel, K., and D. Johnston. 1995. *Children of Incarcerated Parents.* New York: Lexington Books.

Garland, D. 1990. *Punishment and Modern Society: A Study in Social Theory.* Chicago: University of Chicago Press.

———. 2001. *Mass Imprisonment: Social Causes and Consequences.* Thousand Oaks, CA: Sage.

Gaudin, J. 1984. "Social Work Roles and Tasks With Incarcerated Mothers." *Social Casework* 53: 279–285.

Geis, G., A. Mobley, and D. Shichor. 1999. "Private Prisons, Criminological Research and Conflict of Interest." *Crime and Delinquency* 45, 3: 372–388.

Gendreau, P. 1996. "The Principles of Effective Intervention With Offenders." In A. Harland (ed.), *Choosing Correctional Interventions That Work,* pp. 117–130. Beverly Hills, CA: Sage.

Gendreau, P., and R. Ross. 1979. "Effective Correctional Treatment: Bibliotherapy for Cynics." *Crime and Delinquency* 25: 463–489.

———. 1980. *Effective Correctional Treatment.* Toronto: Butterworth.

———. 1989. "Revivication of Rehabilitation: Evidence From the 1980s." *Justice Quarterly* 4, 3: 349–407.

Gerber, J., and E. Fritsch. 1995. "Adult Academic and Vocational Correctional Education Programs: A Review of Recent Research." *Journal of Offender Rehabilitation* 22, 1/2: 119–142.

Gilbert, M. 1997. "The Illusion of Structure: A Critique of the Classical Model of Organization and the Discretionary Power of Correctional Officers." *Criminal Justice Review* 22, 1: 49–64.

Gilbreath, A., and J. Rogers. 2000. "A Deadly Game." In R. Johnson and H. Toch (eds.), *Crime and Punishment: Inside Views,* pp. 183–193. Los Angeles: Roxbury.

Gilliard, D., and A. Beck. 1994. *Bureau of Justice Statistics Bulletin: Prisoners in 1993.* Washington, DC: U.S. Department of Justice.

———. 1996. *Bureau of Justice Statistics Bulletin: Jail Inmates in 1993.* Washington, DC: U.S. Department of Justice.

———. 1998. *Bureau of Justice Statistics Bulletin: Prisoners in 1997.* Washington, DC: U.S. Department of Justice.

Gilligan, C. 1982. *In a Different Voice: Psychological Theory and Women's Development.* Cambridge, MA: Harvard University Press.

Gilligan, J. 2002. "How to Increase the Rate of Violence and Why." In T. Gray (ed.), *Exploring Corrections,* pp. 200–214. Boston: Allyn & Bacon.

Girshick, L. 1999. *No Safe Haven: Stories of Women in Prison.* Boston: Northeastern University Press.

Gladstone, M., and M. Arax. 2000. "Prisons Audit Cites Excessive Overtime Pay." *Los Angeles Times,* Thursday, January 27, 2000.

Glaser, D. 1994. "What Works and Why It Is Important: A Response to Logan and Gaes." *Justice Quarterly* 11, 4: 711–723.

Glenn, L. 2001. *Texas Prisons: The Largest Hotel Chain in Texas.* Austin, TX: Eakin Press.

Government Accounting Office. 1996. *Private and Public Prisons—Studies Comparing Operational Costs and/or Quality of Service.* Washington, DC: U.S. Government Printing Office.

Graves, R. 2002. "War on Drugs Nets Small Time Offenders." *Houston Chronicle,* December 15, 2002, B1.

Greene, J. 2001. "Bailing Out Private Jails." *American Prospect* 12, 16: 23–27.

Greene, J., and V. Schiraldi. 2002. *Cutting Correctly: New State Policies for Times of Austerity.* Washington, DC: Justice Policy Institute.

Greenfield, L., and T. Snell. 1999. *Bureau of Justice Statistics Special Report: Women Offenders.* Washington, DC: U.S. Department of Justice.

Greer, K. 2000. "The Changing Nature of Interpersonal Relationships in a Women's Prison." *Prison Journal* 80, 4: 442–468.

Gross, G., S. Larson, G. Urban, and L. Zupan. 1994. "Gender Differences in Occupational Stress Among Correctional Officers." *American Journal of Criminal Justice* 18, 2: 219–234.

"Guards Acquitted of Staging Gladiator Fights." 2002. *New York Times,* June 10, 2000, A16.

Guy, E., J. Platt, I. Zwerling, and S. Bullock. 1985. "Mental Health Status of Prisoners in an Urban Jail." *Criminal Justice and Behavior* 12, 1: 29–53.

Hairgrove, D. 2000. "A Single Unheard Voice." In R. Johnson and H. Toch, *Crime and Punishment: Inside Views,* pp. 147–149. Los Angeles, CA: Roxbury.

Hairston, C. 1991. "Family Ties During Imprisonment: Important to Whom and for What?" *Journal of Sociology and Welfare* 18, 1: 87–104.

Hamm, M., T. Coupez, F. Hoze, and C. Weinstein. 1994. "The Myth of Humane Imprisonment: A Critical Analysis of Severe Discipline in U.S. Maximum Security Prisons, 1945–1990." In M. Braswell, R. Montgomery Jr., and L. Lombardo (eds.), *Prison Violence in America,* pp. 167–200. Cincinnati, OH: Anderson.

Hammack, L. 2000. "Lawmakers Say Investigation of Supermax Prisons Needed." *Roanoke Times.* Retrieved February 1, 2000 from *http://www.roanoke.com/roatimes/news/story87170.html.*

Hanley, C. 2002. "Infamous Punishment: The Psychological Consequences of Isolation." In L. Alarid and P. Cromwell (eds.), *Correctional Perspectives*, pp. 101–170. Los Angeles: Roxbury.

Harding, R. 1998. "In the Belly of the Beast: A Comparison of the Evolution and Status of Prisoners' Rights in the United States and Europe." *Georgia Journal of International and Comparative Law.* Retrieved July 2, 2002 from *http://web.lexisnexis.com/universe/document?_m=45fbb5ec0315e188cb3baabef7e3a9f8&.*

Harer, M., and D. Steffensmeier. 1996. "Race and Prison Violence." *Criminology* 34, 3: 323–355.

Harland, A. 1996. *Choosing Correctional Interventions That Work.* Beverly Hills, CA: Sage.

Harlow, C. 1999. *Bureau of Justice Statistics Report: Selected Findings: Prior Abuse Reported by Inmates and Probationers.* Washington, DC: Department of Justice.

———. 2003. *Bureau of Justice Statistics Report: Education and Correctional Populations.* Washington, DC: Department of Justice.

Harrison, P. 1999. *Bureau of Justice Statistics: Correctional Populations in the U.S. 1998.* Washington, DC: U.S. Department of Justice.

Harrison, P., and A. Beck. 2002. *Bureau of Justice Statistics: Prisoners in 2001.* Washington, DC: U.S. Department of Justice.

Harrison, P., and J. Karberg. 2003. *Bureau of Justice Statistics Bulletin: Prison and Jail Inmates at Midyear 2002.* Washington, DC: U.S. Department of Justice.

Hartstone, E., H. Steadman, P. Robbins, and J. Monahan. 1999. "Identifying and Treating the Mentally Disordered Prison Inmate." In E. Hartstone, H. Steadman, and L. Teplin (eds.), *Mental Health and Criminal Justice*, pp. 279–296. Thousand Oaks, CA: Sage.

Hassine, V. 1999. *Life Without Parole: Living in Prison Today.* Los Angeles: Roxbury.

Haycock, J. 1991. "Capital Crimes: Suicides in Jails." *Death Studies* 15: 417–433.

Hayes, L. 1996. "Prison Suicide." *Corrections Today* 58, 1: 88–94.

Hayner, N., and E. Ash. 1940. "The Prison as a Community." *American Sociological Review* 5: 577–583.

Hemmons, C., and J. Marquart. 1998. "Fear and Loathing in the Joint: The Impact of Race and Age on Inmate Support for Prison AIDS Policies." *Prison Journal* 78, 2: 133–152.

Hench, D. 2002. "Report Demands Prisons Changes to Help Mentally Ill." *Kennebuc Journal Online*. Retrieved on September 25, 2002 from *http://www.centralmaine.com/news/stories/020925jail_kj_.shtml*.

Hendricks, B. 1999. "Prison-Building Tied to Decade's Drop in Crime." *San Antonio Express*, Friday, February 4, 2000.

———. 2000. "Prisons Chief Faces Woes." *San Antonio Express News*, Wednesday, January 19, 2000.

Henriques, Z. 1996. "Imprisoned Mothers and Their Children: Separation-Reunion Syndrome Dual Impact." *Women and Criminal Justice* 8, 1: 77–97.

Henry, P., J. Senese, and G. Ingley. 1994. "Use of Force in American Prisons: An Overview." *Corrections Today* 56, 4: 108–110.

Hensley, C. (ed.). 2002. *Prison Sex: Practice and Policy.* Boulder, CO: Lynne Rienner.

Hensley, C., C. Struckman-Johnson, and H. Eigenberg. 2000. "Introduction: The History of Prison Sex Research." *Prison Journal* 80, 4: 360–367.

Hepburn, J. 1985. "The Exercise of Power in Coercive Organizations: A Study of Prison Guards." *Criminology* 23, 1: 146–164.

Hepburn, J., and P. Knepper. 1993. "Correctional Officers as Human Service Workers: The Effects of Job Satisfaction." *Justice Quarterly* 10, 2: 315–337.

Hocker, C. 2002. "More Brothers in Prison Than in College?" *Blackenterprise.com*. Retrieved on October 10, 2002, from *http://www.blackenterprise.com/ExclusivesOpen.asp?Source=Articles/10082002ch.html*.

Houston, J. 1999. *Correctional Management: Functions, Skills, and Systems.* Chicago: Nelson-Hall.

Human Rights Watch. 2000. *Punishment and Prejudice: Racial Disparities in the War on Drugs.* Available through website: *www.hrw.org/reports/2000/usa/*.

———. 2001. *No Escape: Male Rape in U.S. Prisons.* Available through website: *www.hrw.org/reports/2000/usa/*.

Hungerford, G. 1993. *The Children of Incarcerated Mothers: An Exploratory Study of Children, Caretakers and Inmate Mothers in Ohio.* Ph.D. dissertation, Ohio State.

Hunt, G., S. Riegel, T. Morales, and D. Waldorf. 1993. "Changes in Prison Culture: Prison Gangs and the Case of the 'Pepsi Generation.'" *Social Problems* 40, 3: 398–409.

Hunter, M. 2000. "The Sixth Commandment." In R. Johnson and H. Toch, *Crime and Punishment: Inside Views*, pp. 193–196. Los Angeles: Roxbury.

Immarigeon, R. 1994. "When Parents Are Sent to Prison." *National Prison Project Journal* 9, 4: 5 and 14.

Inciardi, J. 1999. "Drug Treatment Behind Bars." In P. Carlson and J. Garrett (eds.), *Prison and Jail Administration*, pp. 312–320. Gaithersburg, MD: Aspen.

——. 2002. *The War on Drugs, Part III.* Boston: Allyn & Bacon.

Irwin, J. 1970. *The Felon.* Englewood Cliffs, NJ: Prentice-Hall.

——. 1980. *Prisons in Turmoil.* Boston: Little, Brown & Co.

Irwin, J., and J. Austin. 1994. *It's About Time: America's Imprisonment Binge.* Belmont, CA: Wadsworth.

Irwin, J., and D. Cressey. 1962. "Thieves, Convicts, and the Social Inmate Culture." *Social Problems* 10: 142–155.

Jacobs, J. 1977. *Statesville: The Penitentiary in Mass Society.* Chicago: University of Chicago Press.

——. 1980. *Crime and Justice.* Chicago: University of Chicago Press.

Jacobs, J., and L. Kraft. 1978. "Integrating the Keepers: A Comparison of Black and White Prison Guards in Illinois." *Social Problems* 25: 304–318.

Jenkins, H. 1999. "Education and Vocational Training." In P. Carlson and J. Garrett, *Prison and Jail Administration*, pp. 87–93. Gaithersburg, MD: Aspen.

Jenne, D., and R. Kersting. 1996. "Aggression and Women Correctional Officers in Male Prisons." *Prison Journal* 76, 4: 442–460.

Johnson, R. 1981. "The Complete Correctional Officer: Human Service and the Human Environment of Prison." *Criminal Justice and Behavior* 8, 3: 343–373.

——. 1997. "Race, Gender, and the American Prison: Historical Observations." In J. Pollock (ed.), *Prisons: Today and Tomorrow,* pp. 26–51. Gaithersburg, MD: Aspen.

——. 1996/2002. *Hard Time: Understanding and Reforming the Prison.* Belmont, CA: Wadsworth.

Johnson, R., and H. Toch. 1982. *The Pains of Imprisonment.* Prospect Heights, IL: Waveland.

——. 2000. *Crime and Punishment: Inside Views.* Los Angeles: Roxbury.

Johnson, S. 1999. "Mental Health Services in a Correctional Setting." In P. Carlson and J. Garrett (eds.), *Prison and Jail Administration,* pp. 107–116. Gaithersburg, MD: Aspen.

Johnston, D. 1995a. "Parent-Child Visitation in the Jail or Prison." In K. Gabel and D. Johnston, *Children of Incarcerated Parents,* pp. 135–143. New York: Lexington Books.

———. 1995b. "Effects of Parental Incarceration." In K. Gabel and D. Johnston, *Children of Incarcerated Parents*, pp. 259–263. New York: Lexington.

———. 1995c. "Intervention." In K. Gabel and D. Johnston, *Children of Incarcerated Parents*, pp. 199–232. New York: Lexington Books.

Jones, R. 1999. "High Tech Prison Designed for 'Toughest of the Tough.'" *Milwaukee Journal Sentinel*. Retrieved August 31, 1999, from *http://www.jsonline.com/news/state/aug99/max01083199.asp*.

Josi, D., and D. Sechrest. 1998. *The Changing Career of the Correctional Officer: Policy Implications for the 21st Century*. Boston: Butterworth-Heinemann.

Jurik, N. 1985. "Individual and Organizational Determinants of Correctional Officer Attitudes Toward Inmates." *Criminology* 23, 3: 523–539.

Justice Policy Institute. 2002. "Cellblocks or Classrooms: The Funding of Higher Education and Corrections and its Impact on African-American Men." Report available through the Justice Policy Institute website: *www.riseup.net/jpi*.

Kamerman, J. 1995. "Correctional Officer Suicide." *Keepers' Voice* 16, 3: 7–8.

Kaplan, D., V. Schiraldi, and J. Ziedenberg. 2000. *Texas Tough? An Analysis of Incarceration and Crime Trends in the Lone Star State*. Washington, DC: Justice Policy Institute.

Kaplan, S. 1999. "State Prison Costs Up 83% in Six Years Report Shows." *Stateline.org*, Retrieved August 24, 1999, from *http://www.Stateline.org/story.cfm?StoryID=44823*.

Kasindorf, M. 2002. "Three Strikes Laws Fall Out of Favor." *USA Today*, February 28, 2002, A1.

Kauffman, K. 1988. *Prison Officers and Their World*. Cambridge, MA: Harvard University Press.

Keeton, K., and C. Swanson. 1998. "HIV/AIDS Education Needs Assessment." *Prison Journal* 78, 2: 133–152.

Kennedy, D., and R. Homant. 1988. "Predicting Custodial Suicides: Problems With the Use of Profiles." *Justice Quarterly* 5, 3: 441–456.

Keve, P. 1991. *Prison and the American Conscience: A History of U.S. Federal Corrections*. Cabrondale, IL: Southern Illinois University Press.

King, R., and M. Mauer. 2001. *Aging Behind Bars: Three Strikes Seven Years Later*. Washington, DC: Sentencing Project. Retrieved August 12, 2002 from *http://www.SentencingProject.org*.

———.2002a. *Distorted Priorities: Drug Offenders in State Prisons*. Retrieved September 21, 2002 from *http://www.SentencingProject.org*.

——. 2002b. *State Sentencing and Corrections Policy in an Era of Fiscal Restraint.* Washington, DC: Sentencing Project. Retrieved August 12, 2002, from *http://www.SentencingProject.org.*

Kleindienst, L. 1999. "Florida Prison Guards Twice As Likely As Police to Commit Violations." *Sun-Sentinel,* August 25, 1999.

Kleiner, C. 2002. "Breaking the Cycle." *U.S. News and World Report,* April 29, 2002, 48–51.

Klofas, J., and H. Toch. 1982. "The Guard Subculture Myth." *Journal of Research in Crime and Delinquency* 19, 2: 238–254.

Knight, K., D. Simpson, L. Chatham, and L. Camacho. 1997. "An Assessment of Prison-Based Drug Treatment: Texas In-Prison Therapeutic Community Programs." *Journal of Offender Rehabilitation* 2, 3/4: 75–100.

Kondo, L. 2001. "Advocacy of the Establishment of Mental Health Specialty Courts in the Provision of Therapeutic Justice for Mentally Ill Offenders." *American Journal of Criminal Law* 28, 3: 255–337.

Krebs, C. 2002. "High Risk HIV Transmission Behavior in Prison and the Prisoner Subculture." *Prison Journal* 82, 1: 19–49.

Kupers, T. 1999. *Prison Madness: The Mental Health Crisis Behind Bars and What We Must Do About It.* San Francisco: Jossey-Bass.

——. 2001. "Rape and the Prison Code." In D. Sabo, T. Kupers, and W. London, *Prison Masculinities,* pp. 111–117. Philadelphia: Temple University Press.

Langan, P., and D. Levin. 2002. "Recidivism of Prisoners Released in 1994." *Bureau of Justice Statistics Special Report.* Washington, DC: Bureau of Justice Statistics, Department of Justice.

Lanza-Kaduce, L., K. Parker, and C. Thomas. 1999. "A Comparative Recidivism Analysis of Releasees From Private and Public Prisons." *Crime and Delinquency* 45, 1: 28–47.

Latessa, E., and H. Allen. 1999. *Corrections in the Community.* Cincinnati, OH: Anderson.

Latessa, E., A. Holsinger, J. Marquart, and J. Sorenson. 2001. *Correctional Contexts: Contemporary and Classical Readings.* Los Angeles: Roxbury.

Lawrence, R., and S. Mahan. 1998. "Women Corrections Officers in Men's Prisons: Acceptance and Perceived Job Performance." *Women & Criminal Justice* 9, 3: 63–86.

Leary, W. 2000. "Violent Crime Continues to Decline." *New York Times.* Retrieved August 28, 2000, from *www.nytimes.com/library/national/082800crime-rate.html.*

Leduff, C., and A. Liptak. 2002. "Defiant California City Hands Out Marijuana." *New York Times*. Retrieved September 18, 2002, from *www.nytimes.com/library/national/9C05E1D91530F93BA2575AC*.

Lerner, J. 2002. *You've Got Nothing Coming: Notes From a Prison Fish*. New York: Broadway Books.

Lewis, M. 1999. "Corcoran Guards Launch Ads." *Fresno Bee*, September 17, 1999, A1.

Light, S. 1991. "Assaults on Prison Officers: Interactional Themes." *Justice Quarterly* 8, 2: 242–261.

——. 1999. "Assaults on Prison Officers: Interactional Themes." In M. Braswell, R. Montgomery Jr., and L. Lombardo (eds.), *Prison Violence in America*, pp. 207–223. Cincinnati, OH: Anderson.

Lin, A. 2000. *Reform in the Making: The Implementation of Social Policy in Prison*. Princeton, NJ: Princeton University Press.

Lock, E., J. Timberlake, and K. Rasinki. 2002. "Battle Fatigue: Is Public Support Waning for War-Centered Drug Control Strategies?" *Crime and Delinquency* 48, 3: 380–398.

Logan, C. 1987. "The Propriety of Proprietary Prisons." *Federal Probation* 53, 3: 35–40.

Lombardo, L. 1989. *Guards Imprisoned: Correctional Officers at Work*. Cincinnati, OH: Anderson Press.

MacLeod, C. 2002. "Through the Narrow Gate." In L. Alarid and P. Cromwell, *Correctional Perspectives: Views From Academics, Practitioners, and Prisoners*, pp. 72–85. Los Angeles: Roxbury.

Mallaby, S. 2001. "Addicted to a Failing War on Drugs." *Washington Post*, January 8, 2001, A19.

Man, C., and J. Cronan. 2001. "Forecasting Sexual Abuse in Prison." *Journal of Criminal Law and Criminology* 92: 127–185.

Manocchio, A., and J. Dunn. 1982. *The Time Game: Two Views of a Prison*. Beverly Hills, CA: Sage.

Mariner, J. 2001. "Body and Soul: The Trauma of Prison Rape." In J. May and K. Pitts (eds.), *Building Violence*, pp. 125–131. Thousand Oaks, CA: Sage.

Marks, A. 2001. "A Spiritual Approach to Time Behind Bars." *Christian Science Monitor*. Retrieved on April 18, 2001, from *http://www.csmonitor.com/durable/2001/04/16/p1s4.htm*.

Marquart, J., and B. Crouch. 1985. "Judicial Reform and Prisoner Control." *Law and Society Review* 16: 557–586.

Martin, D., and P. Sussman. 1993. *Committing Journalism: The Prison Writings of Red Hog*. New York: Norton.

Martin, M. 1997. "Connected Mothers: A Follow-up Study of Incarcerated Women and Their Children." *Women and Criminal Justice* 8, 4: 1–23.

Martin, M. 2001. "Pot Clubs Bracing for DEA Crackdowns." *San Francisco Chronicle*, November 13, 2001. Retrieved November 14, 2001, from *www.sfgate.com/cgi-bin/article.cgi?f=/c/a/2001/11/13/MN190086.DIL*.

Martin, S. 2000. "Texans Have a Passion for Punishment." *Austin American Statesman*, August 28, 2000, A9.

Martin, S., and S. Eckland-Olson. 1987. *Texas Prisons: The Walls Came Tumbling Down*. Austin, TX: Texas Monthly Press.

Martinson, R. 1974. "What Works? Questions and Answers About Prison Reform." *Public Interest* (Spring): 22–54.

Maruna, S. 2001. *Making Good: How Ex-Convicts Reform and Rebuild Their Lives*. Washington, DC: American Psychological Association.

Maruschak, L., and A. Beck. 2001. *B.J.S. Special Report: Medical Problems of Inmates, 1997*. Washington, DC: U.S. Department of Justice.

Masters, J. 2001. "Scars." In D. Sabo, T. Kupers, and W. London, *Prison Masculinities*, pp. 201–206. Philadelphia: Temple University Press.

Mauer, M. 1999. *Race to Incarcerate*. New York: Free Press.

Mauer, M., M. Chesny-Lind, and T. Clear. 2001. "The Causes and Consequences of Prison Growth." In D. Garland (ed.), *Mass Imprisonment: Social Causes and Consequences*, pp. 4–14. Thousand Oaks, CA: Sage.

——. 2002. *Invisible Punishment: The Collateral Consequences of Mass Imprisonment*. New York: New Press.

May, J. 2001. "Feeding a Public Health Epidemic." In J. May and K. Pitts (eds.), *Building Violence*, pp. 133–137. Thousand Oaks, CA: Sage.

Mayhew, J. 2002. "Corrections Is a Male Enterprise." In B. Gaucher (ed.), *Writing as Resistance: The Journal of Prisoners on Prisons Anthology— 1988–2002*, pp. 151–159. Toronto, Ontario: Canadian Scholars Press.

McCarthy, B. 1991. "Keeping an Eye on the Keeper: Prison Corruption and Its Control." In M. Braswell, B. McCarthy, and B. McCarthy (eds.), *Justice, Crime, and Ethics*, pp. 239–253. Cincinnati, OH: Anderson.

McCorkle, R., T. Miethe, and K. Drass. 1995. "The Roots of Prison Violence." *Crime and Delinquency* 41, 3: 317–327.

McGowan, B., and K. Blumenthal. 1978. *Why Punish the Children? A Study of Children of Women Prisoners*. Hackensack, NJ: National Council on Crime and Delinquency.

McLaren, J. 1997. "Prisoner Rights: The Pendulum Swings." In J. Pollock (ed.), *Prisons: Today and Tomorrow*, pp. 338–377. Gaithersburg, MD: Aspen.

Merlo, A. 1997. "The Crisis and Consequences of Prison Overcrowding." In J. Pollock (ed.), *Prisons: Today and Tomorrow,* pp. 52–83. Gaithersburg, MD: Aspen.

Messemer, J. 2003. "College Programs for Inmates: The Post-Pell Grant Era." *Journal of Correctional Education* 54, 1: 32–39.

Monitoring the Future Study. 2002. Monitoring the Future Study. University of Michigan. Retrieved from www.monitoringthefuture.com.

Montgomery, R., and G. Crews. 1998. *A History of Correctional Violence: An Examination of Reported Causes of Riots and Disturbances.* Lanham, MD: American Correctional Association.

Morain, D. 2002a. "State Prison Guards Union Endorses Davis." *LATimes.com.* Retrieved August 28, 2002 from *www.latimes.com/news/ local/la-me-endorse28Aug28.story?coll=la-headlines.*

———. 2002b. "Overtime Pays Off at Prison." *LATimes.com.* Retrieved February 11, 2003, from *www.latimes.com/news/local/la-me-overtime10feb10,1,5548722.story.*

Morash, M., and T. Bynum. 1995. *Findings From the National Study of Innovative and Promising Programs for Women Offenders.* Washington, DC: U.S. Department of Justice.

Morash, M., D. Har, and L. Rucker. 1994. "A Comparison of Programming for Women and Men in U.S. Prisons in the 1980s." *Crime and Delinquency* 40, 2: 197–221.

Morash, M., and P. Schram. 2002. *The Prison Experience: Special Issues of Women in Prison.* Prospect Heights, IL: Waveland.

Moritz, M. 2001. "Ruling May End Prison Lawsuit." Retrieved March 20, 2001 from *http://www.star-telegr.../1:AOLNEWS4/ 1:AOLNEWS40320101.html.*

Morris, J. 2002. "It's a Form of Warfare: A Description of Pelican Bay Prison." In L. Alarid and P. Cromwell, *Correctional Perspectives,* pp. 181–183. Los Angeles: Roxbury.

Morris, R. 1995. *Penal Abolition.* Toronto: Canadian Scholar Press.

Muir, W. 1977. *Street Corner Politicians.* Chicago: University of Chicago Press.

Mullen, J., et al. 1980. *American Prisons and Jails, Vol. 1.* Washington, DC: National Institute of Justice.

Mumola, C. 1999. *Substance Abuse and Treatment.* Washington, DC: Bureau of Justice Statistics, U.S. Department of Justice.

———. 2000. *Bureau of Justice Statistics Special Report: Incarcerated Children and Their Parents.* Washington, DC: U.S. Department of Justice.

Murphy, K. 2002a. "State Prisoners Often Return, Report Shows." *Stateline.org*. Retrieved June 10, 2002, from *www.stateline.org/story.do?storyID=240988*.

———. 2002b. "States Get Grants to Help Ex-Offenders." *Stateline.org*. Retrieved July 17, 2002, from *www.stateline.org/story.do?storyID=248888*.

Muse, D. 1994. "Parenting From Prison." *Mothering* 72: 99–105.

Nagy, J. 2001. "State Budgets Battered by Substance Abuse." *Stateline.org*. Retrieved January 29, 2001, from *stateline.org/story.do?storyID=111585*.

National Center on Institutions and Alternatives. 1998. *Imprisoning Elderly Offenders: Public Safety or Maximum Security Nursing Homes*. Alexandria, VA: NCIA.

National Institute of Justice. 1993. *Sourcebook of Criminal Justice Statistics*. Washington, DC: GPO.

Nelson, M. 2002. "Arkansas Prison Still Shackled to Dark Past." *Los Angeles Times*, January 6, 2002, A1.

New York State, Department of Correctional Services. 2001. *Female Offenders 1999–2000*. Albany, NY: DOCS, Division of Program Planning, Research and Evaluation.

Occupational Outlook Handbook. 2002–2003. Online from *http://www.stats.bls.gov/oco/ocos156.htm*.

———. 1998–1999. Online from *http://www.stats.bls.gov/oco/ocos156.htm*.

Ogle, R. 1999. "Prison Privatization: An Environmental Catch 22." *Justice Quarterly* 14, 3: 579–600.

Olson, D., A. Lurigio, and M. Seng. 2000. "A Comparison of Female and Male Probationers: Characteristics and Case Outcomes." *Women & Criminal Justice* 11, 4: 60–78.

Open Society Institute. 2002. *News Release: Majority of Americans Think U.S. Criminal Justice System Is Broken*. Retrieved August 14 from *http://www.soros.org/crime/CJI%20Poll-PR.htm*.

Owen, B. 1985. "Race and Gender Relations Among Prison Workers." *Crime and Delinquency* 31 (January): 147–159.

———. 1988. *The Reproduction of Social Control: A Study of Prison Workers at San Quentin*. New York: Praeger.

———. 1998. *"In the Mix": Struggle and Survival in a Women's Prison*. Albany, NY: State University of Albany Press.

Owen, B., and B. Bloom. 1994. "Profiling the Needs of California's Female Prisoners: A Study in Progress." Paper presented at the meeting of the Western Society of Criminology.

———. 1995. "Profiling Women Prisoners: Findings From National Surveys and a California Sample." *Prison Journal* 75, 2: 165–185.

Paboojian, A., and R. Teske. 1997. "Pre-service Correctional Officers: What Do They Think About Treatment?" *Journal of Criminal Justice* 25, 5: 425–433.

Padron, E. 2000. "The Long Awaited Day of Freedom." In R. Johnson and H. Toch, *Crime and Punishment: Inside Views*, pp. 196–220. Los Angeles: Roxbury.

Palmer, T. 1994. *A Profile of Correctional Effectiveness and New Directions for Research.* Albany, NY: SUNY Press.

Parenti, C. 1999. *Lockdown America: Police and Prisons in the Age of Crisis.* New York: Verso New Left Books.

Parker, K. 2002. "Female Inmates Living in Fear: Sexual Abuse by Correctional Officers in the District of Columbia." *American University Journal of Gender, Social Policy and the Law.* Retrieved July 2, 2002, from *http://web.lexis-nexis.com/universe/document?_M=294eb9c811969dbd76bf1cb0b76f7473&.*

Patrick, E. 2000. "Meaning of 'Life' in Prison." In R. Johnson and H. Toch, *Crime and Punishment: Inside Views*, pp. 141–143. Los Angeles: Roxbury.

Pearson, F., D. Lipton, C. Cleland, and D. Yee. 2002. "The Effects of Behavioral and Cognitive-Behavioral Programs on Recidivism." *Crime and Delinquency* 48, 3: 476–496.

Pelz, M. E., J. Marquart, and C. Terry Pelz. 1991. "Right Wing Extremism in Texas Prisons: The Rise and Fall of the Aryan Brotherhood of Texas." *Prison Journal* 71, 2: 38–49.

Perez, E. 2001. "For Profit Prison Firm Wackenhut Tries to Break Shackles to Growth." *Wall Street Journal.* Retrieved May 15, 2001, from *www.msnbc.com/news/570728.asp?cpi=1.*

Perkins, C. 1994. *National Corrections Reporting Program: Bureau of Justice Statistics Bulletin.* Washington, DC: U.S. Department of Justice.

Peters, R., and M. Steinberg. 2000. "Substance Abuse Treatment in U.S. Prisons." In D. Shewan and J. Davies (eds.), *Drugs and Prison*, pp. 89–116. London: Harwood Academic Press.

Petersilia, J. 1999. "Parole and Prisoner Reentry." In M. Tonry and J. Petersilia (eds.), *Crime and Justice: A Review of Research*, vol. 26., pp. 30–45. Chicago: University of Chicago Press.

Pollock, J. 1984. "Women Will Be Women: Correctional Officers' Perceptions of the Emotionality of Women Inmates." *The Prison Journal* 64, 1: 84–91.

——. 1986. *Sex and Supervision: Guarding Male and Female Inmates.* New York: Greenwood Press.

——. 1990. *Women, Prison and Crime.* Belmont, CA: Wadsworth.

——. 1995. "Women in Corrections: Custody and the 'Caring Ethic.'" In A. Merlo and J. Pollock (eds.), *Women, Law, and Social Control,* pp. 97–116. Needham Heights, MA: Allyn & Bacon.

——. 1997a. *Prison: Today and Tomorrow.* Gaithersburg, MD: Aspen.

——. 1997b. "The Social World of the Prisoner." In J. Pollock (ed.), *Prison: Today and Tomorrow,* pp. 218–258. Gaithersburg, MD: Aspen.

——. 1997c. "Rehabilitation Revisited." In J. Pollock (ed.), *Prison: Today and Tomorrow,* pp. 158–208. Gaithersburg, MD: Aspen.

——. 1998a. *Counseling Women in Prison.* Beverly Hills, CA: Sage.

——. 1998b/2003. *Ethics in Crime and Justice: Dilemmas and Decisions,* 3rd ed. Belmont, CA: Wadsworth.

——. 1999. *Criminal Women.* Cincinnati, OH: Anderson.

——. 2000. *A National Survey of Parenting Programs in Women's Prisons.* Privately published monograph available from the author.

——. 2001. *Women, Prison, and Crime.* Belmont, CA: Wadsworth.

——. 2002. *Women, Prison, and Crime,* 2nd ed. Belmont, CA: Wadsworth.

Pranis, K. 2001. "Sodexho to End Support for Right Wing Lobby." News Release. Retrieved April 20, 2001, from *www.nomoreprisons.org.*

Pratt, T., and J. Maahs. 1999. "Are Private Prisons More Cost-Effective Than Public Prisons? A Meta-Analysis of Evaluation Research Studies." *Crime and Delinquency* 45, 3: 358–371.

Prendergast, M., J. Wellisch, and G. Falkin. 1995. "Assessment of and Services for Substance Abusing Women Offenders in Community and Correctional Settings." *Prison Journal* 75, 2: 240–256.

Raeder, M. 1993. "Gender Issues in the Federal Sentencing Guidelines." *Journal of Criminal Justice* 8, 3: 20–25.

Rafter, N. 1985/1990. *Partial Justice: Women in State Prisons, 1800–1935.* Boston: New England University Press.

Raspberry, W. 2002. "Prison Sentences Devastate a Community." *Austin American Statesman,* October 14, 2002, A13.

Redifer, K. 2000. "Big Trouble in 'Li'l Chilli.'" In R. Johnson and H. Toch (eds.), *Crime and Punishment: Inside Views,* pp. 143–146. Los Angeles: Roxbury.

Reichel, P. 1997. *Corrections.* Minneapolis, MN: West Publishing.

Reimer, H. 1937. "Socialization in the Prison Community." *Proceedings of the 67th Annual Conference of the American Prison Association* 1: 151–155.

Reisig, M., and T. Pratt. 2000. "The Ethics of Correctional Privatization: A Critical Examination of the Delegation of Coercive Authority." *Prison Journal* 80, 2: 210–222.

Rich, W. 2002. "Prison Conditions and Criminal Sentencing in Kansas." *Kansas Journal of Law and Public Policy.* Retrieved July 2, 2002, from *http://web.lexisnexis.com/universe/document?_m=294eb9c811969dbd76bf1cb0b76f7473&.*

Richards, S. 2003. "My Journey Through the Federal Bureau of Prisons." In J. Ross and S. Richards (eds.), *Convict Criminology,* pp. 120–149. Belmont, CA: Wadsworth, ITP.

Richards, S., C. Terry, and D. Murphy. 2002. "Lady Hacks and Gentleman Convicts." In L. Alarid and P. Cromwell, *Correctional Perspectives,* pp. 207–216. Los Angeles: Roxbury.

Richey, W. 2002. "Bans on Ex-Con Voting Reviewed." *Christian Science Monitor.* Retrieved October 1, 2002, from *http://www.csmonitor.com/2002/1001/p02s01-usju.html.*

Rideau, W., and R. Wikberg. 1992. *Life Sentences: Rage and Survival Behind Bars.* New York: Times Books.

Riley, J. 2000. "Sensemaking in Prison: Inmate Identity as a Working Understanding." *Justice Quarterly* 17, 2: 359–376.

Robinson, C. 2000. "Disenfranchisement of Blacks Hurt Gore." *Dawn: The Internet Edition.* Retrieved May 30, 2003, from *http://dawn.com/2000/11/13/int11.htm.*

Robinson, R. A. 1992. "Intermediate Sanctions and the Female Offender." In J. Byrne, A. Lurigio, and J. Petersilia (eds.), *Smart Sentencing: The Emergence of Intermediate Sanctions,* pp. 245–260. Newbury Park, CA: Sage.

Rogers, K. 2000. "A True Story." In R. Johnson and H. Toch (eds.), *Crime and Punishment: Inside Views,* pp. 67–69. Los Angeles: Roxbury.

Rohde, D. 2001. "A Growth Industry Cools." *New York Times,* August 21, 2001.

Rolland, M. 1997. *Descent Into Madness: An Inmate's Experience of the New Mexico State Prison Riot.* Cincinnati, OH: Anderson.

Roots, R. 2002. "Of Prisoners and Plantiffs' Lawyers: A Tale of Two Litigation Reform Efforts." *Willamette Law Review.* Retrieved July 2, 2002, from http://web.lexisnexis.com/universe/document?_m=294eb9c811969dbd76bf1cb0b76f7473&.

Ross, D. 1996. "Assessment of Prisoner Assaults on Corrections Officers." *Corrections Compendium* 21, 8: 6–10.

Ross, J., and S. Richards. 2003. *Convict Criminology.* Belmont, CA: Wadsworth, ITP.

Rothman, D. 1971/1990. *The Discovery of the Asylum: Social Order and Disorder in the New Republic.* Boston: Little, Brown.

Rouse, J. 1991. "Evaluation Research on Prison-Based Drug Treatment Programs and Some Policy Implications." *International Journal of the Addictions* 26, 1: 29–44.

Rusche, G., and O. Kirchheimer. 1939. *Punishment and Social Structure.* New York: Russell and Russell.

Rydell, C., J. Caulkins, and S. Everingham. 1996. *Enforcement or Treatment? Modeling the Relative Efficiency of Alternatives for Controlling Cocaine.* Santa Monica, CA: RAND Corporation.

Sabo, D., T. Kupers, and W. London. 2001. "Gender and the Politics of Punishment." In D. Sabo, T. Kupers, and W. London, *Prison Masculinities,* pp. 3–20. Philadelphia: Temple University Press.

Salant, J. 2002. "More Americans on Parole in Jail by the End of 2001." *Austin American Statesman,* August 26, 2002, A5.

Salladay, R. 1999. "Prison Guard Union, Davis Cozy Pairing." *San Francisco Examiner,* September 14, 1999, B3.

Samaha, J. 1997. *Criminal Justice.* Minneapolis–St. Paul: West Publishing.

Sampson, R., and J. Lauritsen. 1997. "Racial and Ethnic Disparities in Crime and Criminal Justice in the U.S." In M. Tonry (ed.), *Ethnicity, Crime and Immigration: Comparative and Cross-National Perspectives,* pp. 311–374. Chicago: University of Chicago Press.

Sandifer, J., and S. Kurth. 2000. "The Invisible Children of Incarcerated Mothers." *Families, Crime and Criminal Justice* 2: 361–379.

Sanger, B. 2001. "Bush Names a Drug Czar and Addresses Criticism." *New York Times.* Retrieved May 11, 2001, from *www.nytimes.com/2001/05/11/politics/11DRUG.html.*

Sapp, A., and M. Vaughn. 1990. "The Social Status of Adult and Juvenile Sex Offenders in Prison." *Journal of Police and Criminal Psychology* 6: 2–6.

Saylor, W., and G. Gaes. 1994. "The Post Release Employment Project: Prison Work Has Measurable Effects in Post Release." In P. Kratcoski (ed.), *Correctional Counseling and Treatment,* pp. 535–542. Prospect Heights, IL: Waveland.

Schemo, D. 2001. "Students Find Drug Law Has Big Price: College Aid." *New York Times.* Retrieved May 3, 2001, from *www.nytimes.com/2001/05/03/politics/03DRUGhtml.*

Schiraldi, V. 2002a. *Cellblocks or Classrooms? The Funding of Higher Education and Corrections and Its Impact on African American Men.* Washington, DC: Justice Policy Institute.

——. 2002b. "Tough on Crime, but Hardly Smart." *Albany Times Union,* April 17, 2002, A1.

Schiraldi, V., and J. Greene. 2002. "Ripe for Cutting: Prison Budgets." *Los Angeles Times,* February 10, 2002, A2.

Schiraldi, V., and V. Jones. 2001. "New Youth Movement Organizing to Fight Consequences of Their Parents Mistakes." *Pacific News.* Retrieved August 24, 2001, from *www.pacificnews.org/content/png/2001/Aug/0817youth.html.*

Schrag, C. 1961. "Leadership Among Prison Inmates." *American Sociological Review* 19: 37–42.

Sentencing Project. 2001. *U.S. Surpasses Russia as World Leader in Rate of Incarceration.* Washington, DC: The Sentencing Project.

Sharp, S. 2003. *The Incarcerated Woman.* Upper Saddle River, NJ: Prentice-Hall.

Sheehan, S. 1978. *A Prison and a Prisoner.* Boston: Houghton-Mifflin.

Sherman, M. 2001. *California's Three Strikes Law Fails to Reduce Crime.* Washington, DC: The Sentencing Project.

Shichor, D., and D. Sechrest. 2002. "Privatization and Flexibility: Legal and Practical Aspects of Interjurisdictional Transfer of Prisoners." *Prison Journal* 82, 3: 386–407.

Shuler, M. 2001. "Senators Vote to Relax Prison Terms." *The Advocate Online.* Retrieved May 3, 2001, from *www.theadvocate.com/news/story.asp?storyID=21206.*

Siegal, N. 2002. "Stopping Abuse in Prison." In T. Gray (ed.), *Exploring Corrections,* pp. 135–139. Boston: Allyn & Bacon.

Silberman, M. 1995. *A World of Violence: Corrections in America.* Belmont, CA: Wadsworth, ITP.

Singer, S. 1996. "Essential Element of the Effective Therapeutic Community in the Correctional Institution." In K. Early (ed.), *Drug Treatment Behind Bars: Prison Based Strategies for Change,* pp. 75–88. Chicago: Praeger.

Snell, T. 1992. *Women in Jail: 1989.* Bureau of Justice Statistics Special Report. Washington, DC: U.S. Department of Justice.

——. 1994. *Women in Prison: Survey of State Prison Inmates, 1991.* Bureau of Justice Statistics Special Report. Washington, DC: U.S. Department of Justice.

———. 1995. *Correctional Populations in the United States, 1992.* Bureau of Justice Statistics Special Report. Washington, DC: Bureau of Justice Statistics.

Solomon, A. 1999. "Wackenhut Detention Ordeal." *Village Voice.* Retrieved March 5, 1999, from *villagevoice.com/features/9935/solomon.shtml.*

Sorensen, J., and D. Stemen. 2002. "The Effect of State Sentencing Policies on Incarceration Rates." *Crime and Delinquency* 48, 3: 456–475.

Souryal, S. 1999. "Corruption of Prison Personnel." In P. Carlson and J. Garrett (eds.), *Prison and Jail Administration: Practice and Theory,* pp. 171–177. Gaithersburg, MD: Aspen.

Spencer, D. 1997. "The Classification of Inmates." In J. Pollock (ed.), *Prison: Today and Tomorrow,* pp. 84–115. Gaithersburg, MD: Aspen.

Stanton, A. M. 1980. *When Mothers Go to Jail.* Lexington, MA: Lexington.

Stephan, J. 1997. *Census of State and Federal Correctional Institutions, 1995.* Bureau of Justice Statistics Reports. Washington, DC: Department of Justice.

Stohr, M., N. Lovrich, B. Menke, and L. Zupan. 1994. "Staff Management in Correctional Institutions: Comparing DiIulio's 'Control Model' and 'Employee Investment Model' Outcomes in Five Jails." *Justice Quarterly* 11, 3: 471–497.

Stojkovic, S. 1990. "Accounts of Prison Work: Corrections Officers Portrayals of the Work Worlds." *Perspectives on Social Problems* 2: 211–230.

Stone, W. 1997. "Industry, Agriculture and Education." In J. Pollock (ed.), *Prison: Today and Tomorrow,* pp. 116–157. Gaithersburg, MD: Aspen.

Stratton, R. 1999. "Skyline Turkey." In B. Chevigny (ed.), *Doing Time: 25 Years of Prison Writing.* New York: Arcade.

Struckman-Johnson, C., L. Rucker, K. Bumby, and S. Donaldson. 1996. "Sexual Coercion Reported by Men and Women in Prison." *Journal of Sex Research* 33, 1: 67–76.

Stumbo, N., and S. Little. 1991. "Campground Offers Relaxed Setting for Children's Visitation Program." *Corrections Today* 53, 5: 162–173.

Sullivan, L. 1990. *The Prison Reform Movement: Forlorn Hope.* Boston: Twayne.

Sung, Hung-en. 2001. "Rehabilitating Felony Drug Offenders Through Job Development." *Prison Journal* 81, 2: 271–286.

Susswein, G. 2000. "Report: Reading Class Aids Inmates." *Austin American Statesman,* August 30, 2000, B1, B6.

Sutner, S. 2002. "Glodi's Bill Would Charge Prisoners for Keep." *Telegram News.* Retrieved July 12, 2002, from *www.telegram.com/news/inside/jailfees.html.*

Sykes, G. 1956. "The Corruption of Authority and Rehabilitation." *Social Forces* 34: 257–265.

——. 1958/1966. *The Society of Captives.* Princeton, NJ: Princeton University Press.

Sykes, G., and S. Messinger. 1960. "The Inmate Social System." In R. Cloward, D. Cressey, G. Grosser, R. McCleery, L. Ohlin, G. Sykes, and S. Messinger (eds.), *Theoretical Studies in the Social Organization of the Prison,* pp. 5–19. New York: Social Science Research Council.

Taylor, W. 1993. *Brokered Justice: Race, Politics, and Mississippi Prisons, 1798–1992.* Columbus, OH: Ohio State University Press.

Teepin, T. 1996. "For Private Prisons, Crime Does Pay." *Austin American Statesman,* December 12, 1996, A15.

Teplin, L., K. Abrams, and G. McClelland. 1996. "Prevalence of Psychiatric Disorders Among Incarcerated Women." *Archives of General Psychiatry* 53, 2: 505–512.

Terry, C. 2003. *The Fellas: Overcoming Prison and Addiction.* Belmont, CA: Wadsworth, ITP.

Texas Department of Criminal Justice. 2001. *Statistical Summary: Fiscal Year 2000.* Austin, TX: Texas Department of Criminal Justice.

Theis, S. 2002. "New Tact Pushed in War on Drugs." *Plain Dealer-Columbus,* Ohio, August 8, 2002, A1.

"Three Guards Acquitted." 2002. *New York Times,* February 16, 2002, A13.

Timms, E. 2001. "Judge to Lessen Oversight of Texas Prisons." Retrieved June 20, 2001, from *http://www.dallasnews.*

Toch, H. 1975. *Men in Crisis: Human Breakdowns in Prison.* Chicago: Aldine.

——. 1977. *Living in Prison: The Ecology of Survival.* New York: Free Press.

——. 1980a. *Therapeutic Communities in Corrections.* New York: Praeger.

——. 1980b. *Violent Men.* Cambridge, MA: Schenkman.

——. 1981. "Is a 'Correctional Officer,' by Any Other Name, a 'Screw'?" In R. Ross, *Prison Guard/Correctional Officer,* pp. 87–103. Toronto: Butterworth.

——. 1982. *Mosaic of Despair: Human Breakdowns in Prison.* Washington, DC: American Psychological Association.

Toch, H., and K. Adams. 1989. *Coping and Maladaption in Prison.* New Brunswick, NJ: Transaction Press.

Toch, H., and J. Grant. 1982. *Reforming Human Services: Change Through Participation.* Beverly Hills, CA: Sage.

Toch, H., and J. Klofas. 1982. "Alienation and Desire for Job Enrichment Among C.O.'s." *Federal Probation* 46: 35–47.

Treaga, W. 2003. "Twenty Years Teaching College in Prison." In J. Ross and S. Richards (eds.), *Convict Criminology,* pp. 309–324. Belmont, CA: Wadsworth, ITP.

Trout, C. H. 1992. "Taking a New Look at an Old Problem." *Corrections Today* (July): 62, 64, 66.

Trulson, C., and J. Marquart. 2002a. "Inmate Racial Integration: Achieving Racial Integration in the Texas Prison System." *Prison Journal* 82, 4: 498–525.

——. 2002b. "Racial Desegregation and Violence in the Texas Prison System." *Criminal Justice Review* 27, 2: 233–255.

Uniform Crime Reports. 1965. Washington, DC: Federal Bureau of Investigation.

——. 1995. Washington DC: Federal Bureau of Investigation.

——. 2001. Washington DC: Federal Bureau of Investigation.

——. 2002. Washington, DC: Federal Bureau of Investigation.

——. 2003. Washington DC: Federal Bureau of Investigation.

United States Substance Abuse and Mental Health Services Administration. 2001. 2000 National Household Survey on Drug Abuse. Available through website: *www.samhsa.gov/oas/nhsda.htm.*

——. 2002. 2001 National Household Survey on Drug Abuse. Available through website: *www.samhsa.gov/oas/nhsda.htm.*

Useem, B., and P. Kimball. 1989. *States of Seige: U.S. Prison Riots: 1971–1986.* New York: Oxford University Press.

Useem, B., and M. Reisig. 1999. "Collective Action in Prisons." *Criminology* 37: 735–759.

Vaughn, M. 1993. "Listening to the Experts: A National Study of Correctional Administrators' Responses to Prison Overcrowding." *Criminal Justice Review* 18: 12–25.

Vaughn, M., and L. Smith 1999. "Practicing Penal Harm Medicine in the U.S.: Prisoners Voices From Jail." *Justice Quarterly* 16, 1: 175–231.

Verhovek, S. 1996. "Texas Caters to a Demand Around U.S. for Jail Cells." *New York Times,* February 9, 1996, A1, A10.

Von Hirsch, A. 1976. *Doing Justice.* New York: Hill and Wang.

Wacquant, L. 2001. "Deadly Symbosis: When Ghetto Prison Meet and Mesh. In D. Garland, *Mass Imprisonment,* pp. 82–120. Thousand Oaks, CA: Sage.

Walker, S. 1980. *Popular Justice: A History of American Criminal Justice.* New York: Oxford University Press.

Wall Street Journal. 2001. "Prisons as Profit Centers." *Wall Street Journal,* March 15, 2001, A17.

Wallace, D. 2001. "Prisoner Rights: Historical Views." In E. Latessa, A. Holsinger, J. Marquart, and J. Sorenson, *Correctional Contexts: Contemporary and Classical Readings,* pp. 229–238. Los Angeles: Roxbury.

Walters, G., M. Mann, M. Miller, L. Hemphill, and M. Chlumsky. 1988. "Emotional Disorder Among Offenders: Inter- and Intrasetting Comparisons." *Criminal Justice and Behavior* 15: 433–453.

Ward, D. 1999. "Super-Maximum Facilities." In P. Carlson and J. Garrett (eds.), *Prison and Jail Administration,* pp. 252–259. Gaithersburg, MD: Aspen.

Ward, G. 2001. "CCA Majority Shareholder to Sell Stocks." *Tennessean.* Retrieved May 23, 2001, from *www.tennessean.com/business/archives/01/04/05094888.shtml?Element_ID=50948.*

Ward, M. 2002a. "State's Prison Vacancies May Be Costly to Counties." *Austin American Statesman,* March 22, 2002, A1, A22.

———. 2002b. "UT Calls for Independent Review of Prison Medical Care." *Austin American Statesman.* Retrieved on October 12, 2002, from *http://www.austin360.com/auto_docs/epaper/editions/saturday/news_5.html.*

Ward, P. 2002. "So the Crime, Do the Time . . . And Lose the Right to Vote, Too." *Savannah Morning News.* Retrieved August 19, 2002, from *http://www.savannahnow.com/stories/081902/LOCFELONVOTE.shtml.*

Warren, J. 2000. "When He Speaks, They Listen." *Los Angeles Times.* Retrieved August 22, 2000, from *http://www.latimes.com/news/state/20000821/t000078505.html.*

———. 2001. "Inmates Health Care Focus of Suit." *Los Angeles Times.* Retrieved on April 10, 2001, from *http://www.latimes.com/news/state/20010406/t000029385.html.*

———. 2002. "State to Spend Millions on Better Inmate Care." *Los Angeles Times.* Retrieved on February 4, 2002, from *http://www.latimes.com/news/printededition/california/la-000007549jan30.story?coll=la.*

Webb, G., and D. Morris. 2002. "Working as a Prison Guard." In T. Gray (ed.), *Exploring Corrections,* pp. 69–83. Boston: Allyn & Bacon.

Webb, V., C. Katz, and T. Klosky. 1995. "Drug Use Among Traditional Versus Non-traditional Female Offenders: Findings From the National DUF Project." Paper presented at the American Society of Criminology Meeting, Boston, 1995.

Weinstein, C. 2002. "Even Dogs Confined to Cages for Long Periods of Time Go Berserk." In J. May and K. Pitts (eds.), *Building Violence,* pp. 119–124. Thousand Oaks, CA: Sage.

Welch, M. 2000. "The Correctional Response to Prisoners With HIV/ AIDS." *Social Pathology* 6, 2: 149–157.

——. 2002. *Detained: Immigration Laws and the Expanding I.N.S. Jail Complex.* Philadelphia: Temple University Press.

Wellisch, J., M. Prendergast, and J. Wellisch. 1994. *Bureau of Justice Statistics Report: Drug Abusing Women Offenders: Results of a National Survey.* Washington, DC: U.S. Department of Justice.

Welsh, M. 2002. "The Effects of the Elimination of Pell Grant Eligibility for State Prison Inmates." *Journal of Correctional Education* 53, 4: 154–158.

West, W., and R. Morris. 2000. *The Case for Penal Abolition.* Toronto: Canadian Scholars Press.

Whitehead, T. 2001. "The 'Epidemic' and 'Cultural Legend' of Black Male Incarceration." In J. May and K. Pitts (eds.), *Building Violence.* Thousand Oaks, CA: Sage.

Widom, C. 1989. "Child Abuse, Neglect, and Violent Criminal Behavior." *Criminology* 27, 2: 251–366.

——. 1996. "Childhood Sexual Abuse and Criminal Consequences." *Society* 33, 4: 47–53.

Wilkie, D. 2002. "Three Strikes No Deterrent to Drug Crimes." *San Diego Union-Tribune,* August 11, 2002, B1.

Williamson, H. 1990. *The Corrections Profession.* Newbury Park, CA: Sage.

Wilson, P., C. Gallagher, M. Coggeshall, and D. MacKenzie. 1999. "A Quantitative Review and Description of Corrections Based Educational, Vocational, and Work Programs." *Corrections Management Quarterly* 3, 4: 8–18.

Winfree, T., G. Newbold, and S. Tubb. 2002. "Prisoner Perspectives on Inmate Culture in New Mexico and New Zealand: A Descriptive Case Study." *The Prison Journal* 82, 2: 213–233.

"Women in the Criminal Justice System." 1998. *http://www/ojp.usdoj.gov/ reports/98Guides/wcjs98/chap4.htm.*

Woolredge, J., and K. Masters. 1993. "Confronting Problems Faced by Pregnant Inmates in State Prisons." *Crime and Delinquency* 39, 2: 195–203.

Worldcom Must Refund Prisons. 2001. Newstory. *The New York Timesonline.* Retrieved May 4, 2001 from *http://dailynews.yahoo.com/h/ ap/20020503/bs/prison_phones_1.html.*

Wright, K. 1994. *Effective Prison Leadership.* Binghamton, NY: William Neil.

Wright, K., W. Saylor, E. Gilman, and S. Camp. 1997. "Job Control and Occupational Outcomes Among Prison Workers." *Justice Quarterly* 14, 3: 525–546.

Wright, R. 1999. "Governing—The Human Side of Personnel Management." In P. Carlson and J. Garrett (eds.), *Prison and Jail Administration: Practice and Theory*, pp. 151–157. Gaithersburg, MD: Aspen.

Wright, R., and W. Saylor. 1992. "Comparison of Perceptions of the Work Environment Between Minority and Non-minority Employees of the Federal Prison System." *Journal of Criminal Justice* 20, 1: 63–71.

Zamble, E., and F. Porporino. 1988. *Coping Behavior and Adaption in Prison Inmates*. New York: Springer-Verlag.

Zimbardo, P. 1982. "The Prison Game." In N. Johnston and L. D. Savitz (eds.), *Legal Process and Corrections*, pp. 195–198. New York: Wiley.

Zimmer, L. 1986. *Women Guarding Men*. Chicago: University of Chicago Press.

Zimring, F., and G. Hawkins. 1995. *Incapacitation: Penal Confinement and the Restraint of Crime*. New York: Oxford University Press.

Zimring, F., G. Hawkins, and S. Kamin. 2001. *Punishment and Democracy: Three Strikes and You're Out in California*. New York: Oxford University Press.

Zupan, L. 1992. "The Progress of Women Correctional Officers in All-Male Prisons." In I. Moyer (ed.), *The Changing Roles of Women in the Criminal Justice System*, pp. 323–343. Prospect Heights, IL: Waveland.

Name Index

Subject Index